# THE ENDURANCE ARTIST

# THE ENDURANCE ARTIST

## Lazarus Lake, the Barkley, and a Race with No End

JARED BEASLEY

PUBLISHING

80/20 Publishing, LLC
1073 Oberland Drive
Midway, UT 84043
www.8020books.com

Distributed in the United States and Canada by Simon & Schuster

Library of Congress Control Number: 2025939790
ISBN 979-8-9907958-2-2 print
ISBN 979-8-9907958-3-9 ebook
Cover and interior design by Vicki Hopewell
Cover photo: Tamara Reynolds

*For my wife, Hikaru*

*"There was no hope in the world,*
*so why was there always*
*this endless battle for survival?"*

—STEPHEN KING, *THE LONG WALK*

*"Harold's father had a similar sense*
*of the absurd. I remember once in Paris*
*he just stepped out for cigarettes and the next*
*I knew he was arrested by the police for*
*floating nude down the Seine—experimenting*
*in river currents with rubber water wings."*

—MRS. CHASEN, *HAROLD AND MAUDE*

# Contents

## Part I
## DIARY OF A LITTLE DOG


1. Assorted Life-Threatening Injuries 3

2. The Leonardo da Vinci of Pain 13

3. Die on the Course 23

4. A Grueling, Grim, and Hazardous Event 31

5. Spirit of a Wild Thing 41

6. Where Were You When It Got Dark? 53

7. Make Peace with Your God 61


## Part II
## THE ORDEAL


8. Nothing but Love and Puppies 77

9. No Cop Cars 89

10. All of Them 99

11. Endgame Tricks 111

12. Don't Go Away Easy 123

## Part III

# DIARY OF A BIG DOG


13. My Name Is Big **137**

14. The Unfortunates **145**

15. Houdini **155**

16. Count Backwards **163**

17. Just Lie to Us **171**

18. The Business **183**

19. Normal Rules Don't Apply Here **195**


## Part IV

# LAST ONE STANDING


20. Happy Time! **209**

21. I Think It Will Catch **217**

22. Heredity **227**

23. Rules Are Not Suggestions **235**

24. There Might Be a Body in There **247**

25. Can We Go Get Him? **259**

26. Speed Kills **267**

27. The Barricade **275**

Epilogue **285**

Author's Note **293**

About the Author **295**

Part I

# DIARY OF A LITTLE DOG

# 1

# Assorted Life-Threatening Injuries

**FOR OVER A CENTURY,** Brushy Mountain State Penitentiary was the end of the line. Built in the shape of a Greek cross, the pale limestone structure had housed the worst of the worst—murderers, madmen, monsters. It sat hunched beneath a crown of scarred mountains the guards called the Fifth Wall—in an area so remote, so rugged, the Civilian Conservation Corps lost four men building trails here in the 1930s. Eventually, they abandoned their field office due to an infestation of rattlesnakes. Snakes the locals said were "as thick as a man's arm."

Now it stands empty—cracking and molding and dying. But each spring around April Fool's, on a cold, crisp day like today, a retired accountant appears at its gate. He carries a book with an ominous title and plants it against the back wall. Then sometime between midnight and noon the next day, he lights a cigarette, and the world's most grueling footrace begins.

He came at dawn, in a large U-Haul coughing diesel smoke into the Tennessee frost. After crawling out, he leaned on a cattle prod and lit a cigarette in front of the prison gate. He wore faded flannel, red-and-black checked, and a bright sock hat that said *Geezer*. The rest of him was almost deceptive: a tangly grey beard, perfectly manicured nails, and eyes like two-way mirrors—they observed everything and revealed nothing.

To some he is Lazarus Lake. To others "the Leonardo da Vinci of Pain." His Social Security comes to Gary Cantrell. Most call him Laz.

He looked on while a grey truck pulled up to the gate and sat gurgling. When I mentioned the polarizing attitudes toward his race creations, he just shrugged. "Most people think fair is what's best for them. The purpose of a challenge is to find differences. If you don't fail," he said on a long sigh of cigarette smoke, "how will you know how far you can go?"

A young man climbed out, gave us a nod, and worked the lock with a hoop of keys. They rattled against the metal gate until the whole thing, all two stories of it, screeched and unfolded like a zipper.

Laz got back in his vehicle without a word. I followed.

Outside my frosty car window, the mountains loomed up to a series of tall ridges, dull like the color of deer in winter. They were strewn with jeep roads and blown-down timber. You had to think—forty of the world's toughest against mountains the Cherokee deemed too inhospitable to mess with.

The U-Haul circled a parking lot the size of a football field before lumbering to a halt in a puff of exhaust. Laz leaned against the front fender and began to piss. It steamed and splattered till it formed a dark patch on the concrete. I looked away, shaking my head at the fact that it was now 2023, and I'd spent the past year convincing *The New York Times* to let me profile him. "I do two things well," I heard him say behind me. "I sleep well, and I piss well."

I was beginning to wonder if I'd wind up like the rest. *Outside* magazine had tried to do a deep dive on him but were flummoxed when he told them, "Wrong information out there is OK. It just makes the truth harder to find." When Red Bull's writers asked how he started running, he answered "with my left foot" before launching into a lecture on Osage oranges and wild bear fatalities.

One rumor has it that he'd been shot in a marathon. Another that he'd pulled his own teeth. Many are convinced he's diabolical, a man who breaks people for the fun of it. Others see a "bearded saint" who pushes limit-seekers in a way that borders on genius. But most agree his ultramarathons defy convention.

"There's ultrarunning," one runner remarked, "then there's this weird stuff." Tour buses, ferry rides, conch shells, a chair of honor called a "thrown," races with no finish lines, races where older runners beat the pants off competitors half their age—Lazarus Lake filled a gap few realized needed filling. But it was here he first flipped the sport on its head—at least, it is believed—with the Barkley Marathons. It started with how to get in. If you belonged here, you'd find out how to get here, he'd say. And getting here meant finding an email address, sending an application to Idiot, including $1.60, and writing an essay on why he should allow you in.

According to longtime Barkley fixture Frozen Ed, in his book *Tales From Out There*, "The Barkley entry application form is usually a joke in itself." He recalled having to give his age in non-Earth planetary years on a form that began, "Start making excuses." If chosen, Laz sent you scrambling above the prison through briar-laced thickets—to find the books he set out in the wilderness—with no course markers, no aid stations, no tracking devices.

Stories of the depleted souls who stumbled back to camp were legend. Shredded legs. Separated clavicles. Exposed kneecaps. One runner was close to finishing but turned back at a mad flow of mountain water. "If I cross," he told himself, "they will be finding my body."

Another runner hopped 20 miles on a broken ankle just to get to a place where he could quit. The few who triumphed here were names whispered over cookfires with awe and an almost alien reverence. In the last five years no one had even finished the Barkley. In its 36-year history, only 15 ever had.

I trailed Laz toward the back of the prison, where he limped past a ditch, a towering wall of sandstone, and stopped at a conjunction of metal pipes. He produced the book, *Last Will and Testament*, and with little fanfare duct-taped it to the center.

To prove you'd run his course, he had you bring back a page from each book, thirteen this year. The order of the books formed one loop—five loops total—sixty hours to finish. "Sixty hours of Hell," wrote one magazine. He added sections to the Barkley every year, mostly off-trail, yet the distance somehow remained 100 miles. Those in the know say it's nothing short of 125. Not knowing, Laz maintains, is part of the fun.

He also doesn't allow pacers—"that's cheating"—and if you get lost, no one's coming for you—for at least thirty hours. He wants you alone against all that Out There. "If you're going to face a challenge," he once told a documentarian, "it has to be a real challenge."

After lighting another cigarette, he moved to a break in the earth where a swollen stream barreled into a tunnel beneath the prison. Naturally, he sent the runners through it. At night, they reported hearing radios, television sets, even voices calling their names. They swore they were being watched, though no one ever mentioned by whom.

"They'll come up through here," Laz said with some glee and pointed to a shaft lined with slick, glistening stones. Getting up or down would require a chimney climb, wedging feet and arms against opposing walls. "Then, they'll head up *that*," he said and gestured with his cattle prod to a sheer wall of Tennessee jungle.

The slope didn't rise, it lunged at the sky—sixty degrees of winter-stripped trees so densely pushed together they seemed to fight each other for air. There was a flare in Laz's eyes as he studied it. "We call that The Bad Thing."

The cliffs here bound up so steep that a deer once tumbled off and into the prison yard. The inmates kept it and named it "Geronimo." It became one of the boys, a guide told me, and claimed he could still hear its footsteps. "The whole place is haunted," he said, his voice dropping. He described the six-by-six dungeon, the hooks where they'd hang inmates by their thumbs, and the mines in the mountains where hundreds were buried alive. When they collapsed, the guards would just leave them. "No, no," he said, shaking his ball-cap-covered head. "This is not a good place. And I don't do night tours."

"Jesus, you'd need a rope," I whispered, craning my neck up at The Bad Thing.

A thick, congested laugh burrowed up from Laz's chest. "Aw hell," he said. "That's just the first pitch."

Most big trail races have a monster, that one signature, gut-sucking climb. At the Barkley, there are a dozen, each loop, and The Bad Thing isn't even one of the worst. The total elevation gain soars over 68,000 feet, roughly two Everests and a Kilimanjaro—from sea level. Many of the climbs are littered with long thatches of briars—the kind country people used to call "wait-a-minutes" because it wasn't until you got a step past them that you realized you'd been snagged.

"God, one wrong move and you'd come down it alright, like a bowling ball," I thought but actually said out loud.

"Oh, you'd smack into a tree long before you hit the bottom," said Laz, without a hitch. "It'd mess you up a bit. But you'd live." He laughed till he groaned, then stilled for a moment before fixing his eyes on me. "Failure has to hurt."

I let that roll over in my head for a moment. "Doesn't it usually?"

He didn't respond to that but scanned the hillside with his large green eyes. "What makes people quit?" he said, blowing a long column of smoke back toward the prison. "Everybody is born a quitter. It's the default setting. Hell, even fish quit! You can put 'em in an artificial stream with a fake scene, and they'll swim upstream as long as it looks like they're moving. But make it stationary, and they'll quit and go with the water."

He turned to head back to the parking lot but paused. "Life can be a damn good metaphor for sports," he said. "Adapt or die."

---

The U-Haul was moving again, this time along a tight patch of pavement deep inside Frozen Head State Park. The road curved and rolled into a tunnel of trees toward the trailhead. There, the next phase of the Barkley would begin, checking in those Laz had called at various times penitents, fools, and sickos.

The farther we went, the more the forest seemed to want its space back—dark patches of moss slowly overtook the road and boulders crowded the edges. Laz liked to talk about the park's mercurial microclimate, how the air compressed through the gaps like a thumb held over a garden hose. Temperatures could swing from 80 to 15 degrees in a single loop. "First-timers think it's hyperbole," he said, "but you only have to get caught by it once."

Soon, the bars on my phone dwindled to an *x*, and the road began to climb. Finally, a smudge of yellow appeared ahead and became a gate. Set between two stone pillars, this flaking pole was where the ordeal would begin and end. Here, Taps would play on a squeaky bugle for the fallen. Like most things in Frozen Head, one got the sense it was sentient. A cracked sign adorned its middle: "Do Not Block Gate."

By early afternoon, the ritual check-in was underway. A line of forty trail runners twisted up to a large white tarp, a virtual who's who of ultrarunning. The veterans carried items for Laz that he was in need of: cigarettes, socks, shirts. The virgins (first-timers) produced license plates from their home states and countries. Hundreds of these plates hung from yellow ropes strung between the trees—a dangling gallery of far-flung places like Liberia, South Africa, Australia, Antarctica.

There were also unfamiliar faces in line, wide-eyed and wrapped in weather-faded gear. They stood quietly, taking it all in. Every so often, one would lean forward for a glimpse of Laz. You got the sense they weren't here for the mountains. Not even the pain. They were here for *him*—for Laz and his gate and his cigarette, daring them to come undone.

His gravelly laugh echoed through the trees from behind a picnic table, where he greeted the entrants. "We look forward to seeing you suffer," he said to one, before "You might as well go ahead and hit your head on a rock" to another. The runners and crews got green and blue wristbands. The media got pink.

"Any advice?" a runner asked.

"Go home," Laz laughed and handed him this year's shirt.

While most race swag is fairly standard fare, this shirt boasted an illustration of a runner, terror etched across his face as he dashed up a tree. A monstrous black bear was charging him from behind, while above, a cougar crouched on a limb, ready to pounce. At the bottom was this year's theme—*The worst-case scenario is just the starting point!*

After the last runner checked in, they studied the master map. Laz made one of the course each year, and once it was set out, the runners and crews did their best to copy it by hand. They were also given a creatively useless set of instructions. "If the trail you see appears to be too steep to go down," Laz wrote one year, "then it is probably the right trail." Even the veterans got lost. One runner was heard to say, "I'm not sure where I was, but it was hard as hell to get to."

Later in the night, there'd be a chicken dinner and, some years, a birthday cake with "Good Luck, Morons!" written in icing. But when the race would actually start, only Laz knew. Sometime in the next twelve hours, he'd blow a conch shell. If you heard it, you had one hour. If you missed it—and someone always did—you were shit out of luck. Secrecy in all things was absolute; no one outside the camp—save close family members—even knew we were here.

Suddenly chilled by a damp breeze, I made my way back toward my SUV but bumped into Johan Steene. The Swedish ultrarunner was a magnificent sight—long brown hair pulled back into a ponytail, a kind, angular face, and a gentle nature that was easy to read. Whether floating over gnarled roots, rutted mud, or fields of scree in Oman, Steene made technical trails look effortless. The Barkley? Four starts and zero finishes. "I'm excited to finally see you run," I said when we shook hands.

"Oh, you don't *run* the Barkley," he said in a melodic lilt and smiled. When he stepped away, I noticed a laminated sign I could've sworn was not there before. It was taped to a pole with words written in black magic marker. MEDICAL, it read, *for instances of DEATH, near-dying, and other assorted life-threatening injuries.* Below was a phone number.

I revved the engine of my rental, held my numbed hands over the vents, and thought about something ultra-phenom Courtney Dauwalter had told me. She managed only one loop here but insisted Laz didn't want to torture people. One of the greatest ultrarunners of all time, she still felt awkward meeting him at first, not sure if it was a handshake situation or a hug situation. "He's really kind," she said, and found "he makes these crazy-hard events because he thinks we all have more than we think is possible."

Just as I was beginning to get my head around all this and feel my fingers again, the weather shifted. The clouds darkened, and a blistering wind came barreling off the mountains. It whipped and tossed the trees. It was like an unseen hand had pulled a lever. The temperature plummeted, then sleet began to thud off tarps, tents, and scrambling runners.

I spotted Laz by the license plates, gazing up at the sky and sipping a chilled can of Dr. Pepper, a Tennessee license plate swinging in the wind beside him. Its bolded letters read SURVIVE.

# 2

# The Leonardo da Vinci of Pain

**THIS ALL BEGAN WITH A STRANGER** barreling through an icy mud hole the size of a school bus. He was running as if he had minutes to live: face clenched with pain, grey hair matted with frozen dirt, and legs that churned like pistons, spraying water and cinder bits into the air. The damn thing was—the race was already over.

It was an image I couldn't shake. *What was he chasing? What was chasing him?*

It soon led me to a series of seemingly ordinary people who defied normal concepts of endurance—a mother of five who ran the length of Death Valley in flip-flops, and a group of Ukrainian volunteers who avoided curfews to race beneath a sky streaked with cruise missiles. An ailing scientist would ask permission to die in the middle of a race. A Japanese office worker, pushing himself to his absolute limit, nearly did.

They all had one thread tying them together—Lazarus Lake. He was like a gate guardian of some ancient knowledge. He was also the man *Trail Runner* magazine dubbed the "Leonardo da Vinci of Pain," and entry into his peculiar world would be no easy task. He was notoriously cagey. It would take years to get there, but when I did, I'd discover oddities difficult to explain in casual conversation: a body in a bag, a pit bull watching people fight to the death, and something called a "swacket."

But it all started with a stranger back in 2015, in a quiet city park in Decatur, Alabama.

---

The March morning was colder than I expected. My car lights cut through the pre-dawn black and glistened over mirrors of ice. Two days of storms had riddled the one-mile course with pools of water. Then overnight, a wave of Arctic air tumbled south and froze them solid. I huddled at the start line with the rest, sucking in the crisp cold. It spread into your lungs like Icy Hot and came out like a steam engine.

The Delano 12-hour is by no means one of the toughest races in the world. It's a flat, pretzeled course with simple rules: Run as much as you can within the time limit. Set in a landscaped, leisurely park with swing sets, tennis courts, and flower beds, it was where regular people gathered for strolls. But it wasn't an easy spot to come back to. Decatur was my hometown.

At the red-bricked high school across the street, fairness in sport, as a concept, had taken its last gasp for me. My brother used to say I excelled at everything I tried, till it got hard. It wasn't that simple.

When baseball tryouts came, I was the second-fastest kid in Decatur and had a strong arm to go with it. But I wasn't the coach's son. Kneeling in the outfield one night, I watched "his boy" walk fourteen runs in a row. A year of that followed. At one practice, I remember throwing pitches to a catcher in high, floating arcs. And coach taking the ball out of my hands and saying, "You've lost your edge."

In Catholic school, I'd been good at basketball. Good enough to dream about it, anyway. MVP point guard in eighth grade. At Decatur High, though, those dreams didn't matter—I was from the wrong school. They wouldn't even let me try out. Bullying followed, the nasty kind, the relentless kind, and eventually drove me away to another school in another town. There, I could start over. I was always starting over. But ultrarunning, if anything, was about staying the course.

With the belch of an air horn, the Delano 12-hour began, the sound of crystallized grass crunching under our feet. By noon, the March sun had melted the ice into small swamps a foot deep in places. Like most, I went around them, only to get mired in ankle-deep mud—a sucking slurp from holes where my shoes had been. And when the sun finally hung low in the sky, I hobbled stiff-legged to the timing tent. Forty-eight miles showed next to my name on an LED screen. Better than half the field. It was the warmest I'd felt all day. I'd proved something to somebody, though I wasn't sure to whom.

Jon Elmore thought different. "If you run like you ran the last loop, you've got time for one more." The race director's voice matched his face—kind, gentle, welcoming.

"That was pure adrenaline," I said, breathless, and bent down to take the timing chip off my shoe.

"No, no... we got that," he insisted, and he came over to take it off. "You don't want to get all that blood going to your head."

Everyone else had stopped too, it seemed, called it a day. So, I inched over to the screen to get a better look at the results. Not long after, a hardened figure came zooming past in a whir, grunting, grimacing, his head down as if locked in some private war. He plowed straight through the water. I glanced at the LED. There was less than five minutes left.

"Has he run a sub-five mile?" I said, wondering if I was missing something.

"Not even close," Jon replied, oh-so casual. "It doesn't matter. He's just being DeWayne Satterfield."

I scanned the screen for his name and found it, at the top. He'd run 73 miles and was up by three. The race was in the bag! Yet, he was turning the corner and sprinting away through the mud.

When he finally came back around, reduced to a wounded trot, I reached out a hand. I wanted to see this warrior—stone-faced and hard. Instead, he met me with warm eyes, bright and blue, that turned down at the edges when he smiled. He spoke with a voice as gentle as gravy. He was 50, worked as a mathematician, had two smart daughters he couldn't keep up with, and sometimes wished he'd stick to 10Ks. We both played some guitar, but he waved a hand and laughed that he *knew all the chords but couldn't make it cry or sing*. He was the guy next door, and the toughest thing I'd ever come across.

Over the next couple of years, he became almost a figment of my imagination—my own personal superhero. Then, on an utterly ordinary day, he was suddenly in my home. On my television.

---

"DeWayne... you're not doing a reverse loop, are you?" It was a voice I'd come to know well—Laz. His words cut through twenty yards of dark to a ball of bobbing light and the zombie-like figure behind it. The zombie was approaching, head down. Dressed in khakis and carrying a backpack, it lurched left and right like it was sleepwalking. Then it lay down on the side of the trail and curled up in the fetal position.

"How far did you get?" Laz asked.

The zombie replied in a whisper, "The Temple of Doom."

There was laughter, and a voice asked, "Do you feel as good as you look?"

The zombie corrected his mistake. "Pillars of Doom."

"You've still got time to go out," Laz said with a cheerful tone.

The zombie smiled, eyes closed, then nestled its face into the moss and dirt and made a pillow with its hand. A crude version of Taps began to play on a bugle.

This scene was captured in the documentary *The Barkley Marathons: The Race That Eats Its Young*. "It's highly unlikely anyone will die out there," Laz said in the proceeding moments, "because we try to make sure the people know what they're doing, and you have some control over the situation. But they're going to figuratively die because they're going to fail. They're going to get to the end."

This is what the Barkley Marathons had done to my hero. Of the five loops required, DeWayne Satterfield had managed one.

---

Now a writer for *Ultrarunning* magazine, I was up early the next morning to roll over the parameters of this chasm—the one that'd just opened up in my mind between the hard, the really hard, and the downright insane. I headed to my usual haunt, Antoinette's.

The moody, dimly lit espresso café sits fifteen miles north of Manhattan, two blocks up a slope from the Hudson River, nestled deep in the cushy world of Westchester. The usual crowd was already there: the entrepreneurial types at the counter and the mix of Ivy League retirees at the tables. "How far did you go?" one asked about my recent race.

"Fifty-six miles," I said, keeping my eyes on my screen.

"That's over two marathons." I recognized the honey voice of my friend in film props, the one with the witchy long hair, who liked to camp out in the wild and read occult books. "That's like... *insane*," he said.

I smiled awkwardly. "Pretty average," I muttered. "I did see this documentary though. You'd like it. It's in nowhere Tennessee."

He nodded back with a blank stare.

"Are you talking about the Barkley?" Another voice, loud and unfamiliar, was tinged with Brooklyn. "That shit's wrong," it said, and I looked up to see a blur of slick-backed hair, sweatpants, and dress shoes moving toward the door.

The Greek car guru had heard this. Normally, he keeps to himself at the far end by the door with his green jacket zipped up tight, studying his phone. Now suddenly he was in a crouching position on my left. "Ooooh, man," he said in a hushed tone and touched a finger to his lips. "That guy. The Barkley. That race is..." His eyes narrowed as he leaned in closer, whispering. "Man, I love it. You know what I love about it? I'll tell you..." He pointed to his temple and tapped. "It's psychological."

"You run?"

"Never."

A coffee roaster in another café (college kids may bar hop, middle-aged writers hop coffee shops) was a former submarine man turned connoisseur of fast cars and body art. He not only knew the Barkley, he was an expert. "These people actually hunt books, dude, crazy ones like *The Body in the Woods* and *Human Zoo.* But my favorite?" He smiled, running a hand through a hot batch of beans. *"Undead and Unfinished."*

I was shaken. I'm used to eyes glazing over at the slightest mention of ultrarunning. Even the most famous races—UTMB, Western States, Leadville. *Nope*—they'd never heard of them. They'd just stare at me and ask if I'd ever run a marathon. Yet this obscure race in Tennessee they knew and seemed to prickle at the idea of its creator—a puzzling mix of loathing, admiration, and intrigue.

Lost to most of the everyday world was the fact that we were in the middle of an ultrarunning explosion. While marathon participation was flagging, ultras had grown from 293 events in North America in 2010 to over 1,900 by 2019. Trail running was the main culprit, increasing roughly 12 percent year-after-year. With that, entrance fees doubled, then tripled. There were reasons: better medical coverage during events, more comprehensive aid station support, and enhanced timing systems and live tracking.

Lazarus Lake offered none of that.

Every editor I spoke to said getting a press pass from him was as likely as conjuring a ghost. And my emails to him went nowhere. In 2019, *Runner's World* offered me a shot at covering the Barkley... if I could get in. I applied for a press pass over several emails and waited. I finally received a reply—a year later: "i apologize for the delay. things are going nuts here. trying to save the 2020 barkley. some words may have been altered by this stupid phone."

A colleague was playing tricks on me, I thought. Then another message came from the same address. "i think the european media slots may be available. some words may have been altered by this stupid phone." I now felt certain this was Laz and realized, yes—he was purposefully writing in lower-case letters, and "some words may have been altered" was his automated sign-off.

A jolt of excitement shot through me. "I'll be there," I fired back in an email, "rain, sleet, tornado or virus." But the 2020 Barkley was a no-go, shuttered due to the pandemic. His last reply that year was to say that he'd put me on his "Weight List." Journalists I talked to moaned and agreed—it was an open-ended limbo, hopeless.

Two years went by till one day in Antoinette's, sitting under the 1950s film poster *El Gran Houdini*, my phone dinged. I opened it, half awake, and saw the words *The New York Times*. I blinked up at the poster and looked again. They were interested in a story on Laz's latest creation: Big's Backyard Satellite Team World Championship.

The Backyard format "was death by one zillion paper cuts," said Courtney Dauwalter. Deceptively simple, runners had one hour to do a four-mile loop (4.167), every hour, on the hour—last runner standing wins. It attracted runners of all levels. Like the High Striker at a carnival, the bell might not be in danger, but you're curious just how high you can make the puck soar. And what started in the woods behind Laz's house had by 2022 spread to over 70 countries across the globe, each with their own unique courses and eccentric names like the Bullshit Backyard Ultra and God's Own Backyard.

Laz's latest idea was audacious—Big's Backyard Satellite World Championship. He'd ring a cowbell in Tennessee, and 37 countries, from Malta to Morocco to Mauritius—each with a team of 15—would start simultaneously on their loops. Last nation standing.

"the press passes are all taken," he wrote back, thwarting me again. I felt the sudden urge to throw my computer against the wall. Then I clicked on another email from him to find—not a press pass but a math problem:

$$ABCDE \times A = EEEEEE$$

The problem glared at me from my inbox, haunted me from a notepad on my desk, and ran on a repeat loop in my brain. After days of overclocking my brain, I did what any self-respecting journalist would do: I panicked and passed the damn thing off to my wife. She took one glance, pulled out paper and a pen, and spat the answer out in fifteen minutes flat. I was shell-shocked. Out of curiosity, I ran it by an astrophysicist friend as well. His reply took longer than expected. "It's actually quite complicated," he explained but came up with the same solution.

"Did you give it to somebody?" Laz's reply was almost too quick.

Full of dread, I told him the truth.

His response was predictably blunt. "You always let someone else do your homework?"

I slumped onto my couch and rubbed at my throbbing forehead. I could see Laz, triumphantly taking a No. 2 pencil and scratching my name off his Weight List with a flick of the wrist. Three years trying to get a press pass to his races. Four years before that tracking down leads. Gone.

When another email hit my inbox, I was terrified and elated. What was next? "well..." he wrote, "why don't you come down to little dog's and run? it's two weeks before big's and y'all can beat the trail down for the real runners."

The door wasn't exactly open, but it was cracked.

# 3

# Die on the Course

**I PULLED INTO BELL BUCKLE,** population 399, late on an October afternoon and found it alive. Not bustling, not busy—just alive, in that small-town, apple-pie way where you half expect the local sheriff to be whittling a stick on the corner. Families and teenagers hopped along storefronts right out of a 1950s postcard. An old man in overalls read a paper beside a mural of an animated RC Cola. And a freshly painted red caboose sat in a parking lot across from an old-timey general store.

Naturally, everyone nodded and said "hi" as if they'd known you your whole life. But the lady making my iced latte smiled politely and tilted her head—*nope*, she'd never heard of Lazarus Lake, Gary Cantrell, or the Barkley Marathons. "Taylor Swift" at the Bell Buckle Café gave me the same blank stare. When I asked her where she was from, she brimmed with pride. "Right here."

I ambled over to the antebellum B&B next door as the sun was beginning to creep low over the hills. I climbed the long, creaky staircase to my room—a cozy little nook with floral wallpaper, a stack of quilts in a chair, and a dozen pillows on the bed that smelled like my grandmother's soap. I still wasn't sure what Laz expected of me in what he was calling his "B-team event." Since becoming a full-time writer, I was mostly a three-mile-a-day, run when the weather's nice, feel-good runner. I laid out my running gear on the floor in the shape of a body and glanced at my phone—Laz's place, ten minutes away...

Initially, the road out of town was lined with restored Victorian homes, all gingerbread trim and pastel paint. That quickly gave way to more modest housing, and one got a clearer sense of a per capita income just above the poverty line. The occasional trailer and abandoned house peeked from the shadows as the road swerved into native forests and rolling, limestone-pocked fields.

Oaks and maples flared with bursts of yellow and red—it was the time of year when, as a boy, I would camp with my father along a creek in southern Tennessee. The days were mild, but the nights had the bite of approaching winter. A fleeting season when the air felt clean and charged.

Around a corner an opening appeared, where a smattering of tents sat hunched against a screen of trees. Between them, a gravel driveway snaked up a hill and vanished. At the entrance, there was a stone mailbox built without mortar, and fluttering along a row of barricades were the bright flags of Mexico, Cambodia, Sweden, and a dozen more. An old man with a farmer's cap was meticulously tying on another. It was Laz.

He was a highly asymmetrical figure—big head, bulging belly, and a Walt Whitman beard the color of grits. His flannel jacket, black and red checked, looked so thoroughly lived in, I imagined an ash from his cigarette dropping on it and the old man spontaneously combusting.

I introduced myself with an ice-cold Dr. Pepper (his favorite), still dripping from the slush of my cooler. "I see," he said, deadpan. "You must be the Alabama version." His green eyes shifted behind wire-rimmed glasses—alive and devious one moment, sleepy and ambivalent the next. He laughed and said he knew a runner with the same name but from a good state. His accent was surprising—not hillbilly at all, but from many places, only lightly varnished in Southern.

He limped over to an ashy firepit and rested his foot on a stone. "Get over here, Little," he barked, and a small Jack Russell, white and speckled with black spots, darted out of the woods. "She likes to get into things she doesn't need to," he cooed in a gravelly voice. "And she eats poop. But she's a good little girl."

Her counterpart lumbered down the driveway, a large, 14-year-old pit bull named Big. A sack of flesh the size of a pineapple swung from his abdomen. Laz traced him with his eyes. "They're both well past their expiration dates," he said, turning back and smiling deep into my eyes. It was the kind of look that made you wonder if he was talking about himself.

"Oh me," he groaned, cracking open the can of Dr. Pepper. "How far you gonna go tomorrow?"

I shrugged. "Not very far." The little voice in my head was already negotiating: *Just do three loops. That's respectable enough.*

"Well," he said, eyes on Big, as if trying to remember how many lives the dog had already burned through. "You can go further than you think you can."

---

Dawn came with the smell of coffee and cedar floating on a chilly breeze. All eyes were on Laz—a cigarette glowing between his lips—a cattle prod and cowbell gripped in each hand. He blew a long plume of smoke toward a digital timer and winced at the red numbers ticking down. When the butt was on the ground and crushed underfoot, he'd start the madness.

Sixty of us were gathered in his driveway. Some stood motionless on the gravel, arms akimbo, wild stares on their faces like they could run for days. Others were giddy, stretching, smiling, joking. I talked to some. They were teachers, engineers, moms, and dads. But I knew enough to know they were about to morph into something else: hard-nosed, hard-gutted types who wouldn't let crushed arches, hallucinations, or general delirium get in the way of a good time. "It's not about winning or even finishing," I heard one say. "It's will you quit between loops or will you die on the course."

"I'm a writer who runs," I blurted out to the lady standing beside me, hoping to get a smile or a laugh—anything to cool the magma pool rising in my stomach. She didn't hear me. She had the hardened glare of an EMT, with blonde hair pulled so tight into a ponytail that it stretched her eyes into slits. "What I mean is I'm not a runner who writes. You know?"

Laz would get it but wouldn't care. His owl-like eyes were busy probing faces—for weakness—for strength—for a Danny. Twenty-five years coaching kids' basketball had him always on the lookout for The Archetype. This he called a "Danny"—not big, not fast, not necessarily talented—just a tough nut who wants it more than you. This whole Backyard concept, he'd made it just for them—"the common man's Barkley," he called it.

With a last puff, he rang the bell like cowboy dinner and screeched, "Happy Time!" We trotted onto a country road and... down it went like a slide, our hard trail shoes a small chorus of thumpity thump as we bounded and thumped down to the bottom of the hill, bounding and chatting and breathing in the biting cold. A slow stampede around a turnaround marker, then we were back up to where we started. But we hadn't truly started—not yet.

This little out-and-back was designed to thin us out for the real course—the trail—the rock-laden, twisty-hilled trail in the woods behind Laz's house. "The rattlesnakes are asleep this time of year," he'd assured us, "but you don't wanna be out there when the sun goes down."

He stood in the same spot as we passed, his open mouth turned up at the corners, his eyes peeled, soaking up our trepidation. I looked back to see him fall in behind us with his stick. Over his head, an inflated tube arched over the timing mat. He'd duct-taped a makeshift sign to it, covering the usual START/FINISH. It now read, THERE IS NO FINISH.

The trail narrows immediately, and my eyes lock onto a jostling three-foot cone in front of me. A fall at the wrong time and your face is on the serrated edge of a car-sized rock. I jump through a tree built like a tuning fork, dance across a limestone gauntlet of eroded caves, and come to a halt at a hairpin turn. A sign with a crooked arrow points the way but the writing is in Portuguese.

"Why?" I'd later ask him.

"Why not?" he'd reply.

Three hours in, his whistle pierces the air. Back to the corral, back down the hill, back up to the arch by Laz. I nestle behind a clump of runners. I've never felt so ashamed to run, like throwing a football in front of Nick Saban.

Twice a toe-tapper sends me reeling with an *oomph* and the air leaves my body. I hit the ground the first time, headfirst in a neat tuck and roll. The second is a full yard sale. In the sympathetic eyes of the runner who finds me, I see what I must look like—gels and water flasks scattered about, dirt smudged on my reddening face.

Now, the war begins. The war with the voice—the little man inside with the axes, who's convincing me this is all nonsense. *You've already done more than a half marathon.* Around a twist, Laz appears from a stand of brush. "Man," he says in a booming voice, "you are slooow."

I grit out another loop and collapse into my little corner of camp.

"We did that just right," says my tentmate Mark. He's reclined in an ergonomic chair, surrounded by dozens of labeled, plastic containers. "We keep that pace," he says, his smile a cool breeze, "and we'll be fine." His crew person hands him a steaming cup of soup, wafting up smells of rosemary and roasted tomato.

I pry open my faded '80s picnic cooler and scarf turkey cold cuts out of the pack. "Thirty seconds," Laz yells. *Where the hell did the minutes go?* Another loop, and my wobbly lawn chair feels like a boxing corner; the bell, the whistle—coming at me faster and faster.

It's now a hot noon, and my body is in rebellion. The giant latte I had for breakfast is rumbling in my gut like a washer. A full bonk is either on or coming. And I start to dislike the old man standing there with his smirk, his taunting cigarette, and his damn Dr. Pepper. I can't help thinking back to how he'd described Little's to me: "it's a good-old-timey backyard ultra—the kind your momma used to tell you about."

*Tweet!* The whistle glints between his lips. *God almighty.*

My trail shoes are thudding on the road now, skidding and thudding and skidding. When I get to the top of the hill, the old man's not there. I pause.

Under the arch, I scan the area... still no sign of him. So, I sneak behind the tents, expecting him to materialize in front of me. But he doesn't and I collapse into the plastic comfort of my chair—no more loops for me. The weight of five people leaves my body. My life, my dog, my wife, even stupid worries about the stupid political climate come flooding back like a warm shot of heroin.

---

Back in the car, my legs ached and my mind swirled. Ashamed to face Laz, I'd packed up and escaped like a criminal. Now, the road stretched up a hill toward the horizon, and the voice—the same one that convinced me to stop—was back. But the little bastard had changed his tune. *Why'd you quit?*

"Come on," I argued with it. I wasn't delusional. I wasn't here to win. These were real runners, semi-pro types. "I was here to write," I said out loud. "I had deadlines. Yes, I could have done another loop. So?"

*Why did you quit when you did, then?*

I picked at the question like a scab. Whatever the old man's test was, I'd most certainly failed. The winner would go thirty hours. Basically, all I'd done was show up.

I rolled down the windows and let the Tennessee air slap at my face. The scent of pine and fresh-tilled earth filled the car. There's something about the smell of the air you grew up with that reaches deep inside you. It seeps through the cracks and into the buried parts. Laz, I realized, had never said a word to me about running—at all—ever. If his creations weren't about running, then what?

A rush of acid crept up my esophagus. I knew why I'd quit. *I quit because it felt bad.* The thought hung in the air, heavy and silent, as raindrops began to tap and bounce and bead on the windshield. The sound was soft at first, then harder. *Did I back off like that with my writing too?*

Home in New York, I sleepwalked into Antoinette's and slouched into a chair beneath the *El Gran Houdini* poster. I scrolled through my emails and stopped when I came to one from Laz. I hesitated, hovering a finger just above the pad on my Surface Pro.

The PC was brand new—a gift from my wife to help me be more productive—but I left it sitting there. I'd clicked the message and was now pacing around the block, staring down the hill at the Hudson oozing by. "i'm a criminal," Laz wrote, "obsessed with winners and losers." In the email were two press passes—one for the 2023 Barkley and another for the 2023 Big's Backyard World Championship. "if you want to see how the big guns do it," he went on, "you won't find two races more different. man versus course and man versus himself. the barkley is a test of can you do it. the backyard is whether you will do it."

Relieved to find my computer still there, I wrote him back and said I was down, that as long as I wasn't running the Barkley, it should be a glorified camping trip.

"it'll be camping all right," Laz shot back, "with a stick in your eye."

# 4

# A Grueling, Grim, and Hazardous Event

**IN THE SIX MONTHS** leading up to the Barkley, we stayed in touch, first by email then on the phone. Then, in December, he lost his mother; in January, Big. He didn't talk about that much but mentioned more than once that he was 69 and already telling people he was 70. He wanted to prepare himself.

Around this time, he became more reflective, more willing to revisit old stories. He'd call me from the winding Tennessee backroads, his walking stick tapping a rhythm to keep pace with his thoughts. A blocked femoral artery in his left leg had ended his running career years ago. Now, he hoped to stave off an amputation by pumping as much blood to it as he could with long walks.

He gave information in trickles. Generally, he dodged anything personal and followed a track he was comfortable with—his early races, some bad behavior, and a long-held disdain for conformity. His curiosity was boundless—he was a self-taught drystone mason, sketch artist, amateur geologist, and jigsaw-puzzle enthusiast. But asking him anything biographical was like starting a windup toy. Give it a nudge, and it'd walk a straight line for five minutes, then wander off through a garden of its own tangents—from the number of Ritz crackers in a sleeve, to the creeping death of the emerald ash borer, to the three generations of highway guardrails.

So, I'd wait for the chance to wind it up again and return to the one subject he didn't seem much interested in—himself. I also began looking in the usual places, and eventually a picture began to take shape.

"He called me Pops and I called him Son," said veteran race director Bill Schultz. He remembers running with Gary Cantrell in the early '80s in a field house on a frigid January day. "Seven laps to the mile," he said with a fond ring of nostalgia. "On dirt. Hard, hard dirt. He looked like a hillbilly from Tennessee, ran in hospital scrubs, and smoked every chance he could get." But on the persona of Laz, Schultz shifted. "There's been a separation in my view," he said, lowering his tone. "The Gary we all knew is not really Gary anymore." When asked to describe Laz, he had a one-word answer: "P. T. Barnum."

If anyone knew the difference between Gary and Laz, it had to be Nick Marshall—a living legend in ultrarunning, he was also a former bookstore owner with an encyclopedic knowledge of the sport. I walked with the 70-year-old for some miles on a sweltering afternoon, around a pickleball court in New Jersey. He shuffled with a slight lean and spoke in a soft, tempered voice. But beyond the simple basics, he grew tight-lipped, shaking a head of wispy white hair and wrapping himself in a genteel smile. "Gary," he said, "was always a devious trickster."

Laz's first wife, Mary, wasn't surprised he'd created an alter ego. "He wanted everything to not be normal," she recalled. "Gary was the epitome of not normal. He had a frizzy afro of hair, smoked pot to go to sleep, and didn't want to interact with people. And when he did, he said weird shit, often at the worst times. But..." She paused, her voice softening. "He was really, really smart."

They'd met at the University of Tennessee, right before he was asked to leave. "We were pretty much stoners," she said with a laugh. "He never went to class. I think he made a zero point zero." She couldn't recall Gary ever wanting to organize anything other than a good time. He could be detached and unmovable, blanketed by his easygoing indifference. But she remembered the time they watched the film *Harold and Maude*. That had cracked something open.

They were newlyweds, living off campus in the sparse confines of The Sutherland Apartments, just across the street from the flickering lights of the Knoxville Drive-In. One weekend, *Harold and Maude* came to town, a movie whispered about, revered by stoners and oddballs. It was inevitable, then, that they'd sneak through a gap in the fence, stoned and curious. When they settled on the ground, drawing the small speaker between them, Gary's eyes locked on the screen.

The story followed a disaffected youth, Harold, who was constantly faking his own death. His only friend was 80-year-old Maude, a young soul as vibrant as he was morbid. For her, life was a nonstop adventure lived on her own quirky terms. But they shared the understanding that neither of them was considered normal. He drove a modified hearse for shock value while she stole cars to liberate trees from city sidewalks.

"Over the course of my life," Laz would muse to me on a walk, "I've been both of them." As to what part of him might be morose, Mary didn't flinch. "It was the tumor," she said, as if she were waiting for me to ask. Behind Gary's witty humor, life hadn't been an unbroken string of good times. Maybe that's why *Harold and Maude* stuck with him, a defiant laugh in the face of uncertainty. "Ask him about the tumor," she said. "That's what made him."

Though Laz and I had gotten comfortable enough to kid around, I felt it best to file that one away for the right time. Then again, there never seemed to be a right time with him to talk about anything other than his immediate interests.

"Why Lazarus Lake?" I dared one day.

"Well, I never felt obligated to sign the name given to me," he said from his daily walk, his voice suddenly drowned out by the thunder of a big rig roaring by. "I've gone by Mutant, GURM, Idiot." He chuckled when I asked why. "Because shortening Gary wasn't an option. 'Gare'—that just didn't sound right."

He made it all seem like the natural order of things, no explanations needed. Then, the windup toy was off again—to the Alluvial Plain—to the oldest rock in Alabama—to...

"Some say you've changed," I interjected. "That you're not really the same person you used to be." I could hear the *tap... tap...* of his walking stick, tapping against the pavement, rhythmic and slow, like he was measuring out the words he *wouldn't* say. I thought he might hang up, so I retreated to safe ground. "All I know," I offered gently, "is you started putting on races in 1979."

Another pause, longer this time, until finally his gravelly voice came through the line. "Well, I might have started before that."

---

Shelbyville in 1978 was still a quiet town, its streets canopied by pecan trees and its pastures full of sleek-coated Tennessee walking horses. Ordinary people called it home, the kind who got up at sunrise to work the pencil factory, went home to watch the world go to hell on the news, and shed honest tears for its salvation on Sundays. So, when the words "marathon" and "local" appeared in the same sentence, the news was met with slow nods and muttered questions.

The Horseshoe Mountain Runners were sketchy to begin with, an odd sight on the civilized roads of Bedford County, with their tight shorts, bare chests, and sweaty faces. But none stuck out more than the strange hippie figure often spotted running along the backroads, not just of Bedford County but all over the state—without socks. Most times, he had a white T-shirt over his head—the arms hanging over his ears, the rest of the shirt flowing out behind him as he ran. *The Shelbyville Sheik*, they called him—curly shoulder-length hair, bearded chin, always a bottle in hand with a duct-taped handle.

Word was he was a freaky college kid named Gary, who lived over by the Seventh-Day Adventists in that tiny house on the curve. And rumor had it, he smoked dope. But he also headed up the Horse Mountain Runners and had put on the 10K the year before that went over okay. But this Two-Bit Marathon?

He'd told them it would start in the city park on the edge of town, turn up Mountain Road, cross a ford, then come back over Horse Mountain. Entry was cheap—a mere twenty-five cents, two bits—offering local runners a shot at a marathon without having to drive hours to Chattanooga or Nashville.

Race day was everything local runners had hoped for—challenging, hilly, with stunning views of Bedford County—until they got lost.

The leaders checked their watches with frustrated eyes stinging with sweat. *Where was the damn finish line?* They'd been running too good for too long. *Something was off.* The park was nowhere in sight, neither was Shelbyville for that matter. And they were still in the hills!

Confused, they trudged on, marching and bonking till three miles later, they caught sight of the ball fields and a piece of tape stretched between a sign and a fence post. With hands on knees and singlets hanging wet and heavy, they waited for The Sheik to come in. Then, they'd demand answers.

Gary, who was running the race himself, got to the line slower than he'd hoped, and beneath a mess of tangly hair, he listened while the small but boisterous group hemmed and hawed. When they finally stopped talking, he just shrugged. "Precision is less important than having a flow and a logic," he said with a big-toothed grin. "The course we laid out just happened to be twenty-nine miles. We could have stopped three miles before and made you walk back, but I lack that inherent boundary that makes you do things the way they've always done it."

He waited for someone to prove him wrong—to argue that a fixed distance mattered more than the challenge itself. But it was clear his race hadn't gone over. "If you want to run for time," he said finally, "run on a track."

Gary felt more frustrated than disappointed when he got back to his 800-square-foot hovel on Church Road, fired up a joint, and stared at his map. They just didn't get it. Where was their sense of adventure? *The clones are around us*, he thought. *Now we are stuck facing the same PR on a cloned course. And for what, a shirt that makes billboards seem artistic?*

The 10Ks were everywhere now, and the half-marathons. Clones. All the same. The most interesting and challenging races, he thought, were the ones that made running feel alive. They were never standardized. The Redbank 8.24, the Firecracker Chase 9.27, the Old Hickory 11.2. Those races didn't just measure distance; they measured heart. Race directors, he believed, should hunt courses with "a little magic in them."

The Two-Bit was a fail, he had to admit, but the harder truth was his running was too. He'd told himself years before that if he couldn't find a way to break three hours in a marathon, he'd have to reevaluate. He exhaled, leaned back, and let the weed do its work. Soon, he drifted into a familiar daydream, the one he'd have to write down some day.

*Ah, there's my mark. 20 miles, only a 10K to go, and it's time to make my move. For the past five miles I've dogged de Castella's every step; now it's my turn to show the strong man what it's all about. Shifting into a high gear I surge past the famous Aussie, flashing a big grin as I go by.*

*Diggin deep into my reserves of energy, I fairly explode off every stride. Faster and faster with the cold air scaring my lungs and my legs screaming for relief, I gain satisfaction from hearing de Castella's labored breathing slowly receding behind me. Satisfied that I am in control, I relax after a sizzling 2:10 half-mile and allow him to struggle back into my draft...*

*Finally, we enter the Olympic Stadium. I'm in front, floating on long powerful strides; de Castella is behind me, raggedly struggling to maintain contact. There, with the entire world watching, I apply the coup de grace, blasting away from my opponent with a final surge of raw power and speed. As I cross the finish line my arms go up, fists clenched in the ecstasy of victory. Then, it is total collapse.*

When Gary eventually penned it, he'd finish with the cold reality of an Olympic dream fading into the haze. "Utterly spent, I stagger, gasping, up my driveway and lean on my old Camaro. Only a single neighbor mowing his lawn. Once again, I'm just the weird guy down the road."

In his kitchen, Gary raised his eyes back to his map and blew a line of smoke toward its colored lines. He hadn't been in town more than a few months when he bought it and decided to run every street. Highlighting new roads with an orange magic marker felt almost as good as running them. Soon, he got a county map, then three, taping them together till it looked "damn impressive," and he hung it like a piece of art above the kitchen table.

Not long after the Two-Bit, Gary was flipping through the newspaper on the table till he got to the sports page. Before he got there, a word caught his eye. It was mixed in with the usual garbage of cows causing traffic jams and thieves breaking into homes only to end up cleaning them. It was "ultramarathon." Soon, it seemed the word was everywhere. When his monthly subscription to *Runner's World* arrived, there were two articles on ultras. One highlighted the Comrades Marathon in South Africa, a 55-mile race that changed directions every year. The other, titled "Super-Lap," detailed a 72-mile race around Lake Tahoe. The words and pictures jumped off the page with bad, bold climbs and stretches of iconic scenery.

This crowd, they were rule-breakers. And both races favored the idea of courses as distinct within themselves. He found two on the East Coast, but they were serious drives, one in Miami, the other in Brooklyn. When he caught wind of the Stone Mountain 50 in Atlanta, he couldn't apply fast enough.

Smoke barreled out of his Dodge Hornet as he sped to the post office with his application, and two weeks later, a letter came back. He thumbed it open, brimming with excitement. But his eyes fell reading it. The race was cancelled, not enough interest, only four had shown the year before. Looking up at his marked-up map, the realization seemed inevitable—if he wanted to run an ultra, he'd have to build it.

He found part of the answer staring him in the face—the orange lines of his training routes. From that, he strung together a makeshift course, a figure eight with a defining narrow pinch in the middle like "a wasp's waist." He envisioned a tactician's race, one that forced choices of when to conserve, where to push, and what ground to give.

One weekend he and fellow Horse Mountain runner Henry Hulan were coming off a particularly hilly stretch of gravel when his friend ran a hand over his balding head and said, "Those aren't hills. Those are walls." Gary laughed. He liked the sound of that. A name for what those final stretches could be, and a good 10 miles on gravel would make things more... exciting. The Walls were in.

He set out in his Hornet to get the distance, the car sputtering and gasping over the hills. The odometer was reliable, but not much else. Back in Wartrace, his meter showed 41.2 miles. He'd double down on what he pulled at the Two-Bit; he'd call it an even 40.

With autumn came marathon season, and he was at every pre-race dinner, toting a 2-by-3-foot piece of posterboard he'd hand-lettered "Ultramarathon." He smiled and teased when runners squinted to read the details. "A grueling, grim, and hazardous event," it read. "A true test of willpower." Most chuckled, but by spring, twenty or so had agreed to give it a go; half were doctors. "You'd think, of all people," he'd joke, "they'd know better."

When May arrived, twelve showed up the day before, ready for whatever lay ahead. There was an easy camaraderie that night in the basement of the old hotel, a piano roaring while kegs of beer were passed around. There was laughter, conversation, and that tinged atmosphere that comes when you dare to celebrate before a challenge.

The start would be classic, simple, unassuming, with a dash of history. They'd line up at the old well house on Church Street, a single room made of wood, balanced on four red brick columns; and end at the Walking Horse Hotel, beside the grey sign commemorating Strolling Jim. Jim had been the state's first champion walking horse. Now, Gary was going to give a race in his honor—The Strolling Jim 40.

He kept the logistics simple, hoping to lose no more than a hundred dollars on the race. That way, he might be able to do it again next year. The entry fee was set at four bucks, and that included a chicken dinner provided by his new neighbor, Barry Barkley. "Gary wasn't interested in money," Mary remembered with some frustration. "That was part of the problem."

Race day saw runners plodding through the countryside, wildflowers scenting the air, gravel crunching underfoot. They ran up the hills and by the farms, often chased and charged by dogs. They jumped creeks and hit not one wall but several. Every five miles, they came to a water stop, so when they reached the seventh, they guzzled extra to get to the end. But when they spotted another one five miles later, the realization set in—there was an extra mile.

As for Gary's own race, the ultradistance didn't prove to be the boon to his running that he'd hoped for. He came in next to last, ten minutes behind his wife. But as an organizer, something clicked. The pre-race mood in the hotel carried over afterward, and he joined the other runners on the grass for a picnic. Come Sunday morning, they were still perched on the hotel porch, drunk, watching Wartrace families stare back at them from car windows on their way to church. This time there were no complaints about his shenanigans; the ultrarunning crowd, it seemed, *got* whatever he was about.

In the following years, when he took to spray-painting what he called "little motivational messages" on the roads, they loved it. The leaders would be the first to see; just getting their legs for the first climb, the words would appear, "This is not a hill." And when they reached a bigger incline, one that strained legs and tightened chests, there was, "My 86-year-old grandmother wouldn't walk here." It wasn't until they faced a truly punishing grade, one that felt as if it would never end, that they came to the final note. "This," it read, "is a hill."

Despite the quirkiness of the event, or maybe because of it, the locals embraced it. They looked on in wonder at runners, some stripped down to almost nothing, bathing in the town fountain. They cheered by the well house like they were watching something special, something uniquely their own.

Standing on the porch of the hotel after that first Strolling Jim, Gary never could've imagined that forty-five years later, it would still be going on. He was just 24.

# 5

# Spirit of a Wild Thing

**"TO RUN IT, YOU'D HAVE TO BE AN IDIOT!"**

In September of 1981, twelve huddled in the early dark by an old clapboard church deep inside Noblitt Hollow. They shifted like nervous specters in the headlights of an idling truck, waiting. Each runner had paid five dollars to be here but had gotten it back. Gary returned the fee "just for showing."

His new creation he was calling the Idiots Run and warned, "If you are seeking a race bordering on insanity, then this is the run for you." He'd laid out 37 hills over a punishing 76 miles of rock-strewn roads and "spiced" it with a couple of creeks. To take it on, he said, "you'd have to be an idiot."

Around five a.m., he stepped forward, smiling while he kept the runners on edge. He stared at his watch, and they fidgeted. A warm breeze blew in, heavy with the scent of dew, and at exactly 5:04, Gary's eyes lit up with excitement. "Okay, go." And they moved—into the dark, miles from anywhere.

By mile two, several were lost. Jay Birmingham was in the lead group and remembers "passing the first turn in pitch dark." They doubled back, trying to find their way to the course, till a black Dodge Charger gurgled up to them. It was Gary's friend Barry Barkley, in someone else's car, crewing for the frontrunners. "He was exactly what I expected coming to Tennessee," said Birmingham. "Dark, unpolished, and wore all black like Johnny Cash. He just told us to take the next left." Birmingham, a fast speaker, slowed for a second. "Yeah, that's all I remember him saying—the whole race."

At the end of the day, only five returned; the rest were still scattered across the Tennessee hills. David Kerrick led from the get-go, but with just six miles left, he was in a heap on the side of the road, in last place, so thoroughly whipped he couldn't move another step. John Wallis had come over a series of hills Gary had said was part of the Strolling Jim course, The Walls, but from the opposite, more diabolical direction. He now lay on the gravel, beneath a blanket of stars, vomiting.

Birmingham was the first one back to the church and lay sprawled out on the grass. A track coach from Florida, he'd run across the United States the year before. And in the weeks leading up to the Idiots Run, he'd become the second ever to finish a notorious route across Death Valley that would later become Badwater. "I was pretty tired," he remembered about his finish at the Idiots Run, "but more relieved that I'd gotten in before dark."

He stayed on Gary's floor for two nights but couldn't remember any conversations with him other than his first words. "I don't have any blankets. I hope you brought some." But he recalled with vivid precision his award for winning. Gary presented him with twelve acrylic boxes. "They were well-made," clear, and inside each rested a pair of Gary's old, smelly running shoes. Each runner would get one. Birmingham chose the red Nike flats.

If the illusion that Gary might become a great ultrarunner was beginning to fade, so too was the idea that he could run and direct at the same time. Suffering in the heat, his legs throbbing, he opted for a quick joint to dull the pain. He'd never tried it before and never would again. It focused his mind on the agony even more. If anything, it was "a performance de-enhancer." He quit before mile 50.

While he'd laid the course out with his running ambitions in mind, it proved to be at the far spectrum of his capabilities—more a test of what some of the best regional runners were capable of. He watched them with detached admiration when they collapsed in the church yard. Still, as he saw it, the first Idiots Run was an unmitigated success.

His personal life was another matter.

---

Sitting alone in an empty house one cold afternoon after the race, Gary punched a hole through the wall of the living room. He had far too much time now to dwell on his "problems" and a life that felt like it was coming apart at the seams. The usual ways to break the spell: frenetic activity and planning, the self-medication of substances, the pure physical exertion of running—nothing could stop the slide. He could feel it—he was spiraling out of control. He got in his car and sped off.

There had been signs the breakup was coming. Gary and Mary's plan had been simple—he was going to be a nurse, she a physical therapist. Then, he changed his mind, finishing college and taking a job at Precision International as an accountant. He cut his hair, kept his fingernails immaculate, and wore a tie.

No one was more surprised than Mary. She was a neat freak. He couldn't care less. "Household chores were an irritant," she'd remember. Once, she tried to wait him out, to see how long he'd go without cleaning up after himself. She gave up after a week. "I couldn't take it," she said, but felt the main problem was that she'd grown up and he hadn't. "He just didn't have any ambition."

They'd separated in the spring. Now the divorce had become an annulment. He peeled open a letter full of probing personal questions by the church, ones he wasn't prepared to answer. He was also alone for the first time since he was nineteen. And with no races to distract his mind, the empty house had become a prison.

Too much time to reflect had never served him well. Even as a child he'd struggled with negative emotions. They'd swirl up, grow, and spill out over trivial things. He was never sure why the normal teenage angst weighed on him more than others. Or if it did, how everyone else hid it. But an old, familiar feeling threatened to pull him down—that he was a failure.

Trees passed by in a blur of browns and yellows as Gary barreled toward Tullahoma. He drove by the family house, then his old high school, and pulled into the small parking lot of Trinity Church. He cracked a window to smoke. Going to need help this time—he could feel it. Still, talking to someone was only so much relief. It might let some of the internal pressure out, but it couldn't stop the whirlpool sucking him down. People never drown splashing about in terror. They drown from exhaustion, quietly slipping under the surface.

Outside the church, Gary fiddled with a cigarette, looking up at the greying winter clouds, and thought about what to say. It wasn't that Pastor Smith was an old friend; they'd barely interacted when Gary was growing up in Tullahoma. But he knew him to be a trusted advisor and confidant to others—always distinguished, collar on, approachable. He also knew he would offer more than just platitudes.

Gary shifted inside the doors. Why was it all churches smelled the same? He found Pastor Smith sitting in his office. He had that same warm expression he always had—calm, caring eyes, soft voice. He listened while Gary explained, his bald forehead nodding with understanding. “Pastor,” Gary said finally, “I really think I’m losing it.”

Smith suggested he talk with a man named Murphy Thomas. *A head doctor!* Gary never thought he would go for that. But desperate times called for desperate measures.

Gary spent several days with Murphy, talking over a wide range of issues. And he realized something—the world is full of good advice. And the world is full of people who need to hear it. But for good advice to take effect, the right thing has to be said at the right time and for someone ready to listen. He must have been ready the day that Murphy said it, because it was like being thrown a life preserver. “You cannot control what happens,” he told him, looking Gary in the eyes. “But you can control how you respond. You cannot control what other people do, but you can control how it affects you. No one else can make you mad, or sad, or happy. You do that yourself.”

Everything didn’t change overnight, but he’d always look back at this as a turning point in his life. The hold of spiraling negative emotions was broken once and for all. Rock Bottom had been reached, and the rebound had begun—for Gary, it would be like a superball hitting a concrete floor.

Ultras began to make sense in a different way. Suffering didn’t have to be meaningless—it could be what you needed to see things more clearly. More than just added distance, they presented the chance to find the limits of one’s will. “There are aches and pains and outright injuries, bruised and bloody feet,” he’d write for *Ultrarunning* magazine. “There is exhaustion and collapse. But there is also the spirit of a wild thing. A fierce, proud, independent inner toughness. A sense of greatness, invincibility. The conviction that one can withstand anything... the goal is to reach that frontier.”

The next year, he promised, anyone who dared enter the Idiots Run would find exactly that. He threw in more hills, stretched the course to 108.6 miles, and set the start in front of a 200-year-old log cabin. This race would be something altogether different, an "authentic Southern experience," and truly impossible.

*So... who was up for it?* As it turned out, not who he expected.

---

Two plaques hung on the wall of Peter Riegel's office at Battelle Memorial Institute—a mechanical engineering degree from Purdue and a master's from Villanova. Tucked inside a drawer somewhere he also had patents for a non-drip nozzle for gas station hoses and an exhaust regulator valve for scuba gear. But it was his endurance predictor formula that made him a name in track and field.

He introduced his breakthrough in *Runner's World* in 1977 as "a simple formula for comparing relative performances at different distances." In short, it predicted your finish time for one distance based on your performance at another. By 1981, he'd published it again in *American Scientist.* Science, numbers, an understanding of human capacity through study—this was Riegel's world.

But in 1982, the Columbus, Ohio, native was captivated by the unpredictability of what Gary Cantrell was doing in Tennessee. And the idea of trying his formula on the Idiots Run—a course spread over varied terrain that offered more punishment than reward—was alluring. The drive, however, would be a slog. So, when Riegel's friends Mary Urbanek and Gene Dillahunty offered not only to crew him but to fly them all down to Tennessee, he was over the moon.

Riegel had run Strolling Jim earlier in the year and come away impressed by Cantrell. The voice on the phone had been gruff, but in person, he struck him as more of a "happy young mountain man." Gary had a sharp wit, he liked that, and he showed a genuine care for the runner's experience. Not everyone would agree with that, but Riegel felt he'd been a welcome guest.

He studied the map anxiously on the plane, and it became clear what Gary had done. He'd included every possible hill in three counties. Nineteen major climbs and fifty minor ones. Riegel, at 47, felt a rise in his throat. He'd never run more than 50 miles. This was twice that, and he wasn't sure his formula would be accurate in such a race. But looking over the topo map, one thing was clear: It was going to be a beast of a run.

On the ground in Tennessee, a disarming reality sank in. The meet-up spot was not the church he'd read about the year before. Instead, it was now a shack at the top of Noblitt Hollow, land granted to the original Noblitt back in the 1700s for services rendered during the Revolutionary War. The family never left. "The things we saw," one handler (crew) would write, "were from an era long since gone."

Riegel's crew pulled up a rocky driveway, tires spitting pebbles, till a crooked porch came into view. Lounging beneath it in the shade was a pack of dogs, and they were now coming toward the car. "They won't hurt you," said an old man sitting under a tree, sipping a clear liquid in a clear mason jar.

When Gary sputtered up in a green Datsun, he led them on a tour of the course. Riegel watched intently as rough hills, steep and relentless, rolled by—each one more daunting than the last. And the mood among his crew grew somber. At one point, Gary slammed on the brakes, bringing the caravan to a sudden halt. He jumped out with a wild glare and hoisted a six-foot king snake over his head and yelled, "If anyone kills one of these, you're automatically disqualified!"

---

Gary got a kick out of it—easing them down a series of forgotten roads. He wished he could see their faces up close when they forded Flat Creek. He took them up to Chestnut Hill, to the old general store, and its intersection of gravel roads. The pavers hadn't gotten there at least—but they were coming.

Back at the Noblitt place, he lit a large fire in a stone pit and eyed the runners. The Noblitts brought out lawn chairs and whiskey. Marvin Skagerberg of New York caught Gary's eye. He'd flown first to Cincinnati to save money, but a sports car was all they had available at the rental office. Gary grinned when it scraped the large rock coming up the driveway. "That's Oil Pan Rock," he told Marvin. "And the starting line for the run." Now, the New Yorker was sitting across the fire, looking on in horror while a pup "not a year old" scarfed up chicken bones till its belly was bulging.

Marvin had no crew, so Gary lined him up with one of the Noblitt brothers. Dressed in overalls and chewing tobacco, he was talkative and familiar with every twist and turn of the local roads. At least Marvin wouldn't get lost.

The mood brightened when Barry arrived. He brought with him chickens from the Tyson plant where he worked. You could always count on Barry. He lived three doors down from Gary, and the two had bonded right away, drinking beer and playing Monopoly, Risk, Booray. A hippie, stoner type, Barry had gotten into some trouble back in Arkansas. Given the choice between jail and Vietnam, he chose the latter and came back a little rough around the edges. "He had to be de-burred by life," Gary would say, smoothed over "like a jagged piece of shrapnel."

When night fell, the firelight made faces seem devilish—none more so than Gary's as he sized up the field. "I'm an alien observer," he joked, "sent here to find if the development of intelligent life is possible on

Earth." Though he'd comped half of the runners the reduced three-dollar entrance fee and given others travel money, he was thrilled. He'd built it, and they'd come. "If a buzzard starts circling you," he said with mock seriousness, "drop out of the race."

When the conversations died away, his mood shifted. He looked around at the mix of backgrounds and took a snapshot in his mind. He didn't say anything to anyone, but the quiet hum of progress was coming for all this. The State of Tennessee, in its quest for modernization, was launching a crusade against the old gravel roads, paving the way, literally, for the rise of larger, corporate supermarkets. And the country stores, relics of a slower time, would begin to vanish. "You think things are timeless when you see them," Gary mused to himself.

The stores were the community hubs, with the old folks playing checkers in the back, and everything for sale from gasoline to feed and seed. Gary knew all of them in the county and had an account at several. On a run, he'd stop in for water or a candy bar, the wood floor creaking under his steps. In the winter, when he came in dressed like a mummy, he'd warm himself by a potbellied stove in the corner, a hole where the handle went glowing red. The smell of burning coal lingered on his clothes for days. Like the Noblitts, they were a part of a disappearing Appalachia, one you'd never miss unless you first knew it was there.

---

The next morning, the sun rose bright and clear on Oil Pan Rock. A daytime start this year to keep the Idiots from getting lost. A nod from Gary and the eldest Noblitt fired off a hogleg—a double-barreled sawed-off shotgun—and they were off.

Midday, a scorching heat descended on the Idiots, and the air grew thick with the stench of dung and tobacco spit soaking into the dust. But Riegel couldn't help but take in the beauty of it all: the rolling hills, the silence broken only by the occasional rustle of corn stalks. "It's one of the most beautiful places I've ever run," he'd say. A breathtaking, brutal kind of beauty. One that might break him, but if it did, at least he'd be in God's own backyard.

Then came a steep hill, which Gary had warned loomed "three-quarters of a mile straight up, maximum grade imaginable." Flat Creek followed, which now seemed like a small river. Most forded it barefoot or, in one case, in flip-flops.

Marvin prepared for the heat and the creeks by keeping a second pair of shoes on ice. The Noblitt man, who had been good about helping Marvin with his gear and supplies, took them out of the cooler and handed them to him with a smile. But when dusk came with a chorus of crickets, the Noblitt held him back. "Wait a minute, Marv," he said, narrowing an eye. "We're going into the night here now. If anybody takes exception or seems to be upset with you being here, just relax—I'll take care of it." Glinting between the seats in the fading light was "a great big .45 pistol."

Ray Krolewicz, Riegel's predicted favorite, had no such protector. "At dark, a guy came out with a big-ass tractor," he remembers with unfiltered clarity. "It had a thresher or some kind of chopping device. And he came boring up on me. So, I went faster. And he went faster. I went into a field. He went into the field. Finally, I got behind a tree and yelled, 'Come on, you bastard, tear up your blades.'"

Riegel, meanwhile, running without a headlamp, saw constellations he hadn't seen since he was a boy. The night was eerie yet serene. No city lights, the stars bright above, the Milky Way a grand stripe across the void. He was almost lost in the vision when he noticed a glow up ahead, and the silhouette of man beside it. Could be a race official, he thought, and hailed him down. He got closer until, under the lamp, he made out a gaunt, time-beaten soul. The ghostly figure said nothing, just turned his head when the runner passed.

It was all surreal but even-paced at least, until Riegel hit Foster Hill. It went up forever, then some more—the steepest climb he'd seen yet. His legs burned and bitched. At the top, he found a sheet of paper hanging from a branch by a string—Gary's unmanned checkpoint. At the top of the page was a message, "Do it yourself." Riegel signed it and played with a thought. Gary had explained that he could quit here if he had to and still get credit for a finish. It was tempting, but he'd come for the whole experience—and his two handlers had been so diligent—he couldn't just quit because he felt like death.

He pushed on but soon felt his "tide going out." His feet were killing him. These weren't the small, smoothed gravel stones of most places, but "big, one-inch rocks with points like pyramids." Weary and weaving, he couldn't go any farther without sleep.

In the yard of a church, he shivered into some extra clothes and rolled up in his sleeping bag. *Maybe I'm not meant to finish*, he thought fleetingly. *No. Keep moving. Just keep moving.* But he slept. Forty-five minutes. Up again—walking mostly, but moving.

He reached the Walls, the dreaded Walls, and felt as if his cork had been pulled. He slept again, this time on the side of the road beneath a large oak. The sight of the sun was a boost, and one of his crew walked with him. That helped too. But the last stretch to Oil Pan Rock became a death march. He wondered what the country folk thought seeing such an "apathetic shamble" inching up the hill.

When he finally placed his foot on the rock, and it was over, a Noblitt boy came running up. Riegel's crew poured champagne over his head. Soaked, he found a place in the shade to lie down and soon drifted off, "stiff, uninjured, tired, and on cloud nine."

Riegel would write a three-page essay for *Ultrarunning* on his experience and title it "Dear Dad: The Idiots Run." Moved by the wildness and unpredictability of what the race offered, he worked up an elevation profile of the course and suggested ways to make the course even more difficult. Gary was thrilled, declaring the new layout the "perfect loop."

Riegel would go on to measure the marathon courses for the US-hosted Olympics in '84 and '96 and found *Measurement News*, an official newsletter for USA Track & Field. But he would never again attempt a race as long as the Idiots Run. It took him 29 hours, 26 minutes to finish, and that stuck with him. While his predictor suggested he would do much better, his gut feeling was he'd probably collapse somewhere along the way. Then again, the more he thought about it, the more he realized there was something about the whole experience that was... just beyond numbers.

# 6

# Where Were You When It Got Dark?

**ALMOST SPRING, 1985**—and Gary stood on the porch by the Corinthian columns, smoking and pondering his now unrecognizable life. He peeked through the small window by the door. The light was out. Maybe the boy was finally asleep. It was hard to believe Case was already two and growing like a weed. Harder still to believe was they had another one on the way.

Gary had met Sandra Eatherly four years before, spotted her in the front of an accounting class. She was cute in a down-home, feisty sort of way, and he introduced himself by making goofy faces from the back—tongue out, eyes crossed. Over the next few months, he kept asking her out for beer. She told him *no* a dozen times. Finally, she caved. "You never stop," she said, grinning.

He smiled back. "You're not wrong."

Inside his rusty Datsun, she frowned out the window while he snapped open two cans of beer. Yet, he had a way, and they soon married. In '82, she delivered their first child while wearing one of Gary's race T-shirts. She gave birth at home, as she would all her children, but preferred not to in their current house. "It was haunted."

Gary took a final drag, stamped out the cigarette under his heel, and lit another. Not having a calendar full of races had him feeling unmoored. Strolling Jim was all he had left. His Nick Marshall 24-hour track run, started in 1979, had played out. The Idiots Run was buried under black waves of asphalt in '84. And his attempts to start a race across Tennessee hadn't caught on either.

He tried going it alone—left out of West Memphis and crept onto the interstate bridge at three a.m. He made 40 miles a day, retreating to dingy motels at night to recover. It took him six days to get to Lawrenceburg, where he limped into an old general store with clapboard siding to find Time Pilot sitting in the back. He and his buddy Rick had reverse engineered the arcade game. Rick was good at things like that, analytical, could take a problem apart. Rick also presented himself well, always, and Gary tried to emulate that.

In Lawrenceburg, a local hero had seven of the top 10 scores, so Gary threw up an impossible number. He imagined the kid crying when he came in and saw "GRM" at the top, two million points ahead of him. The initials came from "Gurm," something Sandra liked to call him sometimes—one of those nicknames that didn't mean much but stuck anyway. But only when she was happy. And she wasn't happy. For a year he'd been away from home for work, just back on the weekends. Now, he was taking his vacation for *this*?

Gary trudged on anyway, debating whether to stop. *Maybe she was right.* Three days later, he took a ride to Sparta. There, he called her to come get him. From now on, his adventures would have to involve family or be limited to weekends.

Now, Gary was looking up at the portico balcony with its crisscross balustrade railing. Despite the chipping paint and wood rot, he had to admire the place. Fourteen fireplaces, a cellar you could put an army in, and a raised limestone foundation—he was living in a mansion.

Beech Hall sat on a majestic bluff overlooking a 265-acre yard and had once served mayors and senators. The Cantrells, however, were living in it for $160 a month—"and it was a rip-off at that." When the wind pierced through cracks in the walls in winter, Gary and Sandra would sleep with Case squeezed between them to keep warm. The only running water was in a little room tacked onto the back, and they heated water on the stove for baths in a washtub. Though Gary wasn't a believer in ghosts, he admitted the house had all the signs of a haunting—pipes clanking, doors opening and closing on their own, and mysterious footsteps on the creaky floorboards.

Gary strolled down the curved gravel driveway to a long, stone retaining wall. When he kneeled to squint at it in the dark, his knee clicked and crackled like pebbles in a can. Just 30 years old, he'd already accumulated enough miles to have it scoped. Looking back at the house, glowing grey under the moon, he thought it would one day be a pile of timbers. This limestone fence, though, built without mortar, could be here another 200 years. Growth and progress, he mused, didn't always go hand in hand.

That was evident even in ultrarunning. While he was glad to see the sport finally garnering media attention, he couldn't help but feel something was lost. "There was a time when you knew everyone at a race," he'd complain. "If you didn't know them, you knew someone that knew them. Now, I might not know anyone." Many of the newcomers struck him as faddists with a dress code, trendy—and he was allergic to trendy.

The trail ultras were suddenly IT and drawing crowds. Hundred-milers like Western States, Wasatch, Leadville—all offered epic climbs and challenged one another for the title of "the toughest race." Gary didn't want to be overly critical, but the times these runners were bragging about—they just didn't make sense; they were too fast. Were they really putting up these numbers on rugged trails?

One problem he couldn't ignore was pacers. Pacing had never been a part of ultrarunning till the trail boom. He assumed this new wave of runners must not come from a competitive background. It was an unspoken rule of competition—you ran on your own. Add to it plush aid stations, and runners were virtually nurtured to the finish.

The sport was also becoming too self-important, too humorless. "When we get that magic moment in the sun," he teased in one of his columns for *Ultrarunning*, "and the TV camera focuses in on us, the microphone held to our mouth, just remember what the viewers are seeing. A grown adult who has cut the toes off $100 shoes, put band aids on his nipples, and smeared Vaseline between his legs in order to run into a state of total physical and mental destruction."

When he got blowback for that, he bristled. For all the talk about perceived limits, what he saw was a lot of talented runners lining up races like cans to kick over—running on muscle memory. Running safe 100s. Essentially afraid of failing. *Failure had to hurt.*

Besides, "these were footpaths." When he thought of trails, he pictured the kind he and Karl "Raw Dog" Henn used to hike in the Boy Scouts. Karl had always been the closest thing Gary ever had to a best friend. When Gary was flunking out of the University of Tennessee in '73, the two hiked in Morgan State Forest, up and around Frozen Head above the prison. The wilderness was immense, brooding, defiant. They'd talked about it even then, about one day hiking all the way around the perimeter. It would be a mammoth undertaking some weekend. That weekend just never came around.

In '77, Gary had heard like everybody else that James Earl Ray had escaped out of there. The assassin of Martin Luther King, Jr. was caught 54 hours later, shivering under a pile of damp leaves. He'd managed only eight miles against the Fifth Wall. Living in Memphis at the time, Gary mocked Ray with his buddies. "I could run 100 miles in that much time," he'd say with a shit-eating grin. He and Karl joked about it too. Deep down, though, they both knew better.

The fence glistened under the moonlight, and Gary studied it with amazement. It wasn't even leaning. The builders could have used mortar—it would have been easier. Instead, they'd chosen the harder path, fitting each stone just so. And here it stood. He ran a hand over the stones, a thought rolling over fast in his mind. *Frozen Head, the old plan, to assault the entire perimeter—almost a marathon in distance...*

Gary was back up the driveway in a sprint. Inside, he lit a kerosene lamp and set it on the table. It whined softly beside him while he spread out a topographical map. Morgan State Forest—the Boundary Trail. Gary ran his fingers over contour lines so thick, so bunched together, "they looked like shading"—steep places that said *do not come here*.

The next minute he was on the faded rotary-dial phone. "Karl?"

---

*"I didn't create it. I discovered it..."*

When they arrived in Frozen Head in the summer of 1985, Gary and Karl walked into a small trailer. That was new. Inside, the rangers sipped steaming hot coffee and laughed—the pair's idea of attempting the Boundary Trail was pure foolishness. Besides, there had been others, and every time they'd end up going out to rescue them.

Gary wouldn't relent. They had nothing to worry about, he said. They were both highly skilled woodsmen.

Staring at the first climb up Bird Mountain, blowdowns littered the switchbacks every fifty feet, big ones—"four or five feet thick." Weeds and brush rose chest high, and the trails were so neglected, the only way you knew you were on them was if you weren't slipping down the hill. The two had to continuously pull out the map to reassure themselves that they weren't lost.

Soon, the sky ripped open without warning and unleashed a torrent of rain, and the pair slowed to a standstill. They bushwhacked their way forward till they came to a landslide—the path that was there a minute ago had disappeared into raw earth. They crawled over it, slipping and sliding on loose shale, saw briars clawing at them from long, spindly arms.

After ten hours they'd covered only seven and a half miles, and Gary couldn't stop thinking about it. Finally, when they made camp at Coffin Springs, he said it. "What a fucker of a race this would be."

Karl cut his eyes back at him. "No, Gary," he declared. "You'll kill somebody."

Gary looked up through fat droplets of rain at the gnarled peaks, looming steep, one after the other, the gorges cut between them roaring with fast-flowing water. Remnants of coal mines dotted the slopes: dynamite shacks, rusting equipment, and lumps of coal—all sitting defeated by this forest. It was the land that time forgot, eroded by millions of years into "the perfect course."

Any race worthy of it, Gary thought, would have to match it—unpredictable, punishing, absurd, on the very edge of the possible. The kind of crucible that belonged on a day like April Fool's where runners would be called "penitents," the slowest among them given Bib #1, and the whole thing would have to start with, of course, a cigarette. Frozen Head would force runners to adapt. It would demand endurance, planning, and woodsmanship. Failure would be guaranteed, and success would be relative, defined only on personal terms.

And Gary would make it Raw Dog's idea. In the future, any course changes would be blamed on him as well.

Most wild places Gary had hiked as a boy were now full of roads and parking lots. But Out Here, the land was still feral, reliable in a way that made him think of Barry. The man who never missed a race, always bringing the chickens. *They were one and the same*, Gary thought. *Thorny on the outside, but worth getting to know.*

The next year, he'd unleash the Barkley Marathons on thirteen runners.

Until that point, Gary Cantrell had been known only by a fringe family of ultrarunners in the East—the smoking runner and the writer of clever columns. But when no one finished his new creation the first year, in 1986—or the year after—endurance junkies, expert orienteers, and military specialists from around the world began to take notice.

They pilgrimaged to Frozen Head from Switzerland and Germany and Russia. Gary observed them obsessively—how they failed, why they failed, where they succeeded. He incorporated ideas from the runners who got it and also probed them. "Where were you when it got dark?" he'd ask eagerly, then tweak the start time so next year he'd have them where he wanted them and when he wanted them there.

By the time I arrived in 2023, the Barkley was widely regarded as the toughest footrace in the world. Notorious enough for me to secure an article with *The New York Times*. But they were more interested in its architect, who'd transformed into his own creation—Lazarus Lake—a figure as obscured by the fog of Frozen Head as by the smoke of his cigarette. So was I.

# 7

# Make Peace with Your God

**IT STARTED AS A COUGH,** or... maybe a sneeze. Something in the night air of Frozen Head pierced the uneasy quiet of camp. I sat up quickly, heart thumping, imagining the conch. But it was only the wind, cutting through the hills, stirring something metallic in the distance. Around three a.m., I was sure I heard it again. I bolted upright and peered through the frosty SUV window at the Jeep next to me. Photographer Mike Trimpe had blown his nose and was looking over at me from under a small reading light.

The night dragged on like this—false alarms scraping at nerves, nerves frayed like wire—every sigh, sneeze, cough, gust of wind, tent rustling, van squeaking was a conch.

Then, just as the grey light of morning was warming me into a peaceful doze, a low, mournful bellow echoed through the trees then trailed off. I pushed myself up and looked over at Mike. *It must be.* His camera was already around his neck.

Camp came alive like a disturbed anthill. Crews scurried out of vans and tents, carrying gear, lighting cook stoves, and running down lists with their runners. By the time I shuffled into the cold, biting air, the smell of sausage and potato soup was wafting into my nostrils.

For those who'd made peace with uncertainty, the night had passed with relative ease. But for the rest of us it was ten hours of hell. A piercing wind lashed the camp all night, frigid and restless, finding its way into my SUV with frightening ease. Laz once referred to Frozen Head as Icehouse Delirium. That seemed about right.

Layered up, I made my way toward Kowalski Manor, the large white tarp that served as a makeshift headquarters. Along the way, I passed runners shifting foot to foot, hands buried deep in their pockets, mumbling to their crews. Others stayed hidden in their tents, peeking out with red, agitated eyes. A few jogged the length of the pavement, trying to fend off the cold or maybe just clear their heads.

Laz, meanwhile, was standing at the edge of the tarp, a thin wisp of smoke curling up from his fingertips. There was no rush in him, just stillness, his shiny eyes locked on the first victims approaching now to get their race watches. And for a second, you could see it: a glint of anticipation and devilishness, the kind that comes from carefully laying a trap, then lying in wait to see who springs it.

Inside Kowalski Manor, a large box sat on the picnic table, center stage. It held dozens of smaller white boxes waiting to be chosen. He didn't hand them out, no, the runner had to reach in and choose their fate. Since Laz allowed no GPS, phones, or electronic devices, he bought cheap Walmart watches for the runners, ten bucks a pop. He then set them to tick down to the secret start time that no one knew but him.

This year, by chance or fate, Walmart had been one watch short, so he picked up the next cheapest one—a godforsaken touchscreen. Amidst the briars and treacherous footing, it would be a nightmare to deal with the infinite misdirection of menus. Which unfortunate soul would it be?

Karel Sabbe had the best odds. The Belgian dentist was first to arrive and had almost Shakespearean features—tall, a tight-trim beard, almond eyes, and an angular face. He reached a hand into the box, and those gathered around seemed to hold their breath. Last year, he'd come close, closer than anyone in five years to finishing. He was on loop four when he lost his brain and was brought back in a police car. This time, he was already battling food poisoning from the plane ride over. *Surely he wouldn't get it.*

Keith Dunn, the Barkley Twitter man, seemed to be thinking the same thing. He glanced at me with a twitch of his eyebrow and giggled under his breath, "That would be so cruel."

Keith was a man of many interests. A private attorney for the government, he lived outside DC, was head usher at the Kennedy Center on weekends, and was a devout Phish fan who wore light pink hair. Once, when interviewing for a promotion, he made it clear that he would be in Frozen Head every spring, or he would consider other options. He was surprised to get in the Barkley in 2005. Defeated after two books, he took Quitter's Road, a jeep trial that led back to camp. "I was as cold as I've been in my lifetime," he'd say, and after returning to camp, he sat in the showers for a half hour, hot water pouring over him.

His dream was to finish one loop. Laz gave him two more tries, but he never made it. Instead, he became head of communications at the Barkley, the only link between the race and the outside world. "Most years I want the course to win," he confessed to me, one side of his mouth twisting up. It was easy to see he fit in well here—a dry wit and the practiced ease of someone at home with irreverence.

He looked on now like a smirking bird of prey as Karel took the small white box without ceremony and started back to his tent. "Open it up!" Laz said with a wide grin. The dentist paused, thumbed at it, and raised the watch. Just the normal dud.

Joe McConaughy half expected to draw the sucker watch. He was finally in the race after five years on the Weight List, and perhaps the watch had been planned for him all along. He rubbed his chilled hands together and hoped for the best.

"Maybe you'll get the lucky touchscreen," Larry teased, a barrel-chested volunteer from Iowa. Along with Keith, he was part of what some called the Inner Circle—a title they seemed to wear lightly but with a certain understanding that they were gatekeepers of a sort, each with their own role. Larry was the enforcer of the pack, not afraid of confrontation, but softened and reined in by his fondness for friends.

*Ohhh*, moaned the Inner Circle, a Greek chorus in perfect unison—Joe had dodged the bullet.

"Has anyone seen John?" asked Naresh Kumar. "We're at T-minus twenty minutes to Cigarette Launch." No one had to ask which John. John Kelly was the last one to finish the Barkley, back in 2017. *Nope,* nobody had seen him. Half the field now had their watches, yet the dud remained.

Naresh was Laz's Mr. Fix It, a tech wiz and an integral part of the Circle. From Chennai, India, he greeted everyone with the same bright-eyed smile. He was tall, thin, soft in demeanor, and gave you his undivided attention. He exuded a palpable feeling that if you were at the Barkley, you were family.

Then there was Bad Mike Dobies, always ready with a jab. His sarcasm cut clean and sharp. While most of us were shuffling in place, trying to stay warm, he was perched at the picnic table in shorts, his knees thick and red, as he looked through tiny glasses at a computer screen—the data man. You had to get to know Bad Mike. But here, it seemed, you had to get to know them all. It was a strange initiation, and one that didn't come with a guidebook.

The night before, however, The Circle surprised me. We were sheltering from the wind inside Kowalski Manor when I noticed them passing a phone around and speaking in hushed tones. There was a weight to their movements, as if they were deciding something important. They stole glances in my direction, perhaps wary of "the writer guy." But when they handed me the phone, I felt the tide shift. A small gesture of trust.

I recognized the runner on the screen immediately, a high-profile Barkley veteran. Yet here he was, grinning in a selfie, standing brazenly in front of the gate. Posting it to social media was a rookie move. It was a Barkley faux pas of the highest order. It could send ripples online through the fanbase and alert the world that the Barkley was about to start. Like a *Fight Club* in the woods, rule number one was tell no one. I'd held onto the date with some amount of pride and thought for sure Laz would disqualify this runner on the spot.

The Inner Circle, however, moved differently. Most had run here before, and they knew what it took just to make it to Frozen Head. They debated amongst themselves, rubbing their chins, passing the phone back and forth, each weighing the risks. Their caution made sense—a slip-up could invite spectators, or worse, park rangers. The course crossed into protected areas, and one wrong move could jeopardize the race. The tension grew thick till after a few beats of silence, one of them spoke, his voice low but sure. "Don't let Laz see it."

Eighteen watches left now, and a young woman was holding her small box. *Open it!* the Chorus clamored. *Ohhh*... and their shoulders fell. "Best odds were with the first watch," Laz speculated, nods echoing all around. "But wouldn't you feel doomed if you got it?"

"At least you'd know the inevitable was going to happen," said Keith, and Laz erupted—a full-bellied, no signals blocked, pure explosion of laughter. When that receded, Laz shrugged and said casually, "Most of them are doomed anyway."

Next was Harvey Lewis. He joked that he was bound to get the lemon. The tall, balding 47-year-old vegan taught AP government to high schoolers in Cincinnati. His friendly, everyman demeanor belied a hardcore competitive streak, a power that got him through several of the toughest races in the world and made him the world record holder in Backyards. Still, I couldn't help but wince when he reached his hand in the box, his eyes nervous through his smiles.

"Harvey's a Danny, isn't he?" I asked Laz, quietly.

I didn't think he'd heard me, then there was a small ripple across his eyes. "Harvey?" he said without emotion. "He's the quintessential Danny."

---

Harvey never wanted to be told something was wrong with him. But from the first grade on, he was singled out as different. After the divorce, he moved with his mother to Berea, Ohio, and entered school. Immediately he was behind in reading, math, everything. Kids picked on him for being stupid, and the teacher, not sure how to deal with him, stuck him in a corner in the back of the room.

Today, he'd be counseled for ADHD. But back then, the answer was Special Education, and from the day they put him in, he dreamed of getting out. *Nothing was wrong with him! He was normal!* Somehow, he had to prove it. First, he had to believe it.

His mother worked full-time as a nurse to keep food on the table, and Harvey liked food—bad food. The kind of food that felt good before it made you feel bad and made you crave more bad food and made you balloon and get picked on for that too.

While he was desperate to prove he was like everyone else, he was scared to do anything about it. If he failed, it would be the most embarrassing thing ever. And by the eighth grade, he was still in Special Ed.

Like most kids of the '80s, he lived in front of the TV screen. While he identified most with "Chunk," the token chubby character in *The Goonies,* when his classmates called him "fatso," it stung. He'd retreat home to the television and look up at his heroes Schwarzenegger and Stallone—they used physicality to overcome adversity. And if they could do it, so could he.

He also related to *The Count of Monte Cristo,* the story of a man, unjustly imprisoned, who methodically chisels his way out. He would chisel too. He started by going out for the football team, a long shot, but surprisingly made defensive tackle, third string. He was picked on there too. But he refused to quit.

He liked the running drills and was soon doing two miles a day in his spare time. Then, a promotion for the Cleveland Marathon caught his eye. That was his answer! But there was a snag. He'd have to go into the city by himself; he'd never done that. Harvey pleaded with his mother. After all, wasn't she the one who told him he was normal, repeatedly, purposefully? Still, this was a big ask. When he was done making his case, she smiled and said okay.

Nine miles in, everything hurt. Still, Harvey wouldn't quit, couldn't quit. If he failed, they'd all be right—the smart-ass kids, the popular crowd, the bullies. He'd never get out of Special Ed, never be like everyone else; life would be a long, slow road to becoming a shut-in.

When he crossed the line in 5 hours, 10 minutes, he felt the "lights turn on." He believed it now, in his gut—*nothing was wrong with him*. He returned to school determined to improve. D's and F's became C's. Hours of study at night in his bedroom followed, and soon he was getting B's.

He'd never say it, but he knew it in his core, the truth, the absolute truth. They didn't let him out of Special Ed. He chiseled out.

---

"What if Nicky gets it?" The Manor paused for a brief second of contemplation after Harvey was gone. Then, there was a howl, higher than any yet. Nicky Spinks of the United Kingdom had been a great hope in 2019. The breast cancer survivor was a multiple record holder in fell running (a British form of off-trail mountain running), and talk was high that she had a chance. After timing out on loop two, she'd commented, "I don't think I've ever felt that cold." She knew what every woman knew: No female runner had ever finished the Barkley. Now, a month away from her fifty-sixth birthday, Laz was giving her another shot, and some extra motivation.

In most races, Bib #1 is an honor. Here, it's an inglorious one bestowed by Laz to the runner he deems least likely to finish a single loop. He calls this runner The Human Sacrifice. "Laz has cheekily given Nicky the number 1 bib for Barkley," her media team would tweet out after the start. "Go prove him wrong, Nicky!"

The fact that no woman had ever finished the Barkley was a sore spot in the sport. Some said Laz didn't even let women apply in the early years, another misconception he never cared to clear up. They'd run the Barkley since year one, but there was no denying he'd made his bed. On numerous occasions, he declared women weren't strong enough to finish. The hard truth was, only three women had ever made three of the five loops of the modern, post-1995 Barkley.

One of them was here. Like Spinks, she was also a fell running champion and multiple record holder from the United Kingdom. She'd bested the men head-to-head in one of the world's toughest races—The Spine. Not only had she won it, she'd smashed the course record by twelve hours while pumping milk for her newborn along the way. Now, she was back in Icehouse Delirium for a second time. Her name was Jasmin Paris, and she already had her watch.

"One in seventeen you get a worthless watch," Laz bellowed, so loud it rifled through camp.

"They're all worthless watches, Gary," Keith snorted, and a delineation appeared between who called him Gary and who called him Laz. Bad Mike used Laz. Naresh called him Gary. Most of the runners addressed him as Laz. Veteran runners said Gary. His mother had used both; Laz when she was teasing him. But he never told anybody what to call him.

"More victims," Bad Mike muttered when another group approached. And so, the game went on. Ten watches left, then nine, and two serious contenders in the race had yet to pick theirs up, John Kelly and Damian Hall. But Dawn Greenwalt was next. She pulled her box, opened it, and the Chorus erupted. *OHHH NO!*

The smile she was wearing a second ago melted. "We're not friends anymore," she said, fiddling with it as it turned on and off. It showed five minutes till the start, then blinked away.

The Inner Circle seemed pleased. "Wow, it's as bad as they say." Naresh laughed like a schoolboy. Larry had a last question for her. "You goin' for a little five-loop stroll with your little six-pack cooler?" Bad Mike cut his eyes at her backpack. "That's one way to get choked up out there. Get caught on a tree and be dangling over the edge." Keith recoiled in disgust. "Jesus, Mike," he said, his face all scrunched up. Then slowly the corner of his eyes creased, and he began to shake with laughter.

---

"Make peace with your god," Laz muttered as he moved toward the gate. And a hush swept through camp—save the dull rustling of runners approaching, lost in their own ritual of preparation, adjusting straps, fiddling with compasses. Where there had been jovial smiles, there were now taut faces—less talk, more whispers.

Karel arrived with his compass attached to his left forearm. He'd taken it out a hundred times in past races. It was a small tweak, but the Barkley was a gambit of tweaks. "That's a hundred seconds."

Laz stood on the other side. Behind him, the gravel jeep road was riddled with grooves in the tan hardtack. Beyond that, a thin trail turned up multiple switchbacks, but only for a moment, till runners were instructed to go left, off trail, and dive down into a gorge and up Wrong Way Ridge. Then, they'd be Out There, fighting the Fifth Wall.

Laz will give runners a new bib with each loop to keep them off guard—turn in the old number, memorize the new one, remember it when you tear out the book page. With the order of this year's loops, there's another cruel twist: clockwise (day), counter (night), counter (day), clockwise (night). Each loop will look different as runners hit them from various directions and time of day. The fifth—if anyone makes it that far—was left to fate. The first to reach it chooses the direction, while the others alternate—a deliberate attempt to isolate them, cut them off from even the smallest comfort of companionship.

But all this, they certainly expect. "The most fascinating aspect for me," says Barkley veteran Jared Campbell, "is there is no required gear. You could argue it's one of the most dangerous races out there. When you read that it will be thirty hours before search and rescue is called, the result appears to be that people show up remarkably prepared."

To get here, they've had to jump through numerous hoops till acceptance came in the form of a condolence letter from Laz, much like this one to ultrarunner Gary Robbins:

> Dear Gary,
>
> It is my unfortunate duty to inform you that your name has been selected for the 2016 Barkley marathons, to be

> held on April 2–4, 2016, at Frozen Head State Park, in the state of Tennessee, USA.
>
> It is anticipated that this enterprise will amount to nothing more than an extended period of unspeakable suffering, at the end of which you will ultimately find only failure and humiliation. At best, you might escape without incurring permanent physical damage and psychological scarring, which will torment you for the remainder of your life. You may, if you so desire, spend the intervening months between now and April in a futile attempt to perform sufficient training to enable yourself to cover a greater distance before your ultimate demise. However, it would probably be better to spend this time putting your affairs in order.

"Alright folks, HEY!" Laz shouts in his coach's voice—a high-pitched screech that raises heads. The heads of the world's best. Camp has dubbed them "the dream team." In a Cerulean blue top, Jared stands in the middle, hands on his trekking poles. Many have their eyes on him, as he's one of two in history with multiple finishes, and the only three-time finisher.

When he was checking in the day before, I caught Laz gazing at him. "Everything you do in your life is a picture of you," he said, glancing back at me. "Anyone that builds their own house likes a challenge, and Jared feasts on challenge. He has this wall, 'a passive solar wall,' he calls it. Huge. Designed it opposite five rows of windows, so the sun hits it. Converts the heat to his heating and cooling system."

The next runner sat down opposite him and waited for his moment, but Laz kept on about Jared. "On one of the windows, there's a dot," he said, pointing a finger in the air. "And the arc of the sun moves it along three lines he drew on the wall to mark the solstice and the equinox. I told him, 'Damn, that must have taken forever.' He just grinned at me and said, 'Where's the fun in that?' He'd painted them in first, calculated it out, and waited to prove himself right."

Several runners settle behind Jared now. A crucial key to success, it's said, is to follow a veteran—if you can keep up. Otherwise, you could be out there for days, just on loop one. While some older vets take pride in stealing away from newbies at opportune moments, Jared is the opposite. If you can stay with him, and most can't, he is running with you, not against you.

John Kelly has the same reputation. He's in yellow by the left pillar—boyish face, dishwater-blond hair, calm eyes. A few runners form around him. Harvey is on his own, tucked next to the other pillar, as close as he can to having a toe on the line. His eyes are bright and twitchy. Behind him is Jasmin. She wears a red shirt over her thermals, her eyes beaming with enthusiasm.

"Listen up for a second," Laz barks. "The last two days we've been up here telling lots of funny stories. The next sixty hours there's gonna be a lot of new funny stories. We don't know what they're gonna be or who's gonna do 'em. But we'll talk about it for years. But every story needs to end with you coming back to camp alive. So, be smart out there." He glances down at a piece of paper in his hand then back at the runners. "When you've done something as long as this," he continues, "some of the people who made it what it is are no longer here. And so, this is our time to recognize the missing Barkers... they're gone but they're not forgotten."

He names them off, and one cuts sharp for me in the bitter cold—DeWayne Satterfield, my hero from the Delano 12-Hour. Gone suddenly at 55, the kind of loss that leaves you shaking your head at the heavens. Then his name bleeds in with the others, a list comprised of decades of runners most now have never heard of. For Laz, they are a reminder: This ordeal isn't about finishing for most but something more obscure, more personal.

He holds his sock hat over his heart, the wispy hairs atop his mostly bald head sticking up like tufts of dried grass in a breeze. The thin, wavering notes of Taps drift through camp on a squeaky bugle—the first time we hear it. Though it will sound again soon enough.

When the last note dies away, the small horde closes in tighter to the gate, and Keith mans a light grey stone the size of a love seat. He lays out three phones in front of him, each with a different cell provider. If he loses signal on one, he always has another. Then Laz cups two hands together, lights a Camel, and blows a stream of smoke toward the sky.

A holler goes up, and Karel darts out front, his yearlong wait for revenge over. He hopes to avoid a bottleneck on the first bit of single track, but John Kelly has the same idea, flashing a wicked smile like Br'er Rabbit in the briar patch. And the rest file in behind. "It's fun time!" the old man yells, and his voice echoes over the runners as they recede into the wilderness.

Some won't be seen again for days.

Part II

# THE ORDEAL

# 8

# Nothing but Love and Puppies

**FOR THE FIRST TIME SINCE THE CIGARETTE**, John Kelly's thoughts were racing faster than he'd like. Leonard's Buttslide was no easy place to keep a bunch of newbs together, but that was exactly what he hoped to do. If he could find it.

Somewhere under Bobcat Rock, along the sweeping curve of a cliff, would be the opening. And down it would go—a forty-five-degree plunge, riddled with boulders, briars, blowdowns, and other impassable impediments. A miscalculation here, even by a few degrees, and he and the group following him could end up in another county. Some had a real chance. But Kelly had what few had: knowledge and experience.

He was the local boy, born and raised right here, and had the confidence that comes with finishing. But that was six years ago…

Kellys have lived around Joyner, Tennessee, for over two hundred years. John's father used to drive trucks in the strip mines, and one of his grandfathers was a prison guard at Brushy. Frozen Head was literally his backyard, and he grew up scrambling over the mountains. On hikes with friends, he liked to point to a long ridge on the eastern edge of the park. "That's Kelly Mountain," he'd say.

Starting in the third grade, his parents sent him to nearby Oak Ridge for the better schools. He ran cross-country but got picked on back in Joyner for it. "That's running cross-city," they'd say. After earning a PhD in electrical engineering and machine learning, he went to work for Lockheed Martin, then chief technology officer at Envelop Risk.

He was also an elite-level *World of Warcraft* player. "A troll rogue," he'd tell me with some pride. "Solid at PvP." It was while he was thoroughly ensconced in reaching the highest levels of the game that he started spending more time running. In 2012, he entered his first 10K, then fell apart in a marathon. But the urge for more escalated quickly. Growing up, he'd heard rumors of the Barkley, but not much beyond that.

He applied for 2015 but knew he had no shot. He had zero trail or ultra pedigree. So, when Laz sent out an email that said a lot of decisions had to be made but one person *has* to get in, he had an odd feeling it might be him. He was both scared and excited. His initial impression of Laz was that he had "the demeanor of a Rhino and the heart of a Golden Retriever."

That year, John entered his first Barkley and went out smart but hard. "It's a done deal from here," Laz teased, taking his pages from the third loop. "Let's call it a gimme."

But Kelly's family, who was helping crew, was mortified by John's condition. They thought he needed an ambulance. He was hunched over a trash can unable to figure out how to put his shirt back on. Veteran runners huddled around him, told him to reset, to "get some chicken soup and he'd be fine." In the end, John just went home.

He returned the next year, determined to go farther. But if some part of him knew what he was in for, no one else did. Not even Laz.

It was after the local boy had made four loops and was sitting and staring out into nothing that camp began to pick up on the fact that something was different about John. His eyes slouched, his mouth hung open, and the gashes on the side of his neck, nasty and maroon, bulged like infected cat scratches—but he wasn't going home.

With twelve minutes left to start the final loop, he hobbled toward the gate, dragging a trekking pole behind him. His face was "as white as paper, expressionless, gone," wrote Sara Estes in an article for *The Bitter Southerner*. Camp came to his aid with shouts and claps. He leaned heavy against the yellow gate, blankly eyeing the forest.

His wife tried to force him to eat. He refused. "I need to sleep," he mumbled to her. "I want to go to sleep."

With the new bib in hand, he trudged up the trail, then circled and slowly crumpled to the ground. He lay forty yards beyond the gate for an hour. It's a rule of the Barkley that no runner can receive aid once out on a loop. His family looked on helplessly from camp; everyone did. Finally, he rose, dry heaved, and disappeared up Bird Mountain.

Photographer Tamara Reynolds went looking for Laz, but he wasn't in his usual spots. She found him in the back of a U-Haul—his eyes teary and bloodshot, his voice quivering. "We just experienced someone giving everything they've got," he told her, wiping underneath his glasses. "I'm sorry. I've got to compose myself."

Again, John failed to finish. But the next year, he came back to hunt what he called "The White Whale of Tennessee." After 59 hours and 30 minutes, he appeared at the bottom of the hill. Wearing the remnants of a white garbage bag wrapped around his torso for warmth, he touched the yellow gate and became the fifteenth finisher.

In subsequent years, he's been unable to repeat his success. Maybe his experience works against him—he knows the bad that's out there. He's also no longer a newbie; he's the veteran. With that comes responsibility.

He'd told me that his first year, he'd "looked Beverly Abs straight in the eye" and said he was planning to latch on to her as long as he could. That was fine. *Remember that tree!* she'd say. Now, when groups form around him early, he's okay with it. In fact, it feels natural, not unlike the guilds he ran in *World of Warcraft*.

The transition from computer-generated puzzles and multiplayer dungeons to hundreds of miles of running and hunting books in the woods—that also seems natural. He lives a relatively cushy life, as he sees it. "I'm not getting chased by predators, the imminent threats are minimal, and these artificial challenges help us grow to reach a potential we wouldn't have otherwise thought possible. It's crazy stupid, but I'm gonna go out there and do my best."

Now, the Buttslide was at John's feet, and all that was left was to get down it correctly—or as correctly as possible. This out-of-control bounding down the mountain could be a deal-breaker. Gotta get the entry point right. Hopefully, he could help those behind him, but there was badness ahead.

First, they'd have to turn around and climb "straight-the-hell-up" the Buttslide. Then there'd be Little Hell—a 1,500-foot climb in a little over half a mile. Ratjaw would follow, a longer incline with mats of saw briars. After that, down it would go again—Zipline, a nosedive of 1,500 feet on wretched footing. If you made a mistake, anywhere, you might not realize it for hours.

John had earned that understanding. But would those behind him get it? *Remember that rock!*

---

Jasmin didn't tell him that she'd gotten a condolence letter for the Barkley, no point to. Instead, she listened as patiently as she could. She respected professionals; she was one herself—a PhD in veterinary medicine from the University of Edinburgh. And as a mother of two, she knew the word of a doctor always went a long way. “If you want to carry on running,” the orthopedist said, reading the MRI on her knee, “stick to soft surfaces and avoid anything undulating.” With that in mind, she boarded a plane two weeks later and headed to Frozen Head State Park.

After Laz lit the cigarette, she ran with the pack “away from the yellow gate, into the quiet forest beyond.” She waited with the others when a log jam of runners formed at book one. It could have been a feeding frenzy but for Jared Campbell. The runners called out their bib numbers, and he handed them the pages. A selfless move. Class.

She spotted John Kelly taking off with a small group and her coach, Damian Hall. So as soon as she got her page, she dashed through the woods to catch up. Staying with them, especially on the first loop, could be the difference between finishing or becoming one of *those stories.*

Before Jasmin came to Frozen Head, her achievements in ultrarunning were already prolific. In 2016, she was crowned female champion of the Skyrunning World Series, extreme division. In 2021, she ran under a full moon in the Eastern Highlands of Scotland to bag as many 3,000-foot mountains as she could in twenty-four hours. Known as Munros, these peaks number among Scotland’s highest. She topped 29, a new record. Three months later, she was first female in the 100-mile Ultra Tour Monte Rosa in Switzerland. But she turned heads by coming to Frozen Head in 2022 and finishing three loops on her first go.

She did her best to ignore expectations. Of course, before she even learned much about the logistics of the Barkley, she’d heard that no woman had ever finished. But something inside her told her she could. She trusted that part. To finish was the goal, the only goal, period.

But now, she’d lost sight of John and Damian and was running alone. She climbed her way up The Bad Thing and trudged up the long slog to Chimney Top. And by the time she reached the gate, they were already gone on loop two. She took advantage of the speed slot, a new system of setting up mini aid stations in front of the gate. (It saved walking fifty yards to your tent.) There, she sat cramming liquid and food down her throat while her husband, Konrad, arranged her night gear.

This would be the year. She knew it. It had to be! The weather forecast was too good. Barkley weather was notorious, could change in a heartbeat, but for now, it was clear, cold, and perfect. Still, loop two was counterclockwise this year. That's always tougher, everything you just did but backwards—and night was approaching.

Then, a streak of blue caught her eye. Jared Campbell. He and Karel were heading down the hill. Decisions have to be made at Barkley, sometimes very quickly. Really, there was no choice—if she couldn't hang onto Jared, she'd be alone in the dark, navigating the Barkley in reverse.

With a mouth full of food, she grabbed up her trekking poles and sprinted away. She caught them by the time they hit the bottom of the hill. Still alive. For now.

---

In camp, Laz decided to spice things up with a new idea, and Keith loved it. They'd play with the dot watchers, the thousands on Twitter refreshing their feeds for any scrap of info. *Let's not tell them who's in the race. No names. Just descriptions. Let them figure it out.*

And so, several unheard-of characters were suddenly a part of the race. There was The Nondescript Man, Guy with Mohawk, Guy with Glasses, Another Bearded Guy, and The Small British Woman. They'd all started loop two, Keith tweeted. And with each new description they invented, a fit of laughter followed between the two. This new wrinkle would stick—and The Watch!

As the sun began to settle on the horizon, camp grew still. I wrapped myself in more layers and made my way to the firepit. Naresh was squatting at it, stirring a gallon of bubbling beans.

"You've done this thing?" I asked, my breath pouring out like frosty smoke.

"The Barkley?" he said with clear eyes that seemed to have slept all night. "Oh, yeah. Once. I'm the guy who dropped the F-bomb on the documentary." He blew on the spoon and took a sip. "You want some beans?"

I waved a no thank you.

"The first time I came, I tell you, I should have turned around and gone home." Naresh laughed, carefully placing more wood on the fire. "You never know what is going to happen here. It doesn't matter if you're in the race or not."

It was still daylight on the first day when Taps began to ring through camp. Two had gone off course and ended up at Gobey Church. Having failed to finish one loop, they lumbered in unannounced from Quitter's Road like stray dogs. They stood at attention while the somber series of three notes was played over a bugle, eight times, in the key of B-flat.

Another did the first loop in under ten hours, but when he went out for the second he was overcome and could barely walk. The more food he put in, the more spewed right back out. Taps played for him too.

The first victim had been 75-year-old Frozen Ed Furtaw. Ed was a staple at the Barkley with his loud, multicolored tights. After becoming the first finisher in 1988, he'd written *Tales From Out There*, detailing the race's history. He tried 22 more times to repeat his success but never could.

In 2018, he was diagnosed with advanced prostate cancer and wondered if he'd ever return to the Barkley. Yet, four months later—and just a month after his last treatment—he showed up in Frozen Head. Too weak to run, he hung around camp just to be near the action. The shirt that year made him smile: "The Barkley Marathons. Nothing Out There but Love and Puppies."

He returned again in 2022, this time to run, but appeared on Quitter's Road after ten hours, having reached less than half the books on loop one. Taps played for him, and he smiled through his tears as the notes echoed through camp.

This year, he emerged from the woods after eight hours and with only three book pages. Part of what doomed him, he thought, was Laz's torturous new start. No more fourteen switchbacks up Bird Mountain. Now it was straight-the-hell-up Wrong Way Ridge—1,500 feet in a mile. His back, his feet, his neck—they were killing him. But he'd run two years in a row, suffering alongside the others, and couldn't be happier. He was back. And when his time comes, he hopes someone will honor his wishes and spread his ashes Out There.

---

Night slammed down over camp like it had something to prove, forcing those of us not hidden away in our cars to the firepit, which burned reluctantly. It was a stubborn little blaze—never quite big enough, never quite warm enough. We leaned in until the smoke filtered out the tops of our jackets. It would reach the low twenties tonight, someone said. "It'll be a hell of a lot colder up on those ridges," Laz growled.

The initial rush of day one was starting to settle, and the chuckling and games had died down. Laz talked little about the race. It was too early. Instead, he spoke about Backyards and the upcoming championship. "It's easy till it isn't," he said, the firelight dancing across his face. I'd heard him say it before, but there was an air of contentment about him now as he eased into a chair and lit a Japanese-made Camel. After a long drag, he fell quiet and listened as Barkley lore was passed around. Most involved spectacular failure.

Somehow, most Barkley stories always came back to Dan Baglione. His inglorious record is stunning on its face: two miles in 32 hours. How he got there—a wrong trail, dead batteries in his flashlight, the flashlight bulb rolling down the hill, a night alone in the dark, and an uncontrollable shivering till he came upon two good ole boys with some weed—was legend.

Another treasured tale was the runner who had led for two loops before he "slumped down to the ground, face down beside the fire, and began weeping in earnest." He staggered bravely to his feet but began to vomit, and Taps played for him.

One runner became so disoriented, he believed he saw a creek flowing uphill. He sat down to recover, taking off his glasses. Moments later, he thoughtlessly got up without them. After crawling blindly back to camp, Taps was played for him.

Then there was Sergeant Stone, who in 1987 assaulted the Barkley with five of his best Marines. "We can finish anything," he proclaimed. His warriors were done on loop one—and so was he.

Another time, two runners ended up too close to Brushy Mountain State Penitentiary when it was still active. Prison guards held them on the ground at gunpoint till they discerned that in fact the two men were—honest to God—in some sort of running race.

Then there was Animal—real name Dennis Herr—spotted on a log, frustrated and delirious. "Gary's gone *too far* this time!" he said.

Veteran Lou Peyton had a similar reaction. "It's too much. It's too much," she said. "You've got to understand, it's just *too much*."

For a moment the laughter settled, and we sat quiet, listening to the wind whistle across the peaks. But the spell didn't last. Soon, the chatter fell back into a rhythm. There were also stories of unthinkable triumph. In 2008, Brian Robinson was back for a third try. But by loop three, his feet were completely macerated, and a fall off a cliff in the dark dislocated his clavicle. He pressed on anyway and not only finished but became the fastest runner to ever do five loops.

And there was Andrew "AT" Thompson. After making only one loop on his first try, he kept coming back. He improved each year until finally, on his tenth attempt, he became the eighth finisher.

Speculation about this year followed, loose, in all shapes and sizes. But there was little debate that loop four would be the real gauntlet, where the race really began. And this year it would be merciless—counterclockwise, at night. That is, if anyone made it that far...

"That a runner?" Laz was by the pillar, the side of his face illuminated by a small LED lantern.

"Kind of." A voice from the dark, meek.

It was Jon Eisen, and when he came into the dim light, he looked like someone who'd wrestled a bear—cuts and scratches on his legs, hair a mess, and wandering eyes that searched for something the mind wasn't sure of.

"I couldn't make decisions," he'd later write. "I told Miranda, 'I'm going to need work.' I don't think she understood my meaning. Quickly, things got bad. I started shivering uncontrollably. I asked to go to the tent. She took me to the car and started it. I broke down in the car, telling her about the battle in my mind. My battle with Past Jon and Future Jon for the rights of Current Jon to quit this stupid race... Finally, after 30+ minutes in the car, I stopped shaking. My mind centered. My thinking became clear again. I would continue."

He wandered off into the night, and Keith tweeted, "A corpse sprang to life joins 30 other runners on loop two."

Not long after, word came that the jugs of water at the Fire Tower left out for the runners were all frozen. The news bounced off Laz like a paper airplane. The tip of his cigarette glowed bright as he took a drag.

"Well," he said, "life isn't always fair."

## 9

# No Cop Cars

**LAZ SAT ALONE IN THE MORNING LIGHT**, drifting off in a lawn chair. Those who were still in his crucible were on loop three. Others were timed out, yet to make it back. And a few Out There hadn't been seen since the opening cigarette.

Overnight, he'd stolen snatches of sleep whenever he could. He'd stretch out in the back of that battered U-Haul, where he kept a cot, a space heater, and a radio. He kept it parked beside the gate, ignoring the groans of the photographers that it was "in every shot!"

After sunrise, some of us ventured out of our tents and vehicles and glued ourselves to the firepit. We blew white puffs into the morning chill and stared solemnly at a sad leg of chicken. It sat alone on the cooking grate, black and sizzled out. Jared's wife, I couldn't help but notice, had a large bulge in her sock. It reminded me of my father on the golf course—Bermuda Shorts, socks pulled up tight, and a pack of Max 100s tucked inside. "What have you got there?" I asked, and she looked down at her ankles. "Oh," she said seemingly surprised. "Just battery-heated socks."

I wrapped myself in that thought for a moment, letting it warm me, until the crack of a can of Dr. Pepper snapped me out of it.

That's when I moved, sitting beside Laz on Keith's stone. Despite shadowing him as much as I could, it was the first time I'd gotten him alone since the start. There were always people around, eager for a piece of his attention, always leading him off into conversations and tangents. He happily obliged. And then there were his duties—every time a runner returned, he was there, standing by the pillar to mark the time or bowing his head while Taps played.

"When I get back, I've gotta up my miles," he said, sipping his drink. "Live hard, die young? Well, I tried that. It's more like live hard, pay for it forever. Oh me..." He groaned and stretched his leg. "I need to be able to do twenty-three miles a day," he said, wrinkling his brow. "Otherwise, I won't make it."

"Make it?"

He looked at me, incredulous, as if I'd missed something obvious. "Across America."

"You're going to walk across America?" I tried to blink the morning out of my eyes and search his face. There must be a hint of a joke, a flicker that he was pulling my leg. But I was also aware that he'd done it twice before, once east to west and another time north to south. But that was years ago and given his current physical state, it sounded like a suicide mission. "You're serious?" I said.

He seemed ready for that. "Doesn't everyone walk across the country when they turn seventy?" he said, then retreated inward, the smile on his lips fading as he took another long sip. "You never know how far you can go until you go as far as you can go."

I was about to ask him more when a voice rang out, "Runner!"

Three were skulking in together, down Quitter's Road. One was female hopeful Nicky Spinks. She'd timed out on loop two but defied the curse of the Human Sacrifice; she'd at least finished one. The night, the navigation, the reverse direction—she just wasn't fast enough. Hats off. Taps played. "A mass burial," Keith tweeted.

By noon, the Barkley had dispatched most of the field. The early ones that slinked in most assuredly had lost their way in the night. Every time one would appear from Quitter's Road, Laz would stir, shuffle to the pillar, call out a time, take his sock hat off for Taps, then return to his chair. And soon, his eyes would be closed again.

He was awake and smoking when Harvey Lewis appeared, his shorts and pack splattered with mud. He'd fallen more times than he could count, and it showed—his once-vibrant eyes had turned dull, exhaustion pulling down a smile. He'd miscalculated, he figured. Halfway through loop two, he'd run out of food, overpacked for a possible bout of freezing rain, only to face hunger instead. It was always a gamble out there, and this time he lost.

Laz had been on Harvey's case even before the race began, poking fun at his vegan diet. At a Mexican joint, Laz had a molcajete, two pounds of meat and veggies and cheese in a bowl of volcanic rock with three little pig's feet. He shot a disapproving look at Harvey's skinny veggie plate. "I'll convince that bear in the Barkley T-shirt to turn *VEE*-gan," he said, stretching out the word for emphasis. "And its first meal," he added, pausing just long enough for a grin, "will be Harvey."

"If people could see what we go through out there, they wouldn't believe it," Harvey said now, crumbled into a lawn chair. "No documentary really shows it—the insanity of running down those mountains. It's absurd—almost like a Dali painting. Just people tumbling, falling, getting back up, falling again. I broke both my poles on the first loop." He leaned over his bloody knees. "I don't see how you can't fall."

Officially, he had one loop to his name.

---

Karel Sabbe's numbed fingers were beginning to lose grip. He was upside down... suspended above a stream, then... a splash and a jet of water over his head... his back cracked on the pointy stones of the creek bed... a rock tore off the tip of his shoe... then ice water, running and rapid, zapped his skin with electric cold... and he bolted out as he'd come in.

The blowdown had seemed like a good way to get across the creek and stay dry. Keeping his feet protected and staving off maceration as long as possible was crucial. So, he'd hopped onto the log, arms outstretched like a tightrope walker, each step deliberate, tense. Until he slipped.

Now soaked from head to toe, he picked up his pace to stay warm. This was nothing, he told himself, and nothing was going to stop him this time. Nothing.

In 2019, Sabbe's required essay explaining why he should be allowed to attempt the Barkley had been characteristically direct. "I find having a suffer-fest every now and then is very important in a man's life," he wrote. "They allow you to get to know yourself in a way that in regular life would take many years. My idea has always been 'do or do not; there is no try.' When we look at the Barkley, it does seem there is a try. I want to experience this try."

But his try ended after three loops. In 2022, he came back and could almost taste the finish, one of only two runners on the fourth loop. Then, it all went sideways...

The first calls came into the Morgan County Sheriff's office at 4:45 a.m., with descriptions both consistent and perplexing: a shadowy figure scampering across lawns—a vagrant leering into windows. One frantic caller claimed she saw a woman "dressed as an Indian" conversing with a trash can.

Investigator C.J. Porter was on patrol when he heard the chatter on the radio. He pulled his cruiser onto Main Street in Petros and immediately spotted a tall figure in the road by the library. But the suspect had a beard, was clad in black tights, and seemed "dazed and confused."

"What's going on?" Porter asked. The man's eyes squinted and shifted in the beam of his flashlight.

"I need help." The voice was weak, the accent strange. He pointed a finger up toward the old prison and explained that he'd come from the wilderness.

"Are you in the Barkley?" Porter asked.

The man, who'd given his name as "Carol," looked confused. He began checking the trekking poles he carried and the clear bag with the torn-out book pages crumpled up inside.

Porter raised his voice a notch. "Do you want me to take you back?"

Carol nodded. He was pitiful—ashen skin, eyes unsettled. When he said he was hungry but didn't have any money, Porter helped him into the cruiser. "Don't you worry about that," he said. "After what you've been through, you deserve something to eat."

"Carol," Porter would find out, was Karel Sabbe, a 32-year-old dentist from Ronse, Belgium, and one of the most accomplished endurance athletes in the world. Sabbe didn't break records; he destroyed them. In 2018, he crossed the 2,189-mile Appalachian Trail five days faster than the previous record of northbound ultrarunning legend Scott Jurek and four days faster than southbound Karl Meltzer. He held that record and the 2,655-mile Pacific Crest Trail record at the same time—the first to ever do so. In 2021, he set a Fastest Known Time (FKT) on an arduous route of climbs known as the Via Alpina, a 1,647-mile stretch of trails over eight countries in the Alps. The record was 44 days. Sabbe did it in 30.

But this race in Tennessee he couldn't crack. In fact, he couldn't even finish. Two attempts, two failures.

Inside the cruiser, Karel replayed what he could remember of the last 14 hours. There was the lady with the two kids. She seemed so nice before she morphed into a trash can. He saw friendly faces in windows but found out they too were hallucinations when he approached them, and they'd disappeared. If only he'd gone back when he first got off the trail. It was against his instinct, but sometimes going forward is the worst thing you can do.

It was still dark when Officer Porter pulled into DD's, a small, two-pump mom-and-pop gas station. He grabbed Sabbe a chicken biscuit, water, and a Gatorade. Pulling up to the trailhead, he saw a series of headlamps moving like strobe lights. "I need to speak with Laz," he said after getting out.

The race director emerged, wearing a long brown duster and balancing on a cattle prod. "Well," he grinned, "this is a first. Where did you find him?"

Now, in 2023, Karel was just trying to hold himself together. His lips were frigid and blue when he jogged into camp from loop three. The icy stream had been a mistake; he couldn't afford another. "Thirty-two, forty-six, thirty-one." Laz called out the time as Karel touched the gate. "Now it's easy, right?"

A few hours of daylight hung on the horizon—he could make up some time, he thought before catching himself. Though loop four was back to clockwise, it would be mostly at night. It was always slower at night. He powdered his pruning feet and did the math—tight, too tight. So, he chewed the burger faster and downed another orange soda, no time for the burrito.

Jo, his crew, stuffed it in his thermal top anyway and showed him a text from Karel's wife, Emma. She was huddled with family and friends in a café in Belgium, following Keith's tweets. She had sent a picture of their son Jack. Karel held the phone with the burger he was still working on and smiled. Then he saw himself in the reflection. He looked unwell. But he felt good. Then again, he'd felt good last year.

His stomach turned over and complained when he stood. *No mistakes*, he reminded himself. He wasn't here to survive—he was here to finish, to put the Barkley behind him for good. With his trekking poles tucked under his arms, he headed to the yellow gate. He'd been in camp 14 minutes.

As he started up the jeep road, he heard the crack of Laz's voice behind him. "No cop cars!"

Karel turned and grinned. He had no way of knowing then that he'd lose his way even before reaching the first book. His try would once again be a vague memory, his mind utterly lost.

---

Not long after, the last bits of daylight were beginning to fade, and a dim figure appeared from the jeep road. It was Jared Campbell. He hobbled in as if the soles of his feet were touching hot stones and leaned against the gate.

Someone jokingly asked if the race had started yet. Jared smiled the best he could. "Oh, it's started."

When he grimaced back to his tent, the mood around camp shifted. He hadn't dropped, but it looked imminent. Keith watched him pass without comment. Naresh stopped what he was doing by the fire. I couldn't help but wonder—if Jared had been reduced to this state, what was the Barkley doing to the rest?

No runner has been as successful here as Jared Campbell. He completed five loops on his first attempt. However, he once shared with me that it was one of his worst runs that stuck with him the most.

The year was 2013, and Campbell was back on a specific mission: He was going to do the whole race on his own. He'd finished the year before like most do; he'd latched onto a veteran till loop five. This time, he was going to prove he could do it alone.

And he was having the race of his life—till loop two, till adversity came for him in a series of waves. First, a fog rolled in, thick as soup, wispy with the wave of a hand but filling in as fast as quicksand. Then, he made a mistake—he skipped a bearing check atop a hill. When he descended, he went into the wrong drainage area, where he thrashed around for hours, in the dark, in a rock-laden gully. The temperature suddenly dropped, and it began to "piss freezing rain."

Next, all his methodical preparations began to fall apart: His headlamp played out, the last of his spare food was gone, and all his batteries went dead. All he had left was a keychain flashlight and a hundred-calorie gel.

The decision he eventually arrived at was to continue farther down the gully. After some time, he spotted a light up ahead—the prison. When he reached it, he remembered, he had "nothing left in the tank. Nothing more to give." Standing there by the prison walls, the rain coming down in sheets, he said he felt as though he'd "just skirted death."

It was then that he started to lose it mentally. He had gone from running at the front of the race to facing an hours-long hike back to finish the loop just to quit. So, he decided he'd bail instead—go to the road, hitch a ride back. It was then that an unfamiliar war of inner voices ensued, jabbing and nipping at him, as he stood in the rain. He pictured the old man's face as he pulled up in a vehicle and listened to Taps for the first time. No, he couldn't do it, he decided. He couldn't go out like this.

Hungry, soaked, and exhausted, he turned and started up The Bad Thing, and hours later, when he finally clambered into camp, all he wanted was for there to be an end. He touched the yellow gate, bent over his knees, and looked up at Laz.

The old man was smiling down at him. In any other race, if a runner had come in five hours late, the race director would be freaking out. Laz, however, seemed calm, smiling even. It was a look Jared didn't expect. There was something in that smile, in his eyes, that understood. That *got* the hell Jared had just gone through. "Bad things happen at the Barkley," Laz said softly. "Don't they, Jared?"

At first, he wasn't sure how to take it. He looked over to his wife, wanting a hug but didn't get one. "Well," she said, matter of fact, "are you gonna get your act together?" He wasn't expecting to feel it. He didn't even believe it was still there. But it was—that push to go on.

While there wasn't enough time to finish the race, there was another option. Laz allowed forty hours instead of the usual thirty-six for those who opted for only three loops, what he called a Fun Run. Jared had never been a "checkdown" runner, but it was the only option forward.

He cleaned up in the bathhouse, refueled, and forced himself to reframe his situation. He returned to the gate, took his bib, and headed back out on a nasty counter loop. When he returned, he had more than a Fun Run, he had a realization: He was around the right kind of people, and he'd married the right person.

That made it all the more surprising when, in this year's Barkley, I watched him limp slowly back to the gate. Wearing a heavy blue coat and a frown, he looked around camp as if taking a picture of things to remember, like he was soaking up this failure too. When he said it was his knee and he was "bowing out," there were no questions. The old man held his shoulders and said, "Appreciate you coming out."

Taps played, the last tinges of light faded, and soon, darkness sat over Frozen Head. Six were left Out There in the gauntlet of loop four, and mere minutes remained for anyone on the third.

The mood shifted after Jared. A reverence seemed to fall over the camp. The runners had been out there two nights now, and those of us by the firepit were weary-eyed and quiet. Even Naresh had grown still.

Laz kept vigil by the stone pillar and was a dark silhouette against it, the faint light of a lamp touching at his back and the unruly tangles of his beard. Bundled in layers, he was ever vigilant, almost maniacal, like Ahab by the mast—bracing on a bad leg and staring out into the dark. The Barkley made some sense that way, a beast of his own making that he could never conquer. Instead, he dared others into the deep and waited to see who surfaced.

"Runner!" A voice cut through the night, and a headtorch lighted in the distance. Laz peeled his eyes. "Which runner is this?"

There was only silence. Then, a small voice. "Jasmin."

After touching the gate from loop three, she slumped into a chair, choking down the food Konrad shoved at her—pasta, Sonic tater tots, chocolate oat milk, sweets. Her stomach began to revolt. Konrad stuffed her pack with food that he hoped she could tolerate. In the Barkley's three-decade history, only one woman had ever dared loop four. With six minutes left till the cutoff, Jasmin disappeared beyond the gate and became the second.

# 10

# All of Them

**HE COULDN'T SHAKE IT**, the sensation of being pulled into a black hole. His headtorch flickered over the loose stones and dirt as he hunted the edge of the ridge. Somewhere below was The Meatgrinder, a treacherous slant ready to hurl him thousands of feet to the river below. Trekking up it was an hour-long slog at best. But going down it at night? As he saw it, one of the worst of Laz's additions, a monstrous mix of all of Barkley's bad things. And John Kelly hadn't slept for forty hours.

But one runner was still with him, Damian Hall, and thank God. Strength in numbers, at least till loop five when the old man would force them in opposite directions. But Damian had complained more than once how dizzy and sleepy he was and would hate for John to miss a cutoff on account of him. Earlier, at dusk, when the shadows were playing tricks on the eye, Damian simply vanished. Convinced his friend's navigation was off, John picked up his pace till a slim figure appeared on a spur. It was Damian—and John realized he was actually the one that was off. But could Damian keep up now, on the fourth loop?

John tilted a foot over the rim and checked his bearings one last time. Every step was a math problem, a calculation he needed to get right every time. With a rush of gravity and adrenaline, he bounded into The Meatgrinder. In an instant, he was in the darkest depths of space. Navigating an asteroid field with a brain beginning to slip. *Frozen Head, nature's hall of mirrors,* he'd later describe it. *Time dilation delirium. The mind floating free, out in space somewhere... observing the body getting sucked into a black hole.*

Boulders whizzed by the size of cars... trees... blowdowns... the world bouncing like an LED strobe as his headlamp jostled and blinked... step, slide, pole, slide... keep your bearing... heel plant and slide... listen for the sound of the creek at the bottom... grab that tree... slow the cannonball... brake... balance... breathe...

Finally down, the world tilted sideways, John's pulse pounding like a jackhammer in his ears. His heart rate slowed but not his mind. Something was off. *Where was the book?* His gut clenched. Had he gotten them off course, again? Had he stopped too soon? *Remember that rock!* But he had. His mind was a mess, fragments of thoughts crashing into each other like bumper cars. *Was it the wrong confluence? Couldn't be. Could it?*

Damian hit the bottom not far behind, and together they stumbled forward, Hardy Boys in the dark, their beams slicing through the gloom. And then—there it was. The book! *Thank God, hallelujah.* The relief was soon snuffed out by the weight of the grinder, the asteroid field, and every sleepless hour—it all came crashing back.

John's lids drooped, his mind moving in some liminal space. A power nap, he suggested. Damian nodded in agreement. *Brilliant.* John jabbed at his Walmart watch, looking for the alarm, but the little plastic bastard just blinked, mocking and lifeless. Damian's wasn't any better. So, they trudged on, dragging their feet and hatching a new plan. Make the next book, then sleep on the thing. Let the next poor, unsuspecting runner wake them when they passed. *But what if nobody came?*

And then, faster than he thought possible, John was at the Garden Spot, a desolate patch of grass perched on an exposed bluff. Lonely and quiet in the night—it was perfect for a nap. Here, many slept in peace, holy ground for those who, for personal reasons, the Barkley just meant more. Like Dr. Stu Gleman. How Stu's remains made it to the Garden Spot was a story unto itself.

A rocket scientist with patents on explosive bolts, Stu had been one of the Barkley's earliest and most devoted supporters. "Seussical" was how Barkley veteran Carl Laniak described him, "in word, thought, and look." Despite dozens of attempts, Stu never finished a loop at the Barkley. And at 71, Stu had no hope of even starting it. He'd been sick for years. So, he approached Laz about entering one of Laz's newest creations—A Race for the Ages. Entrants were allotted hours equal to their age—a 70-year-old got seventy hours, a 40-year-old forty. The oldest runners often won, with the average winner being 68.

"I'd like to die on the course," Stu told Laz, who demurred in his inimitable way. "But Stu, think about what that would do to all the other runners. They'd have to walk over your body." Stu relented and managed to run 110 miles. That night, he went home to the hospital and passed away.

Frozen Ed had agreed to bring Stu's ashes in a baggy to the Garden Spot, but by book two, he felt miserable. When he saw a French runner's headlamp flickering toward him in the dark, he explained the situation. While Ed hobbled back to camp, Stu went on to his final resting place in the hands of a stranger.

As John and Damian searched for the book at the Garden Spot, it was impossible not to think of another veteran—Charlie Taylor. John had spread his ashes here himself. Charlie had longed to complete a Fun

Run. He never made it in life, but in death, he got his three loops with John, moving through the course in a different way—quiet, weightless, slipping through the trees. John had barely known him—saw the request on the Barkley listserv: someone to take Charlie on one last race. "He'll have a good run if he goes with you," wrote a family member.

Book found, and Damian didn't waste a second. He dropped his head onto it, indifferent to the frozen grass and relentless wind, and was out like a light. When John and Damian weren't running themselves ragged, the two were usually locked in a never-ending duel of cultures: sweet tea versus Earl Grey (lukewarm, of course), what qualified as a real biscuit, and the hidden glories of Sonic Drive-In.

John flopped onto the ground beside his friend, and what followed was nothing short of bliss: a plunge into the void—merciful emptiness, stillness, until...

A light—who? Albert... Okay. Albert Herrero Cassas, the Spanish runner with the salt-and-pepper beard and glasses. That made no sense though. He'd stayed in camp and slept like a cat by the fire. No way he could have caught them so quickly. Well, this was actually good, John thought. *Strength in numbers.*

No sense in trying to sleep now, so John shook Damian till the Brit's eyes cracked open, glazed and bloodshot, seemingly unaware of where he was. But no time for explanations. They were moving again. All three of them. Half a loop left. Hours till the sun, till sight, till the mercy of a moment's rest.

Little Hell loomed ahead, and it wasn't just steep—it was obscene: 1,500 feet of vertical madness packed into just over half a mile. Forty-five degrees of straight-the-hell-up! It was the kind of climb that didn't just mock you; it laughed in your face while chewing your legs into pulp.

John took the lead, grunting with each step—grunting and shoving his poles into the earth, digging his toes in, and pressing onward. Up and up and up. His headlamp cut narrow beams through the dark, glinting off scattered metal remnants of a dead mine. Ventilation shafts yawned like cavernous mouths and coal piles sat hunched in the dark like bodies.

Each step was a war, the tips of his poles planting into the hill, level with his eyeballs. Push. Grunt. Push. Robotic repetition—his lungs screaming, thighs burning hot as molten ore. *Keep your bearing. Keep your bearing.*

At last, it was flat. Merciful, impossible flatness. They'd made it. Little Hell was behind them, conquered, destroyed, and left to smolder. For all intents and purposes, loop four was in the bag. John staggered forward, rasping, and reached back for the ultimate punctuation—a triumphant fist bump.

But his hand hit only empty air.

---

Nothing made sense to Karel anymore.

He was here again, the very same spot where last year he'd unraveled into madness. That much he was sure of. He'd pushed on then when he should've stopped to collect himself. That's why he was still sitting here, sitting by this tall, brooding oak stretching toward the stars. It added up—for a minute. Then *poof,* gone. His thoughts slipped through his fingers like sand. He clawed for them, trying to hold onto the one that had been there just a second ago. *Wait. Why was he here?*

He'd made a mistake, sure. Somewhere, somehow. But where? *The book!* That's why he was here. To find the book. It was in these woods, and that's why he was sitting here ruminating by this towering oak. But he needed a beech tree. *Why?* No, wait. *The Barkley.* He was running it. That's why. The thought hit him like a slap. Of course. He pressed his palms to his eyes, trying to rub away the confusion away like a layer of grime. One problem solved.

The whole loop had gone twisty, he remembered, twisty and wrong, right from the start. A navigational blunder on the very first book and then the Frenchman appeared—Aurélien Sanchez. That had been a shock. It was Aurélien's first Barkley and he was only a half hour behind him. *Or was it an hour?* Didn't matter. He shouldn't have seen him before the first book. And yet, there he was, like an apparition.

"Let's work together," the Frenchman had suggested, nice, polite even. But this wasn't some weekend group run. This was about you against all that Out There. No, at some point, you had to stand alone. Be your own man.

And now, under the looming oak in the icy blackness of Icehouse Delirium, Karel knew one thing for sure: He never wanted to come back to this god-awful place. Not ever. That left only one option. He had to finish. But dammit if it wasn't slipping away. He'd been all over this ground. Up and down, back and forth, crisscrossing like a deranged squirrel—the book just wasn't there. At least he had his warm top on. Small victories. Without it, the cold would've sunk its claws into him already. And if he didn't get moving soon, it'd be biting at his bones.

What would Emma say if she could see him now? She'd laugh. No... she'd tell him to get his ass up, get it together. After all, everyone was watching. Jack too. One day, when Jack got tall like him, he hoped to tell him. Tell him his dad had finished the world's toughest race. And he wouldn't be *that* guy anymore—the trash-can guy.

He clutched his cold body a little tighter to himself and that's when he felt it. A lump. *Oh... ha! The burrito!* He remembered now. Jo said he'd pack it. He could almost see Jo's face, flickering in front of him like a film reel gone bad, hazy and strange. Karel reached into his warm outer and ran his chilly fingers over it.

The first bite into the gooey tortilla was a small explosion, real food sloshing around his mouth. The texture, the hearty smell, the chalky aftertaste. And it was—gone. He folded the wrapper into a neat square and put it back in his pack. *Leave no trace.*

Good food paid dividends. He could feel it, kicking in. Even his mind was clearing up. Or maybe it wasn't the calories at all. Maybe it was the ritual, the everyday act of eating, pressing the reset button on the brain. Kind of like how Courtney Dauwalter brushed her teeth during races. *Ha!* Whatever it was had the forest sharpening before his eyes, the blurred lines crisping up.

And that's when he saw it. Wait... it couldn't be. *Could it?* His mind teetered on the edge, threatening to topple into delirium again. But no. *No!* He could swear on it, swear an oath! He adjusted his headtorch till the beam cut through the dark toward it.

Karel shot to his feet, his heart racing. He reached out, and there it was. Solid. Real. The book! It'd been there the whole time—ten feet in front of him.

"This is still possible," he muttered in the dark air. "I'm not gonna let it go anymore." Bow to the burrito. Yes, and at some point, thank Jo. He grabbed his poles and set off, his feet crunching against the trail as he aimed himself toward the prison. *If I can get to the gate in a few hours, light will come.* The thought was like a warm blanket. But the comfort of remembering he was in the Barkley was fast replaced with the reality that he was... in the Barkley.

By the time he reached the prison, every step dragged air from his lungs in shallow, scraping gasps. The coughing started then—short, sharp bursts that echoed through the endless concrete tunnel beneath Brushy Mountain State Penitentiary.

He walked the cement line in the center, each step a delicate dance. *Keep the feet dry. Keep the feet dry.* But when he pressed up The Bad Thing, the infernal bad thing, the coughing came harder, faster.

And then—a light.

A headlamp pierced through the void, its beam trembling, unsteady. It was moving toward him, in the wrong direction, a pinpoint growing brighter and brighter. Karel froze, his body taut.

It was the ghost of Albert. The world record holder for most elevation gain in twenty-four hours was alone and coughing up pieces of lung tissue. He was also quitting. Or at least, he was trying to.

---

To nap or not to nap—it was a damn hard choice. Back in camp, John sat alone, his body screaming for sleep. He always struggled at dawn anyway, and it didn't help that the others seemed so far behind. Something about it—John never did well when things seemed easy.

Coming in alone from loop four, he knew he'd made mistakes—big mistakes. Uncharacteristic, careless. He'd drifted mindlessly off course in an area he knew like the back of his hand. Fortunately, something in his subconscious had jolted him awake—a mental cattle prod—and he'd avoided disaster.

He couldn't afford to do that again. Not now. Here, it always seemed the higher up the mountain you went, the farther you could fall.

Sleep. That was the best bet. A quick thirty minutes. Recharge the batteries. Just enough to face the fifth and final loop.

Not five minutes later, Aurélien stormed into camp. *He must have crushed his fourth loop.* John checked his watch—his stomach dropped. Aurélien had gained nearly an hour on him.

Now, it's a different game entirely. The old man's favorite kind. The first to the gate got the ultimate prize: the choice of loop direction. Of course, John wanted clockwise. No, he *needed* clockwise. The thought of going up The Meatgrinder in the blaring midday sun? Not an option. Forget the nap...

So, he hurries, but in doing so puts his shoes on before taking off his tights. *And where's that food?* He was just picking at it five minutes ago. Never mind—he dashes to the gate, takes the new bib from Laz, and heads out.

He'd been in camp for twelve chaotic, dizzying minutes, and now he was back Out There.

---

"OH MY GOD—you must be so tired." Emma's voice crackles on the speakerphone. "We are rooting for you. I'm so happy to hear you. You've already made us so proud."

Karel sits back in the glory of a proper camping chair, his body sinking into the fabric like a collapsing building. "Yes, but if I don't finish," he says, "it doesn't really matter."

Jo is a blur, his movements sharp and relentless, like a hummingbird. Packing Karel's gear. Shoving food into his hands. Thrusting drinks at him. It's all about time—minutes, seconds, fractions of seconds—and there's no question of sleep. Because only one person has ever started loop five this late and finished. John Fegys. And Jo knows this because Fegys just came over and told him. "Hurry up," Jo says. "You can make it."

Karel knew Fegys's story. So did everyone else at the Barkley.

It was 2012, and John "Fegys" Fegyveresi was at a crossroads. His father had passed away suddenly, just a year before he was set to retire. It was a gut-punch, a harsh reminder of life's short wick. Live for now, never let a chance slip away.

Fegys was a researcher studying ice cores in Antarctica, and by no means a pedigreed runner, but his essay had impressed Laz. He was a true Danny—scrappy, stubborn, all heart.

From the start, Fegys couldn't hang with the veterans. He wasn't built for their pace and ran most of the race alone, a solitary figure against the wild expanse. By loop four, he was unraveling—mumbling to himself, his skin pale, his frame gaunt and shaky. His eyes darted, shifty and paranoid, like a prisoner locked up too long in solitary.

But he didn't stop. Couldn't stop.

By loop five, he was lying in the creek under the prison, water swirling around him as he stuttered gibberish. The world spun beneath him, but he got up. Again and again, he got up. Stumbling forward, he plodded his way toward the gate. He came in bracing himself with a crooked stick, hunched and weary, like Rip Van Winkle waking from a century-long sleep. He was the slowest runner to ever do it. But he finished the Barkley.

"Fegys did it," Jo says coolly, checking everything one more time. "So can you." But Karel doesn't seem to hear him. Emma either, her voice soft but insistent on the phone. "Just one book at a time," she reminds him, before softening her tone, probing. "Are you alright?"

Karel winces at that, looks over at Jo. "I think I've lost all my toenails."

"It doesn't matter," Jo says, sharp and deliberate. "If you finish."

---

The first light reached Jasmin on the summit of Stallion Mountain, "coloring the sky with the promise of a spectacular dawn." It was clear and cold as she slogged on toward the prison, but the beauty, she couldn't ignore it. She'd later write it was "as if Barkley was holding its breath in respect of the morning's splendor."

When her watch ticked over to forty-eight hours, and she was officially out of the race, she didn't linger. She'd expected it—the time had been too short, and she just wanted to get as far as she could. She didn't think of Laz's rules either, to go straight back. There was no debate in her mind about it. Carry on. *Just give it everything.* So, she opened the prison book, *Last Will and Testament*, took her page, then pushed up The Bad Thing.

Later, when the midday sun warmed her shoulders, she saw the sculptures, and they were beautiful indeed. Modern. Spread along the landscape, on spurs and tucked in pockets of quarried stone. *Why put it here? It's going to be so underappreciated.* Soon, she was joined by old friends from school. It was great to see them. Family too. It was kind of them to come all this way and make their way into the woods to find her. The exotic animals in their bright colors? Mesmerizing. Her dream turned finally into flesh. They were much better than the dark humanoid figures, stalking and scampering through the trees, always a look away. While she was aware this was all in her mind, they were unsettling.

She shuffled on through the crunching leaves, wishing her friends would quiet down a bit. She argued with them. "The climb couldn't possibly be so long," she complained. Then, suddenly everything fell quiet, and she was running down a mountain in what she would later say felt like a "a slow-motion movie without sound." It was then she saw the body lying across the path. That couldn't be real either. None of this was. But it sure felt real when she nudged it. Then, it rolled over. Damian.

"Are you okay?" he said, cracking open an eye. He'd been unable to find the last book. It just wasn't there. He had a leaf, though, a small rock too. And he'd spread pieces of biscuit around. That should prove to Laz he'd been in the right spot, he said, confusion crumpling his brow. "That probably wouldn't work, would it?"

---

Late afternoon Thursday, the park seemed to change—less malevolent—the sun out, bright, and small buds of spring pushing through their winter prisons. I was sitting on top of a large boulder when I spotted the figure at the bottom of the hill.

It was black and grey and moving fast in our direction. Then it was Jasmin, pushing on her trekking poles and bounding, determined and smiling, and picking up speed. The talk in camp had died out hours ago, that she was over time. Everyone knew it. Keith had tweeted earlier that morning, making it official: "We are over 48 hours into the race. Jasmin Paris has not completed loop four within the time limit and is out of the race."

She knew it too. Had to. Yet, she was running... running hard till she touched the gate. She looked remarkably fresh, her skin full of blood, and she spoke easy. "It was an incredible morning," she told Laz, her voice full of wonder. "Out of this world."

Frozen Ed appeared, unable to hold back his curiosity. "How many books did you get?"

"All of them," she said with a sheepish grin. Frozen Ed looked around with glee, hoping to catch someone's eye, to share in what that meant—that she was the first woman to complete loop four, albeit over the time limit.

"How far did you get before you timed out?" asked Laz, now down to a white long-sleeve button-up dress shirt, a small ponytail sticking out his sock hat.

"Nine books." Jasmin shrugged her shoulders and rested against the gate. Frozen Ed's eyes glistened. The previous best by a woman was two. She offered her pages to Laz to count, but he had no need for them. "Do you feel like the hundred is still in reach?" he asked.

"I do, yeah," she said and smiled. He smiled back. And Taps played.

## 11

# Endgame Tricks

**JOHN KELLY HURLED A BATTLE CRY** into the trees, a desperate scream to stay awake. Since forgoing the nap in camp, every step felt like something fading, a zombie trying his best not to fall off a cliff. His feet dragged. His eyes dulled. *Finish*, he told himself. Just that. *Finish.*

The trail up Jury Ridge was marked. Too marked. His mind hated that, hated the ease of it. Ease meant drifting. And drifting now meant the end. He screamed again but could feel himself slowing, the fatigue spreading. So, he stopped. Couldn't go on. Couldn't do another step. Not like this.

But taking a dirt nap now was risky. He might never get up—the Walmart watch couldn't be trusted. So, he found a creek, knelt beside it, and laid the back of his head in the icy water. It was a go-to move he'd learned somewhere, during some other endless stretch of exhaustion. At a certain point, the cold discomfort of the water would wake him, keep him from the abyss.

When he cracked his eyes open again, though, he was shivering. He checked the watch. *Six minutes.* Not enough. It never was. *Dammit.* The water had been too cold.

Restless and irritated, he forced his legs to move again. After cresting the ridge, he caught his breath and started down The Meatgrinder. That should keep him awake. Danger, fast and cruel, was better than caffeine. Down he went in controlled chaos till finally at the bottom, he turned and looked back. His eyes traced an imaginary line. Anyone climbing this thing now—counterclockwise, in the midday heat—God help them.

He trudged onto Hillpocalypse. It didn't fight you; it seduced you—a mundane climb that never seemed to end, pressing minutes into hours, hours spent with your eyes inches away from the dirt.

The warming air didn't help either. Soft and heavy, it lulled him into what he called "non-lucid reality." A state not quite here, not quite there, where everything felt untethered and strange. He didn't hallucinate—he lacked that gene—but he started to feel he was inside a video game. "Some people have lucid dreams," he once explained. "They know the fantasy isn't real. When I'm sleep-deprived... I don't know that reality isn't fantasy."

In this video game, he saw a sign ahead, "Park Headquarters." It was in the shape of an arrow and pointed to a trail descending the mountain. "Quitter's Road," he mumbled under his breath. *Endgame tricks*. He wasn't going that way. But the muddy tracks were promising, glistening with thawing ice, inviting like a dream. And dreams came with sleep. Sleep. A luxury he couldn't afford. Not now. Not when this was everything. Not when every step forward, every glance at his watch, became a reminder. He had to keep moving. He had to be the one who didn't quit.

Yet here he was—on his knees in the mud. With deliberate care, almost excitement, he laid himself face down in it, closed his eyes, and time lost all sense of meaning, till...

A sound. Low, indistinct, just enough to pull him back. He lifted his head and cracked an eye open. A face hovered above him. Familiar and impossible. A childhood friend, smiling. *Twenty years? No, more.* He was leaning closer now, and with him a wife perhaps, and a child. John called his name, a croak of recognition, but the wires in his mind sparked and frayed. *This wasn't real. Couldn't be. This was, yes, his first hallucination surely.* He called out again, and the friend laughed, his voice crisp and warm. "That's a John Kelly nap if I've ever seen one."

*Ha! Ha!* John let the laughter roll over him, let it soak in. His friend was walking away now, fading into the ether. Still smiling, John dropped his face back into the thawing mud, as if it were the most natural thing in the world to do.

He squeezed his eyes shut, but sleep was a no-show. Sleep was somewhere else. No matter. He pushed on. He crossed the chasm of Son of a Bitch Ditch and climbed up to the Garden Spot. He was not even halfway through the loop.

Atop the rise, it all came apart in the heat. With the warm sun high in the sky, he surrendered, letting the dark void pull him under. If Aurélien or another runner came through, they'd have to wake him. There'd be no choice. Why? Somewhere, deep inside, John was grinning. In a film of non-lucid reality, he saw himself from above—sprawled out, blissful, dead to the world—right on top of the damned book.

---

The book wasn't there! Aurélien Sanchez's tired brain squeezed with frustration. He circled the cairn, methodical at first, then like a wild man. A wild man with a throbbing knee and three days of candy and cookie dough swirling in his stomach.

Since the conch blew, the Frenchman had slept only ten minutes. That had been on a patch of ground by a van in the parking lot. It all wrapped together and had him here, teetering on the edge of something close to crazy. He couldn't even hike in a straight line anymore. Still, he was absolutely certain this was the right place.

He had come to this cairn four times already. Each time, the book had been here, nestled beneath the stones. But now, it wasn't. And no matter how many times he circled or clawed at the pile or scoured the surroundings, it still wasn't. He knelt beside it, damp earth seeping into his knees, and ran a hand over the smooth stones. For six years, he'd imagined himself here, imagined this fifth loop, these woods. But not like this.

People told him getting into the Barkley was impossible. He was just a hiker, didn't have enough ultra experience, had never even run a marathon. Still, the race became Aurélien's fixation. To get in, he took on FKTs on some of the world's most iconic trails. He attempted The John Muir and failed. The Tower Room Trail? He came up short there too. "It was very difficult," he would tell CNN. "Very tough to fail in some of the ways I failed, but I learned out of it. I learned that I was not the strongest person ever, that I had to deal with my weaknesses."

Every year he sent a request to Laz, and every year, silence. Then, he set the record on the John Muir and hiked 550 miles of the Pyrenees Crossing in twelve days with no crew. When the condolence letter finally arrived, he wept. "Everything I did was for the Barkley," he would say. "I wanted to have the privilege one day to run it."

Now, staring at the empty cairn, he wondered if it had all been for nothing. It felt like the culmination of his fears. But if he allowed himself to linger too long on what this *might* mean, it would undo him. He could hear Laz's voice, sharp and amused: "*Twelve pages? Is one playing hooky?*" He'd be one of those stories they told by the firepit over scalded chicken and beer. The Pageless Wonder.

Aurélien sank to his knees and rubbed his forehead. *Could this be a trap? Another twist in Laz's game?*

The frenzy came on him fast—he ripped the cairn apart stone by stone, dirt caking his hands. Still, no book. In a final act of desperation, he spread the remnants around as if arranging an offering, a message. *This happened. I was here.*

Dusk thickened, the forest dimmed, and he staggered forward, his breath catching in sobs. Everything he'd endured, all of it, would be erased. All over a damn book. Out There had beaten him, but worse than that, it was going to forget him.

Dark fell fast and hard over Aurélien on the final stretch, but he could see the glow of lights flickering through the trees, faint and unreachable. The voices, the cheers, the clapping—they didn't feel real either. Nothing did.

He stumbled in front of the gate, legs like lead, mind swirling. He reached out and touched it, then rubbed at his eyes. Laz was there, red and black checked, lit by an LED lamp. Through its harsh, white light, he barely registered the old man's smirk. But his eyes caught him, the way they glinted with mischief and authority, almost daring him to say something.

"There is a book at Phillips Creek which is missing." Aurélien's words tumbled out in a rush. "I—I don't know what to do about that."

Laz said nothing. Just reached behind his can of Dr. Pepper and lifted a clear plastic bag into the air. Inside, unmistakable, was the black book. Aurélien blinked and staggered back a step. If this was a game—what did it mean? How do you win?

A playful curve came to Laz's lips and that cackle that you were never sure was with you or against you. Next came the story: the hiker who believed the race was over and would do a good deed by picking it up; his fellow countryman, Guillaume Calmettes, begging Laz to let him run the book back up before Aurélien got there; and Laz saying no, "shit happens."

When the explanation was over, exhaustion and relief hit Aurélien at once. His head dropped, and the tears came. He hugged everyone near him. This was what he had dreamed of, fought for. To be here. To finish. And he had.

His crew brought him a chair. He sat, and that felt almost as good.

---

Soon, cheers erupted once more—softer this time, carried on tired voices. And another headlamp bobbed through the darkness but from the opposite direction. It was John Kelly.

He moved steadily toward the gate, eyed Laz, then smacked the yellow pole. His hand lingered for a moment. His second finish; the third to ever complete the Barkley twice. Moments later, he and Aurélien embraced. Laz stood close enough to touch but looked on like the moment unfolding was not his to claim.

Camp settled quickly. This thing wasn't over. Zipped up in a coat, John leaned against the gate, and an unspoken moment passed between him and the old man.

"Do you know where Karel is?" Laz asked finally, his voice now like wet gravel.

"He was at the top going down on Buttslide as I was at the top coming back out," John said, thinking back. "That put me thirty—forty minutes ahead of him. He's coming in."

"I hope so," said Laz. "He's paid a heavy price for two years to get here."

An hour ticked by, and still, no Karel. Laz squinted at his watch. Twenty minutes left. Camp seemed suspended in an uneasy pause, the hum of conversation dissolving into silence. Phones began to light up like fireflies in the dark, fingers darting over screens to relay updates. Jo, Karel's crewman, stood nearby, shifting from foot to foot. "He was forty-five minutes behind at the tower," he said. "But he started an hour behind."

John sank into a chair by the gate while his kids played on it. Part of him wished this would hurry up and end so he could go home. His legs, slashed and bruised, began to throb. But leaving wasn't an option. So, he busied himself with the math. *There's X minutes left, which means we need to see his headlamp up there within Y minutes or down there within Z.*

But the minutes crept by, and it all started to feel too familiar. He had been here before—in this very spot—maybe in this same chair, waiting, hoping, dreading. 2016. Gary Robbins. The thought gripped him, made him shudder. He didn't need to say it either; déjà vu was curling through camp like smoke. A shared understanding that this had all happened before, and a silent prayer that it wouldn't happen again.

---

It was the most memorable finish in Barkley lore.

Laz had already had to remove his glasses and wipe away emotion spilling from his eyes. John Kelly, who once crumbled to the ground on the far side of the gate, had finished. Now, roughly fifty people crowded around the gate, waiting for Gary Robbins.

A prolific runner, Robbins had not only won scores of ultras but set course records on the grueling HURT 100 and on some of the most brutal trails of the Pacific Northwest. But the year before, 2015, the Barkley had stumped him after three loops. So, he trained as if nothing else existed. Overnights in freezing rain, running in snowpack, tackling monstrous climbs and bombing down dangerous downhills. He was determined. Focused. Obsessive.

He arrived in Frozen Head in 2016 looking like a mountain man. A thick red beard curled to his chest beneath a hardened face and penetrating eyes. For three loops, he battled rain and fog but came in each time running fast and fresh. Then out for four and back in, spouting orders to his crew. A tense cloud over his eyes.

On a rain-soaked loop five, word had spread that he was moving well. His wife, Linda, cradled their baby and waited, dark circles under her eyes. Camp had exploded when John came in, but that seemed long ago now. The crowd fell eerily quiet. There was no sign of Gary, and time was getting short. Too short.

They whispered updates and tried to read the tea leaves. But seconds bled into minutes, and the air tightened with a kind of dread, the cutoff time looming ever closer. Then, there he was, sprinting. He reached the gate, gasping, and collapsed backwards to the ground. "I have all my pages, Laz," he said in breathy stops and starts. "I have all my pages."

He lay in a pile of chilled sweat, pain, and exhaustion. He tried to explain that he'd taken a wrong turn. He handed his pages to his wife, who was kneeling beside him, stroking his shoulder. She passed them to Laz, wet and wadded up, and searched the old man's face for some solution.

Glances darted all around. *What just happened?*

But if Laz had an answer to the pain and devastation Robbins was writhing in, he didn't show it. Frozen Ed, curious, asked about the time. "Six seconds," Laz said, with a smile. *Rules aren't rules if they aren't enforced, they're merely suggestions.* And Robbins was six seconds over the 60-hour cutoff.

But the time didn't matter. Laz knew that. Robbins knew it too. He'd come in the wrong way, from the wrong direction. After navigating fifty-nine hours of Barkley—in the dark and the rain and the fog—he'd gotten lost in the daylight, on the easy part.

A collective expression hovered over the onlookers. Surely there was some kind of exception. The veterans knew better, understood what it would mean for Laz to move the goalposts. Robbins wouldn't want that. And his sock hat was off and over his heart as he listened to Taps, his face gaunt, frozen with defeat.

The next year, he trained even harder, came back even more determined, but would ultimately fall short. When he got to the second book, he found a special treat from Laz. The title was just visible through the plastic bag—*Six Seconds.*

---

It was a tour bus—Karel was sure that's what it was. Why and how it had arrived in Frozen Head was another thing. Didn't matter; it was awesome, they probably had sodas and coffee. He'd take one, both, whatever. Then, it was gone, but at least he wasn't alone. There were figures behind the trees, voices calling to him from the dark. When he dropped into the tunnel underneath the prison, he heard televisions playing above, and whispering and laughter.

Then, he was climbing but not sure what. *What am I doing in the woods?* There was something urgent. A task. *What was it?* Another hill stretched up ahead. His instinct was to go up it. Something also told him to *find the book.* It was a compulsion, distant but forceful, and he followed it. And there was a book. He ripped the page out, and a rush of adrenaline surged through him. He put it in his baggy and felt his brain tingle, a cloud parting with some sort of clarity.

Something also told him to run fast, then even faster. He looked at his watch and for the first time in hours, it made sense. He had "forty minutes to reach something." Then, a shot of panic—that *something* was the gate, and it was exactly forty minutes away.

---

"Emma is stressing out," Jo says to Jared. She's texting him nonstop. On edge. It's one thirty in the morning in Belgium, but she's up, unloading on him, waiting on Karel to finish. He must finish. He can't do this again. He can't go back. Not another year of brutal training and pressure and relentless stress about this race.

In the café, she's eyeing screens—Keith Dunn's Twitter feed, a WhatsApp feed, and a sports page. It's too close now. Too close! Jo looks at the messages piling up and stares out into the dark. Emma's right, it is too close.

A small group waits by the pillar. Laz. Sandra. Naresh. Bad Mike crunching numbers on a screen. Keith, on one of his phones, tweets: "The 2023 Barkley Marathons ends in 10 minutes." Laz eyes the bottom of the hill. Nothing. A minute ticks over. Then, one more. Then...

*Runner!*

All eyes in camp move toward a light bobbing side to side. A figure behind it, a hundred yards away, is running toward the gate. Claps, cheers, and whistles urge it on. He's in the pool of light by the gate now. Karel. The lines of his face crunch together as he heaves forward. With one final move, he reaches out for the gate and folds to the ground when he touches it.

Jo is there in a flash. Arms around him. Eases the hydration vest off Karel and lays him flat. The only sound is Karel gasping. He closes his eyes and grabs his chest. His face and neck are red, his mouth hangs open, and his dusty wedding band glints softly. He groans when Jo supports his head with the vest. He struggles to unzip a pocket on the right side of his shorts. "Lights," Laz barks at the media still on site. "Get the lights out of his face."

With his eyes still clenched, Karel presents his collection. "Laz," he wheezes, "these are my pages." He lies back down, and another coughing fit erupts. He checks his watch. Still seven minutes left—he's made it.

He'd always envisioned himself coming in, high-fiving those around. There would be smiles and cheers as he stood there, "taking it all in." Instead, he's on the ground, his face painted with pain. Still, he'd later describe this moment as "the best joy that you can feel."

When he finally raises himself up, claps ring out around him. "I'm sorry for the drama," he says and laughs. "My brain was out, man."

Laz leans over the gate. "One last formality," he says, stretching a red plastic button in front of Karel's face. The Belgian smiles, knows what to do, and presses it. A robotic voice activates. "THAT WAS EASY."

## 12

# Don't Go Away Easy

**"TO SAVE IT," LAZ SAID** in a hollow voice that last day of the Barkley, his bloodshot eyes blinking open...

I'd been sitting nearby, my fingers tapping nonsense into the keyboard as the race dwindled before my eyes. Soon I'd be in a cushy hotel room—light-years from Frozen Head—and I'd gotten next to nothing on the man himself.

It was Thursday in the real world, but here four runners were still alive. The others who'd fallen short were gone or going—tents folded, cook stoves packed, vans and trucks disappearing down the hill. Meanwhile, Laz and his volunteers had been working in spurts to erase any trace that we'd been here at all.

So, when Laz eased into a chair beside me, I shut my laptop.

"You know, one thing doesn't add up," I blurted out, a knot rising in my throat.

"Just one?" Laz's head bobbed with a chuckle.

"For twenty years," I said, "everything from the course map to the start time to the entrant list was secret—zero media, nada. Then suddenly in 2007, it's *The Washington Post.* Not long after, *Runner's World,* Netflix, *The New York Times.*"

His head dipped as if it might tip forward in sleep and stay there. Then, his eyes opened again, resting on a few embers glowing faintly beneath layers of ash. "To save it," he said, like it was obvious, his lips twitching into something like a smile. "Everything changes. People don't like it much, but it happens."

"To save—"

But he was on his feet again before I could finish. A commotion had caught his eye—a small man toting a large camera and a woman pointing a microphone in people's faces. I half expected him to explode—*finally*—to bark like an ogre and send them scrambling down the hill for their lives. The Inner Circle said it was bound to happen when the race went deeper and his nerves began to fray. But instead, he gave the reporter a short interview in front of the license plates.

The remaining hours unfolded in fragments—demands, questions, goodbyes, his presence required at the gate for Taps. Combined with Laz's penchant for going off topic, it was enough to seed a serious doubt as to whether our conversation was punctuated by interruptions, or the other way around. There were also strange hellos from people who seemed to sprout from nowhere like mushrooms after a storm.

It was while Laz was speaking with the local news crew that I noticed a shadow lingering beneath the trees. A short man finally stepped into the light, mid-thirties, a high-and-tight military cut. He fidgeted with his hands and asked if I'd tell Laz that he needed to talk to him. He'd come alone from Germany, he said, rented a car and found his way to the park. A boyish grin spread over his face when he said his wife and kids had no idea he was here. He also told me he worked in the prison system, and I half wondered if he'd busted out. Yet, there was an earnestness in his eyes that gleamed with the shifting light.

Laz didn't blink, just took him aside and talked with him for eight, maybe ten minutes. Afterward, the man lingered for a moment, as if waiting for something more. Then, head down, hands shoved deep in his pockets, he slipped back into the trees.

"What did he want?" I asked.

Laz shrugged. "To know why he hadn't gotten in."

Soon, the license plates were neatly boxed, the barricades leaned against the U-Haul, and Laz began smoothing the flags between his hands, too precious to fold in haste. Watching the Barkley come down, I couldn't help but think of a carnival—the kind that comes like a storm, with thunder and lights, then vanishes, leaving only trampled grass.

It would pop up again in the spring, in Wartrace for Strolling Jim. Then The Last Annual Vol State in the summer, followed by the Last Annual Heart of the South. And in October, Big's Backyard Championship.

I caught Laz again later in the afternoon by the U-Haul, a cigarette hanging from his lips. "The media," I said abruptly, trying to pick up where we'd left off.

He nodded, wrinkled his brow, and studied the end of his cigarette. "To keep it going," he said, watching the smoke trickle toward the sky.

"How do you mean?"

"To show the park service how small our footprint was. The documentary did a good job of that."

"It must've worked," I said.

"For now," he muttered back.

A lone cloud slid across the sun, softening the light on his face. I expected him to veer away again, or someone to ask him something. But he didn't move and set his eyes on me, those sleepy eyes—red and weary a moment ago, now shiny and devious. “You never know with the Tennessee Department of Environment and Conservation,” he said, thumping an ash on the ground. “One day, there’ll be an RV park in Frozen Head, and roads, lots of them, winding their way up to every landmark. The first will be to the Fire Tower. Oh, they’ll want that view.”

He looked amused and gave a slow nod of disbelief. “The Tennessee Valley, the Cumberland Plateau, the Smokies off to the East. But they sure as hell won’t want to walk. Next will be the gorges at New River—cut out the woods, throw up lodges, cabins, restaurants. ‘Amenities,’ they’ll call them. Convenience, drive right up! Government...” His voice sharpened, a hint of scorn creeping in. “It’s what they do. Make everything the same. All parks, all places—uniformity at all costs.”

He took up his cattle prod to walk away. “What? You didn’t know they tried to kill the Barkley?” His voice dripped with sarcasm while his eyes glinted with triumph. “But they made one fatal mistake,” he said, looking up at the trail past the gate.

“They thought we’d go away easy.”

---

For years, officials had expressed concern over the race’s supposed “negative impact” on the park’s sensitive natural areas. Sections of the course were repeatedly being closed off, forcing Laz to retreat and reroute. Finally, in late 2004, the Department officially pulled the plug, notifying Laz that the Barkley would be terminated.

“i’ve been going out there since the ’70s, when it wasn’t even a park,” Laz complained in an email chain. And didn’t the park officials remember? He’d already held the Barkley for two years before Frozen Head even became a state park. If they did, they didn’t care about it, nor about his pleas to work together as allies, with a common interest, to keep the wild spaces wild. He was furious and ready to fight, writing, "i ain't near giving up." He wasn't alone.

According to Frozen Ed's *Tales From Out There*, a group of dedicated Barkley runners circled the wagons around him. Joe Kowalski, a veteran of the race who'd provided the tarp for years, joined with others in a letter-writing campaign. Kerry Trammell worked the local politicians in nearby Oak Ridge. Then there was Stu—a man who knew how to navigate bureaucracy.

Together, they managed to wrangle a stay of execution—barely. The Department would allow the Barkley to go on in 2005, but after that? They'd have to pack up and move on. They offered up three alternative parks, and Laz reluctantly visited one. He returned convinced that his cynicism about the state's idea of progress was justified—even generous. "i have never seen such devastation in my life," he wrote. "strip mines, clearcuts, jeep roads, 4-wheeler tracks, all the remainder of the mountains around frozen head are an enormous waste pit."

When January 2006 rolled around, the mood was dire among the Barkers. Then suddenly Tennessee State Senator Jim Tracy hopped onto their email chain. He explained that he and fellow senator Randy McNally were getting desperate calls about a one-of-a-kind race in imminent danger. In a surprise February move, the legislators took up the matter and drafted a resolution:

> *WHEREAS,* the close relationship between the race's organizers and state park personnel has helped to ensure that the Barkley's participants leave behind no permanent disfigurement of Frozen Head; and
>
> *WHEREAS,* after 20 years of a mutually beneficial relationship, the Department of Environment and

> Conservation has recently informed the race's organizers that the Barkley can no longer be held at Frozen Head, citing the race as an "inappropriate use" of the park; and
>
> *WHEREAS,* this general assembly respectfully disagrees with the Department's decision, believing strongly that not only is the Barkley an appropriate use for Frozen Head, the race is a precious jewel of Tennessee's outdoor recreation that is well worth preserving.

While it was an enormous victory, the resolution was only a recommendation. The Department would naturally obey in the short term, but there were no guarantees for the future. The Barkley would also have to abide by certain concessions: 200 loops run in Frozen Head a year, or roughly 40 runners total. Laz had in fact suggested it—a bureaucratic morsel for the Department to hold onto, something concrete, something they could measure, slap on a report, and call progress.

---

It was the final hours now, and Laz was standing by the gate with his sock hat over his heart as Taps played for Damian Hall. He'd returned just after Jasmin, in an altered state, unable to find even the first book. Seeing Laz stand side by side with him, I couldn't help but think Laz suffered in the comparison.

The old man's eyes were sagging, and his back was hunched. He'd barely slept since lighting the cigarette early Tuesday morning. He had also eaten very little. Eating meant the inevitable bathroom trip, which meant leaving the gate and walking down to the facilities. And he'd be damned if he was going to miss possible Barkley drama for stupid bodily functions. But by Thursday, it was beginning to catch up with him.

Earlier, while dozing in a lawn chair, he'd begun contorting, involuntarily, like a possessed doll. His right leg kicked out straight as a garden hoe. It then bent from the knee and returned to a resting position on the ground. This bizarre yoga repeated itself every five minutes or so but never disturbed the peaceful look on his face—eyes closed, lips turned up at the edges. During that time, the Inner Circle had finished the packing—everything neat—till there was nothing left but the U-Haul.

After Damian retired to his camp, dusk began creeping in, stretching long shadows over the gate, where Laz leaned like the center of a storm. I had the distinct feeling that if I didn't get some insight from him now, I never would, so I approached with a parting gift—two ice-cold Dr. Peppers. The chill made my hands tremble when I set them on the pillar, or maybe it was the gnawing realization that I was on my way back to New York, and my article was going to be a skim job at best. "You know," I said, opening mine with a frustrated snap, "we haven't spent more than five minutes talking about *you*."

He didn't react to that but stretched his left leg with a groan. "The blood doesn't pump in the cold," he said, rubbing at it.

"Yeah, you had a little *Exorcist* thing going on there," I joked. If we had a default language, it was humor. I was beginning to realize just how much the old man laughed. It was almost a tic. I thought back to a column he'd written: "We may experience competition, compassion, companionship, and camaraderie," he wrote, "but the highlight is comedy."

"Graves' disease," he said, wincing and working his leg. Then he took a long drag of soda and slid the can into a black-and-red-checked flannel huggie, a mini-me of sorts, with two little arms sticking out. He adjusted his glasses, and his eyes ballooned up for a second. "You wake up with double vision," he said, "then your brain takes out one of the pictures. It raises the things that matter and shrinks the things that don't."

The doctors gave him a pill to radiate his thyroid, but it took out his parathyroids in the process, and if he doesn't eat right, he runs low on calcium and the spasms come. Stress adds to it, of course, and sleep deprivation doesn't help either. "Discomfort," he says, like the slipped disc in his back and the clogged femoral artery in his left leg. "But not deal-breakers."

One year at the Barkley, he fell off a stump and tore something in his shoulder. A runner's handler, who happened to be a nurse, fixed him up with a sling, and he stayed at the helm of the pillar till the end. Nothing short of dying, and maybe not even that, would pull him away while runners were Out There testing his course.

"The idea that you can do anything you want to do?" he said. "That's an old wives' tale. You can do anything you want to do *that you're capable of.*"

"But doesn't that adage give us the belief to try?"

"Most of us never really try," he said, eyes flittering as if seeing something in the distance. There was nothing there but the purpling of shadows beneath the trees. "We bail on ourselves," he went on. "It's not about winning. It's about trying to win. Big dog exemplified that."

I sipped my Dr. Pepper. "I assume that's why you named the Backyard after him?" I muttered.

"It's really easy to quit the Barkley," he said, out of nowhere.

I cut my eyes at him. He seemed to like that.

"Think about it," he laughed, shifting his weight against the stone column. "You're tired, sleep-deprived, wet, and you look up at a ball-buster of a climb full of briars. Granted, it may take you hours to get back, but the decision is easy. But a Backyard, the real test is not Out There... but in here." He circled a finger beside his temple and laughed till he coughed. "Ohhh me," he groaned. "What gets you to quit—the Backyards are all about it. Takes a different kind of individual when the toughest section on the course is between the chair and the start line. Well, you'll see if you make it this October."

I got tripped up on that thought for a moment. At Little's, I'd looked forward to nothing more than my little green chair. I pictured it waiting for me while I was on the trail, an understanding friend that never judged, only comforted. In the end, it had been my worst enemy.

Laz sounded far away as he rambled on about the trail behind his house and his plans. He wanted to make more bridges so runners wouldn't get their feet wet, to clear off blowdowns so they wouldn't trip, even connect a trail for his neighbor Ben.

"Wait," I said, snapping to. "So, you're going out of your way to make Big's easier?"

"Oh yeah," he said, and his eyes woke up a bit. "The easier course holds the burn longer, makes it harder to quit." He smirked. "Backyards are a blood sport. When Big was alive, I used to say it was the only time you'd see a pit bull watch grown men fight to the death."

Frozen Head was now absorbed in darkness, eerily quiet, and the air rapidly cooling. Laz pulled open an LED lamp, and the sharp light reflected off his glasses, making his eyes that much harder to read. But the weariness that had been hanging on him appeared to be melting away with nightfall or washed down with the fizzy sugar. Either way, he seemed triggered, riled even.

"You need to be able to deal with physical discomfort," he said, leaning a hand on the gate. "I don't like pain, but I learned how to deal with it. Doctors did all kinds of shit to me as a kid, took a large syringe attached to a hose, stuck it up my nose, and blasted water up it till it came out my eyes." His eyes lit for a second, then drifted sideways. "You know, when you're a kid, you think only old people die."

I paused at that, thought about it for a long second, then said it. "Are you talking about the tumor?" When he didn't say anything, I felt the adrenaline rise and tingle in my chest. But he finally nodded a yes, drew a cigarette, and a flame squirted up between his cupped hands.

"People get disabled about pain," he said on a long exhale of smoke. "Only a few times in my life have I experienced pain. There's three kinds: the physical, the emotional, and the kind you can't name. Most of the time it's discomfort—there's a difference. The true application is when you get old." He laughed, shaking his head with a sort of performative bewilderment. "Hell, I can't even get around to set the books out anymore, but if I'd taken disability because of my leg, I'd be dead by now."

"You didn't set out all the books?" I felt dizzy and sat on Keith's stone. "So, who did?"

"Carl did 'em this year," Laz said. "Hell, I haven't been able to do them for years."

"So, why in the world would you try to walk across America?" I said.

"Why *wouldn't* you want to?" There was an uncomfortable pause—his eyes sparkling, enjoying it. Some photographers started gathering near the gate, and Laz scanned the hill. Darkness. "Carl will have to do it all next year," he said, snuffing out his cigarette.

"All of what?" I said.

His eyes stilled. "The Barkley."

I just stared.

He looked at me like he had a dozen other times, shocked that I seemed shocked. "I'm not going to live forever," he quipped. "I'm handing it over to Carl. He's got the right temperament if he can let go of the uselessness of compassion."

I almost choked on my drink. "You're what?"

"Well, I'll be here, but he'll be running it." Laz couldn't have been more matter-of-fact, like he'd said he spilled his drink.

"You're putting me on," I said, trying to gauge him in the shaft of lamplight.

"Things change." Laz smiled wide, revealing a glowing set of perfect dentures. He was doing the windup toy thing again, I thought, going off on an arbitrary vector. Carl was Carl Laniak. I'd talked to him a bit in camp. Quiet. Smart. Good guy. But Laz had to be kidding. The race couldn't go on without him. He *was* the Barkley.

A million possible angles and questions whizzed around but coalesced into none. My can was empty and so was my brain.

"Runner!" A voice cut through camp, high pitched and cracking.

Laz's eyes searched the dark as an orb appeared in the distance, bounding toward us. It was the light of a headlamp. One, it seemed, had survived. And for all we knew… the wilderness had swallowed the rest.

## Part III

# DIARY OF A BIG DOG

13

# My Name Is Big

i used to have a different master and a different name.
one day that master took me in a car.
we drove far away to a place I had never been.
master and i got out,
then master forgot and drove away without me.

i had never been outside before,
and i was very afraid.
so i waited for master to come back for me.
i waited all day.
i got very hungry and thirsty,
but i dared not leave. master left me there.
so that must be where I was supposed to stay.
finally a car came.
it wasn't master, but it was a human.
i needed help, and humans are help.

i do not know why, but he was afraid.
he yelled at me and threw rocks,
so i ran away.
i found another human
and i went to him for help.
this one pointed a stick at me and fire came out of it.
my shoulder exploded with pain and my leg wouldn't work,
so i ran on 3 legs, back to where the master left me.
the rock throwing human was gone, but his car was there.
so i hid nearby, under a fallen tree.
and i waited for master to come back.
all night I lay there.
and all the next day.
my leg was on fire.
i was so hungry, and so thirsty,
but master never came.
i was weak and feverish.
all my world was hunger, thirst, and pain.
i needed my master.

—LAZ, *THE BIG DOG DIARIES*

**TO UNDERSTAND THE SIGNIFICANCE** of the Backyard Ultra and how it was born, I was told, you had to go back to 2010—to a blocked artery, a dying dog under a tree, and a man who'd just lost everything. With that in mind, I returned to Bell Buckle, roughly seven months after the Barkley.

I turned in past the stone mailbox to see Laz looking dumbstruck before a carnival-sized tent, striped green and white. I eased to the bottom of the hill, tires crackling and popping over the gravel, and parked. The little house was now a nerve center. Tall stacks of water jugs leaned against it, and electric cables protruded from underneath, lying over the ground like umbilical cords till they disappeared into a compact timing tent.

Like at the Barkley, Laz offered no greeting. It was as if the moment I left Frozen Head was five minutes ago. He wore his habitual white button-up shirt, complete with a pen protector. Without the sock hat, his hair roamed wild and tangly beneath a farmer's cap as he listened to a man in work pants explain how, when they were staking in the big tent, they'd hit a pipe. "It was a geyser," Laz said, looking at me for the first time. The man and his crew had that tapped down, but the solution meant there would be no water to the main house. He didn't know when he could get out to fix it. In a few days, he "reckoned."

Laz waved at the truck when it pulled away and disappeared behind the trees, then turned and groaned. "Well, we better get the runners' tents up." He'd agreed to let me come down days early if I put in some work. So, a volunteer named Jeremy and I spent the afternoon erecting tents and hauling out aluminum barricades. Everything had to be done Laz's way, the correct way. Open the tents like this, hang the water jugs for ballast this way, latch the barricades like—*no, not* that *way*. By sunset, we had 36 tents up. The vendor had shorted him two. That problem, and tying on the national flags, could wait till tomorrow.

"Well," he said gruffly, "I guess we got a room upstairs you can stay in." He lit a cigarette and limped away from the small green house. I'd assumed he lived there, and that I would be sleeping in my car. But he walked into the woods and up a slope. I followed. At one point, he edged over to a tree and leaned against it, wincing.

"Your leg?" I asked.

He shook his head. "My back. I let the doctors take an X-ray a few years ago. They were like 'God. And you walked here?'" A gravelly laugh followed and trailed off with a sigh.

"Looks like you need a better surgeon."

"Oh no, I just went home," he said after taking a long drag. "How many people do you know who've had back surgery and gotten better? A few weeks ago, I went for my annual checkup. Turns out one of my carotids is 90 percent blocked. I guess I'll have to give on this one."

"The carotid is kind of important," I joked, not knowing what to say.

"Well, I've got two of them," he said. "And they aren't touching me till Big's is over." He blew out a cloud of smoke and craned his neck up at the tree above him. It was riddled with thick cracks and bark that hung like dreadlocks. "You know what this is?" he asked.

I glanced downward, feeling guilty as usual for not knowing everything.

"A shag-bark hickory." With a grunt, he pushed off and continued up the gravel till a modern, grey two-story came into view. It was tucked tight into the woods like a foot in a sock and, on close inspection, was backwards. The front directly abutted a wall of trees while the back served as the entrance. We took a path to a long stone porch, where on one end, a fireplace stood, constructed without mortar. The stacked stones rose on each side, then gracefully curved inward to a single keystone. When I said that it reminded me of the mailbox, Laz said that he'd built them both—the porch too.

Near the door sat a shamble of boxes and equipment and an old broken-down La-Z-Boy that used to be Big's. It sat like a deflated balloon, the guts coming out in yellow stuffing. He'd passed in January, and Laz couldn't bring himself to get rid of it. But he'd lived to be 14, a remarkably long life for a pit bull.

Before we went inside, I noticed a tall cage on the edge of the woods, where a weathered doghouse leaned into the earth. "He got out of that in a day," Laz said, holding open the screen door. "If you want something bad enough, you'll find a way to do it." His eyebrow arched in that way that often signaled something devilish was coming. But instead, he just said, "The plan was to teach him to be a better dog. That was hubris. He showed me how to be a better person."

---

It was 2010, a Sunday, and Laz was certain this was the same pit bull he'd run off two days before. Red coat, thick about the neck and chest, easily 100 pounds, it was sitting underneath a fallen tree that was caught and suspended by two larger trees.

"Get," Laz barked in a throaty growl, picking up a rock and approaching cautiously. He swung his arms in wild, threatening gestures. "Get on home." A pit bull this size could kill him with ease, he knew that. In the shadow of the tree, he could see its greenish-yellow eyes, the kind that belonged "to some sort of demon."

He'd chucked a rock at it on Friday when it first appeared in the yard. Later, on his walk, he stopped some kids on bikes and asked if they'd seen it. "My uncle had a pit bull," said an 8-year-old, proudly. "It was a great dog. It won 26 fights. Then, it lost. When we got home, he threw it in the ditch and shot it in the head."

*God,* Laz thought, *he doesn't even know that this is wrong. What chance does he have in life? About as much as that dog.* None of his neighbors knew of anyone with a pit bull. And there was no sign of it on Saturday. Now, it was back and struggling up to its feet. One of its front legs "stuck out at an angle."

Laz inched forward some more. His eyes adjusted to the shade, and a dark-colored patch of dried blood on its chest explained everything—someone had shot him. The dog wagged its tail, and Laz knelt next to him, searching his large, frightened eyes. There was a gaping hole near the left shoulder, pointing toward the dog's heart. Bits of metal glinted in the flesh around it. It was a kill shot but must have been a hollow point, Laz thought, shattering on impact and spreading throughout his chest. *Some people don't deserve animals.*

He'd have to be put down as soon as possible. The vet, however, wouldn't be in till the morning. He'd do it himself if he had to, had done it before, but it never got any easier. He couldn't stand to see anything suffer, and the dog seemed unable to move the bad leg. Only two months before, Laz had his own leg problems, a blocked femoral artery that led to a stent and an end to his more than forty years as a runner. How could he turn his back on a "leg-issues brother"? he thought. So, he brought it a bowl of Little's food.

She'd also been a stray, showing up in the spring when they were finishing the house. "A puppy skeleton with hide stretched over it," Laz would say. This house out in the woods was supposed to get them away from people and problems. But Sandra took to Little right away. There had been several more since, but he wasn't inclined to keep any. It wasn't the cute puppies that got to him. It was the dogs nobody else would ever want.

The big dog ate the bowl of food greedily and gazed up with pleading eyes. Laz told himself to look away, to not start feeling things. He headed back to the house, but the dog followed behind, limping. At the top of the porch, Laz looked back to see the big dog waiting at the base as if asking for permission. Laz looked up at the darkening clouds. "Come on," he said, reluctantly, "you might as well spend your last night on the porch, where it is dry."

He watched it climb the steps of the porch awkwardly and lie down with a squeal. Against his better judgment, Laz reached out a hand to let it sniff him and felt its hot, moist breath on his skin. Slowly, carefully, he stroked the back of its neck and ran his fingers along indentations where a too-tight collar had been.

The dog stayed on the porch throughout the night, mostly quiet, sometimes moaning. Despite his intention not to worry about the stray, he went to the door every 30 minutes, and each time "the big dog lying on the welcome mat would bob its head with joy and wag its tail." The area around the bullet hole was now the size of a softball. Finally, Laz couldn't take it and called the vet to see if there was something she could do to ease its suffering. Unfortunately, she was out of town for a horse show, she said, but would be in the office in the morning.

Laz couldn't resist going out to pet him again. This time, he let himself look deep into the dog's eyes. There was uncertainty there; he'd either get more water, another bullet, or a beating. "You live until morning," Laz promised him, "and we will see if we can't do something to help you out."

Sunup, Laz awoke with a start and went to the porch. The dog was still there, raising its head when he came to the door. He hadn't even thought about how to get it to the vet. It certainly couldn't get up in the back of the truck. He'd have to take it in the front seat of his car, but the dog couldn't or wouldn't get himself in. He pleaded and tempted him with food, but to no avail; the pit bull seemed to have some trauma with cars. On top of having a bad back, Laz knew grabbing a wounded dog wasn't the best idea. "I hope you know this is an act of faith," he said, grabbing its butt, "that you won't kill me."

They made it to the vet's office, where the pit bull lumbered up the ramp under his own power, albeit slow and strained. Laz could see it was tense entering the examination room. It seemed to sense the fear from other dogs in the air and trembled at the cold touch of the metal table.

Laz watched the vet mouth the words that he'd already played in his head a hundred times; that it was best to put him out of his misery, to end his suffering. But if he wanted, she could do an evaluation to explore any other possible solutions. When she pushed a financial form in front of him, he hesitated. At 55, with a new mortgage and one stray at home already, the last thing he needed was more bills. He signed it anyway—if he was in for a penny, he'd be in for a pound—but when he came to the line for the dog's name, he paused again. Then, he wrote in "big dog."

Later that day, word came from the vet that Big was about 18 months old. *God,* Laz thought, *this Goliath is a puppy*. If he survived, which was doubtful, she'd need another day to see if his leg could be saved. Either way, he'd never be normal, the vet explained. There would be massive scarring, as most of the shrapnel was too close to his heart to be removed. He'd have to live with it or die with it.

After the phone call, Laz could no longer deny that he was on some kind of journey with this dog, one that was becoming increasingly familiar.

# 14

# The Unfortunates

**IT BEGAN QUIETLY,** like most troubling things do. Gary's parents noticed it first, his mouth hanging open, and they got onto him for looking stupid. "But if I close it," he protested, "I'll suffocate."

As the winter of 1966 settled into Tullahoma, Gary's congestion—and his father's frustration—grew worse. "It's just a cold, the flu, or maybe allergies," Frank insisted. Acting sick was annoying and a breach of a Cantrell family rule: If you felt bad, you didn't let on. The answer to "How ya doin'?" was always "Fine." No exceptions—you kept up appearances at all costs.

Frank Cantrell worked on military aircraft for a living, didn't wear safety glasses because you weren't a man if you did, and had a sliver of metal in his eye. But he never complained. So, when Gary wouldn't behave, he threatened to take him to the doctor. To 12-year-old Gary, there was nothing worse, so he kept his mouth as shut as he could and still breathe.

He had a "deathly dislike" for shots, even getting his finger pricked. A few years back, when he had his tonsils removed, he'd squirmed away from the nurse holding a pre-op syringe. An orderly, a large man with big arms, had to scoop him up into a ball while the nurse "pounded it in."

By Christmas, Gary couldn't get any air through his nose at all, and his father's voice cut across the room with authority. "Stop that mouth breathing!" Dinner was on the table, and he'd had enough. "Either you start breathing through your nose," he said, looking into the boy's eyes, "or we're going to the doctor to find out why you can't."

Gary hesitated. Doctors meant pain and waiting and needles. He looked to his mother, Earlene, but she had that *listen to your father* look. They always maintained a unified front, but when he whispered, "Okay, I'll go," he watched their faces change.

Something really *was* wrong.

---

Gary was four when he discovered how quickly you could transition from laughing and playing to screaming in agony. He was chasing his father around a kiddie rocker when his toe caught the corner. His pinky nail split, and in an instant, the thrill of the chase was filled with the terror of a mangled nail. Frank taped it back on, but it eventually grew in sideways and would cause Gary problems the rest of his life. But he didn't go on about it. He was from tough people.

Frank and Earlene were children of the Great Depression, childhood sweethearts from the boomtown of Alluwe, Oklahoma. In kindergarten, they played Red Rover, and Frank always called for Earlene. But they were separated not long after and wouldn't see each other again for more than ten years.

Their parents had come from Arkansas, following the opportunity of oil, and in Alluwe, there was plenty of it—but it came at a cost. Whenever wells were "spudded in," the inevitable whirlwind of disorder came too—bootleggers, wildcatters, and shysters in felt hats. One newspaper marveled that "no bank in Oklahoma suffered as many robberies, in such a short span of time, as the Alluwe Bank."

"I was lucky enough to know someone who lived in the real Wild West," Frank would tell Gary. "The best thing society ever did was to stop letting everyone run around with guns."

The night sky in Alluwe blazed bright with the fiery glow of burning wells, and in the workhouses, the thin walls shook like leaves when oil and gas erupted from the ground. Danger lurked everywhere. Serious accidents on the rigs weren't the exception but the rule. Men wound up burned, scarred, or dead. Out of this chaos came a lineage of hardy self-reliance and larger-than-life ancestors that would shape Gary's ideas of toughness.

One aunt, it was said, was a giant of a woman—six-four, three-hundred pounds—and had yanked a man off a horse and beat him to death, all because he'd heckled her. Then, there were the cousins who lived with bandits up in the Dog Creek hills. One was shot between the eyeballs but was later seen in attendance at the bandit's murder trial. He'd survived. Or so the story goes.

But it was Grandpa Cantrell who stood taller than the rest, Gary's true hero. A roustabout on an oil rig, Allen Cantrell had a sharp mind and calloused hands. Uneducated, he taught himself algebra on a shovel with a piece of charcoal and worked his way up to logging data. During the Great Depression, he was never unemployed. He saved his money, bought land in nearby Foyil, and built a farmhouse by hand—its doorway a perfectly engineered circle.

Gary's maternal grandmother, Mama Lou, was just as rugged and moved her kids to safer ground in Chelsea. She'd come to Oklahoma in a covered wagon but was a widow by the 1940s. She raised Earlene and four boys, all while running a five-and-dime. Mama Lou's side of the family was crazy about sports. One cousin was a pro baseball player and another a successful basketball coach. Mama Lou loved basketball, even moving next to a gymnasium, where she and Earlene would bake pies to sell at the games.

She had very little schooling, as her father didn't believe in it. "Edication," he used to tell her in his Arkansas drawl, "is the ruination of the world." She wasn't big on advice, Gary would remember, and didn't interfere with family. Most who spoke of her said she was the "salt of the earth."

Earlene grew up with church and ball. Before services on Sunday, she'd be at the games on Friday and Saturday, sewing her own clothes while she watched. By the time she finished high school, she was engaged to a soldier serving in Korea. Then, one day on a bus to Claremore, she spotted a thug on the side of the road. Rough, disheveled, and standing next to a doorless truck ("a door and a hole") was her former schoolmate Frank Cantrell. While she didn't believe in fate, it seemed to have its way when they met again at a dance.

A daughter came first, Delana Kathlene. But she was anencephalic, stillborn without the development of her brain. That wasn't talked about much. "Her name was Dianne something," Gary would strain to recall. He came along in 1954, then a brother, Doug, a few years later.

With kids, the finances got tight. Frank had gone into the Army after high school, and while Earlene pitched in with secretarial work here and there, he began to regret not going to college. After everything his father had accomplished with so little, he could do more. While working as an airplane mechanic, he turned over an idea with a buddy. What if he went back to college? Then again, maybe not; he worried he'd stick out. "You know how old I'd be when I graduated?" he said, laughing. When his friend frowned back at him, it caught him off guard. "Well," the man said, "how old will you be if you don't?"

Frank entered college in his thirties, eventually earning a degree in aeronautical engineering. From working mules in the field as a kid and riding a horse to a one-room schoolhouse, he'd carved out a new future like Allen had. And if Gary, as smart as he was, didn't meet or surpass the same expectations, the failure would be his, and his alone.

While Frank presented himself as a "pillar of perfection," Gary was born with an independent spirit, one that would soon be at odds with his father's standards.

---

Born in San Marcos, Texas, he was bounced around when Frank began moving up the engineering ladder. "There isn't anyone who remembers me as a kid," he'd say with a touch of resignation in his voice. "When you move every year, you can't really become part of anything. You're the oddball who comes in the middle of the year and vanishes in the middle of the year."

There was Tacoma, Washington, for a few years before Tulsa, where he went to kindergarten. First grade was in Norman, but by midyear he was in another school. Second grade was Madison Elementary. Back to Tulsa for fourth. Fifth was in Claremore, and when redistricting came in the sixth, he found himself facing yet another set of strange faces. So, when Frank announced a new job in 1966—this time in Tennessee—a familiar sense of unease set in. Unlike skimming around the Tulsa area, however, the idea of coming to the South felt quite different. After listening to his grandparents tell stories of Arkansas and *Missourah*, he would be surprised if people wore shoes.

It was many years before Gary understood the magnitude of this moment for his father—a farm boy from a class of seven, now among the aerospace engineers developing engines that would put man on the moon.

They moved to Tullahoma in October, their mini-caravan of a white F-100 pickup and a brown and tan Ford Fairlane with big fins pulling into town. The plan was to stay at the Holiday Inn for two weeks, while Frank worked and searched for a home. The small town had charm and was steeped in memories of the Civil War, where it proved to be a quagmire for the Union. One general believed Tullahoma must have come "from two Greek words—'Tulla' meaning mud, and 'Homa,' meaning more mud." Since WWII, it had become an aerospace town, home to AEDC, Arnold Engineering and Development Center, one of the most advanced flight-simulation facilities in the world.

The day they arrived, they pulled into a Red Ace gas station. The moment Gary stepped out, the still air hit him—beads of sweat instantly popping up on his skin, his thin shirt stuck to him with the grimy stickiness of a long car ride. When he came around the back, he was shocked to see three bathrooms, the doors flung wide open, and the stenciled lettering of black paint, faded from the Tennessee sun, that read Men, Women, and Colored. The Colored bathroom was neglected and abused: a dilapidated room, walls stained, a sink hanging by a single screw in a single bracket with a broken mirror above it. *You wouldn't send animals in there*, he thought, and covered his nose from the damp, sour smell leaking out into the fall air.

He remembered his Black friend in Tulsa. The schools had already been integrated there, and in fourth grade, the boy became a part of Gary's group—the kids who, for whatever reason, didn't fit in. One morning on the dusty, bare playground, the boy arrived teary-eyed and shaken. He and his father had stopped at the gas station on the way to school like always. Only this time a group of men humiliated his father in front of him.

Gary felt bad for him; he looked smaller than usual, and broken. The image of the boy standing there in the dirt by the jungle gym, with his Levis and scuffed leather shoes, would stay with him the rest of his life. Your father was supposed to be invincible. Struggling to find something to say, 9-year-old Gary muttered, "I'm glad I'm not colored." He regretted it instantly when the boy whispered back, "I wish I wasn't."

Back in the truck, Gary kept quiet but wondered, *What kind of place have we just moved to?* Tullahoma was part of the Jim Crow South and had just integrated the year he arrived. It was a town that held its secrets close, the silence punctuated only by the drone of transport trucks and the occasional roar from the base. While the research labs brought people from diverse backgrounds, personal details were often locked away. "No one knew the details," Gary would remember. "Not until there was a funeral."

For him, it was just another stop—no need to make friends. His plan was to do what he always did when moving to a new town—get a library card, negotiate for extra books, and disappear. When he read, the world and its problems slipped away.

The first book that hooked him was *Curious George*, the story of an orphan and the man in the yellow hat who adopted him. If there was no book at hand, he read the back of cereal boxes. His parents protested. "There's more to life than reading!" they'd say. But it was no use. When he was lost in *The Raft* or devouring *The Lord of the Rings*, his parents resorted to tossing shoes at their son to get him to the dinner table. When he'd finally stand, his legs would be stiff from sitting, his mind still tangled up in the story.

Several books would stick with him at various points in his life. In his late teens, Abbie Hoffman's *Steal This Book* taught him how to break into any vending machine he wanted. He'd reach a hand up, put a small dent in a soda can, then twist it till it came out. Newspaper machines were even easier.

Later, there was the Stephen King novel *The Long Walk*. In it, walkers competed in a last-man-standing competition. They were made to keep a four-mile-an-hour pace or be shot. When one went down, Taps was played. To enter, you had to complete an exam and write an essay on why you should be allowed into The Walk. But what struck him most was the camaraderie between the competitors, the conversations, the bonds of shared suffering.

Tennessee would soon become home after Frank secured a position with the Apollo program, but Oklahoma was never far away, and the family's love for it was common ground. If Sooner football or basketball wasn't on the TV or radio, they retold stories of harder times. There was nothing wrong with being common, his father maintained. All their ancestors got dirt under their fingernails.

Eventually, the wells were capped in Alluwe, the gas companies closed shop, and the housing camps were either moved or abandoned. Though the plan to build a dam and swamp the old ghost town was signed in 1938, bureaucracy held it up for decades.

Frank took Gary to watch it sink beneath the waters, and with it the history of their rugged ancestors who worked the oil fields. To survive that kind of work, as one reporter put it, took "strength, stamina, and toughness of mind and nerve."

---

Back in Tennessee, Gary's mother brought him to Doc Webb's office after school and he sat in the lobby, fidgeting and rubbing his slick palms together. He had only one thought: *I hope I don't have to get a shot!*

The doctor was jovial as usual, but the cold stethoscope against Gary's skin felt like ice. He clicked a pen-like object, and a light came on. Gary leaned his head back. The pen clicked again, and Doc Webb was standing up straight, grimacing. Then he was on the phone, a whispered urgency in his voice. "Thank you," he said, nodding, then smiled at Gary.

Good news, he said. An ear, nose, and throat specialist would see him the next day. Gary was relieved—it was over and there hadn't been any shots. His mother, however, looked far from reassured. After exchanging quiet words with Doc Webb by the door, she gathered Gary up, but her usual stoic façade appeared cracked, her smile painted on.

# 15

# Houdini

hello my name is big.
i am a very sad dog.
i have no master.
i have no important work to do.

i'm so very lonely.
it was not always this way.
i have had many masters, but no one wants to keep me.
i am not a good enough dog.

—LAZ, *THE BIG DOG DIARIES*

**BIG HAD BEEN AT THE VETERINARY CLINIC** for two days when Laz was finally brought in for an update. He was recovering well but not out of the woods. The primary danger was nerve damage if the wound didn't heal properly. Laz would need to isolate him as much as possible and keep an eye on his bad leg to watch for any signs of movement.

The dog was malnourished and riddled with parasites, the vet said, but he was generally docile, friendly, and housebroken. Pit bulls, however, she warned, were very owner-oriented. They made bonds quickly. If he was going to find Big another home, he needed to do it soon.

When they moved past the door where the dogs were kept, one barked loud enough to make Laz's chest vibrate. The vet stopped and smiled. "Your little boy has found his voice."

When he got Big home, he had to wrestle him into the crate. He was like an overgrown child, putting on the brakes with all three of his useful paws. Laz hated to put him in there, but it was for his own good. If the isolation and the antibiotics didn't work, the wound would continue to drain, and that meant surgery to remove the fragments.

Laz did his best to ignore Big's woeful barks after leaving him outside in the crate. That night, he fired off an email to the Ultra List, a social media list serve for ultrarunners. "do any of you listers need a good dog project?" he wrote. "i already have one needy dog, and i don't see how i can do justice to the big dog too—Laz."

Gary had been signing off "Laz" on the Ultra List for some years. He'd found the name in a phone book in a motel room on one of his runs across Tennessee. It belonged to a pastor in the small town of Bolivar. Gary began using it when email race applications became the norm. Increasingly paranoid about identity theft, he deemed a new alias the natural choice for someone who'd gone by Idiot and Mutant.

The next day, he took Big out for a short walk and suspected the dog might have a sense of humor. Unable to put much weight on his bad leg, he leaned against a tree to pee. When a toad hopped in front of him, he pounced, picked it up in his mouth, and quickly spat it back out. "he must have been a house dog," Laz would write for a now growing audience of Big followers on the Ultra List. "i've have never seen a dog pick up the second toad." And the pit bull always seemed eager to get inside. Laz imagined how clueless Big must have been those first few days, left outdoors—terrified—going up to any stranger he met.

Big was too weak to resist the crate the first few days, though he barked prolifically in protest. As he grew stronger, however, he began defeating it with astonishing ease. One night, after Laz crated him, he headed back to the house to find Big on the porch waiting. Laz cocked his head and returned to see what Big had done—he'd popped the latch open.

After working it with a pair of pliers and pushing the hook deeper into the catch, Laz went back inside, satisfied. Out of curiosity, he peeked out the window. Big was sitting in the crate, studying. When he looked again, the dog had his good shoulder on one corner of the crate and his butt on the adjacent corner, pressing till the latch popped. And he was back on the porch, smiling.

Next, Laz tried turning the crate door against the wall. Moments later, there was a racket. He went out to find Big's head lodged between the gaps where the crate sides were attached. He'd pushed his head through and would soon get his entire body out. So, Laz wired the gaps together. But Big took what he'd learned from his shoulder-and-butt trick, and this time gave it his full strength. Laz watched as the whole crate came apart like a piñata burst from the inside. Amazed, Laz was unable to keep from grinning. Big smiled back, as if to say, *I tried to work with you*.

This dog, Laz determined, was an irresistible force. "word was," he wrote to the Ultra List, "after they made big, they killed the mold maker." Sandra, however, was more pragmatic about the pit bull. "Don't get too attached," she'd warn Laz, and generally stayed away from the dog. He could end up costing them a fortune. Not only was he eating them out of house and home, now nearly 100 pounds, he could maul a child, an adult even. "We are not keeping this big, ugly dog," she'd say, and badger him daily to find him a home.

"i just don't know what for sure to do if i can't find big dog a home," he wrote. "if i had a fenced in yard for him it would be different, but i can't afford that. i can't let him run free, he'd just get shot."

The Ultra Listers came to the rescue, sending enough money not only to help with Big's medical bills but also to get him a pen. Laz picked out a 10-by-20 foot chain-link kennel and assembled it on the edge of the trees where the dog could get a look inside the house while staying in the shade.

But Big defeated it in hours, popping the latch with his nose. Laz then jerry-rigged it with a special fastener, a challenging one that took him two hands to secure and came with an instruction manual, which he kept hidden from Big "just to be safe."

Laz was by his computer when he saw the dog smiling at him from the porch. He'd dug out like a mole. So, Laz grounded it with two-inch pipes and put boulders around the bottom. Big unraveled the chain-link with his teeth. He also defeated a dog-proof collar and a body harness. Laz found it on the ground turned inside out, still attached to the cable. Each time Big got out, he'd end up on the porch, looking in with gleeful, ready-for-play eyes. Laz's daughter took to calling him Houdini. The only way to keep him in the pen, Laz found, was to leave the door open.

"he has approached each crate and chain with the measured professional calm of a military sapper," he wrote. "studying, calculating, and testing before implementing the latest plan in his devious mind.

i have come to dread the words, 'big dog is out.' he simply never gives up. free to a good home," he told the list. "one canine genius (with a sense of humor)."

In the meantime, the best he could do for Big, he thought, was to train him. Wherever Big went in the future, as a pit bull, he'd be on the one-strike-and-you're-out program. So, he taught him to sit, not to jump, and to wait for his food. It took several days, but Big finally learned to not pull him like a sled on their walks.

Big insisted on a walk every morning before Laz went to work. At four a.m., Laz would grab the blue leash and head for the pen. Big, now healed up, would jump higher than Laz's head, flipping and spinning and wagging his tail. His favorite walks were on the trails Laz was building behind the house. The first had been to the septic tank, then Laz began clearing footpaths to other points like the rock outcroppings of an old quarry and the cedar glade.

If Laz didn't appear on time, Big would bark to wake him up. If a storm came and Laz skipped his walk, Big took it on his own. More than once, Sandra got a call from a neighbor saying Big and Little had paid a visit.

Little was fearless when it came to her new companion. The terrier in her was undaunted by her diminutive size and would steal Big's bones and food. One morning, Laz was doing yardwork when he noticed Little going in and out of Big's pen. Then came a "snarling and growling and crashing sound." A thrum of adrenaline surged through him when he looked up and saw the two dogs on their hind legs "in mortal combat." In an instant, Big had Little on her back, "her entire neck engulfed in his jaws."

Laz's first instinct was to jump in and try to save Little. But he remembered watching Big snap a cow bone in two to get at the marrow. Even if he could run like he used to, if Big wanted, Little would be a goner before he even reached the pen. Laz turned his head and looked away. He didn't want to watch her die.

But when he heard her high-pitched "war cry," he glanced back to see Big flat on his back, spread eagle. Little was mounted on his chest like a lion, her little jaws at his throat. Big looked over at him, his eyes twinkling with joy. "all i could do was laugh with him," Laz wrote. "big knows how to make a joke."

---

He must have overslept, he thought—Big was barking. It was still dark out when he got to the pen, and Big was doing his usual flips. But on the walk, he seemed to sense something. He was unusually quiet and calm instead of his overzealous, tail-wagging, adventurous self. For most of the walk, Laz did the talking and Big did the listening. He told him how happy he was going to be, about the big fenced yard he was going to have, and all the neat trails he would soon explore. He told him that he was even going to get to sleep indoors.

Tony was a young man, a former college football player, and newly on his own. He seemed responsible in emails and said he had experience with dogs. Though he lived in St. Louis, he spent a lot of time outdoors and was looking for a dog companion. He'd sent his sister Sam the day before to walk along with Big while he went through his routine. Laz proudly showed her the commands Big had learned. "He must have known it was an important test," he would say, "because he performed like a champ."

Soon, Laz and Big passed the curve where Big always noticed the rabbits darting about. Usually, he'd sniff and chase them into the briars, but now he just kept going. Finally, they came to a small rise, and miles of forests and fields spread into the pink glow of sunrise. The two stopped to watch in silence. “You know, don’t you, Big?” Laz said. “Somehow you know.” Big looked up at him and leaned his enormous head against his leg to be petted. Laz wanted to say more but the tears were welling up in his eyes, so he said nothing.

Doing the right thing, he thought, is not always easy.

# 16

# Count Backwards

**IT WAS FRIDAY, EARLY**—early enough that the sun was still hesitant and pale. Twelve-year-old Gary sat in the passenger seat, staring out at the fields blurring by. The drive up to the hospital was like any other trip to Nashville. Gary and his mother talked about the rock walls and old homes along the route. Strangely, the best way to deal with an event that was highly anticipated (like Christmas) or dreaded (surgery) was the same. Think about something else! Regardless, the arrival at the hospital seemed all too soon.

The dreaded finger-prick blood test started things off on the wrong foot. Gary wondered if the blood was taken that way just to maximize the discomfort. For all his dread of needles, the little triangular mini-blade used on the finger was worse. Drawing blood with a needle would have been better, as long as it wasn't drawn from the fingertip!

X-rays were made, followed by a wait, and about midmorning he was taken down a long hallway. The air was sharp, sterile, and minty. He caught glimpses of patients and odd, bulky equipment behind half-open doors. Finally, they came to a small room with walls the color of dull lemons. A chair waited, green and tilted back, with an overhead light that gave the whole room a vaguely alien feel. Gary eyed it, his stomach tightening. It was like the dentist's chair, and he hated the dentist.

Dr. Alley was cordial, grey-headed, calm—and reminded him of Doc Webb when he came in. There was something about his demeanor, too, that had gravity. His voice was smooth, practiced, and he spoke directly to you as he explained what he was about to do. Perhaps, he suggested, the blockage could be dislodged with water.

For the first time in two days, Gary allowed himself to feel some hope. *This could all be over today*. Then, the nurse pulled a tray up beside him and he saw the needle. It was as long as a pipe, like something from a horror movie except the tip was cut off at an angle so that one side came to a point. The nurse connected a hose to it that ran to a rectangular box on wheels, which began to hum, low and steady like a refrigerator.

Gary felt the urge to run out, but the nurse stood behind the chair and got his head in a viselike grip. He had learned after the tonsillectomy experience that struggling only made it worse. When you are a child, whatever they're going to do, they're going to do.

Dr. Alley returned, hands gloved, and told Gary to lean his head back. With a deep breath, he obeyed. First was the touch of cold metal from the probing tool, followed by a strange pressure in his nose. He squirmed a little. To his horror, if not surprise, that massive needle went up his nose. Dr. Alley turned it to the side, and Gary felt the needle going into the flesh of his nostril then his cheek. He could hear the crunching sound of the needle as it was slowly pushed through what felt like the bones of his face. Then came the water, a violent erupting inside, deeper than he thought possible.

The purpose of the nurse holding his head was now obvious as Dr. Alley pushed hard to drive that big needle through Gary's face—pushing, probing, jamming in and out—sending daggers into his brain, his eyes, his cheeks.

The nurse's gaze never faltered, calm and detached, while Gary's knuckles whitened on the arms of the chair. He locked eyes with Dr. Alley, saw kindness there, practiced assurance, eyes that had seen boys his age live through this and be okay.

The world began to mute, voices receding, everything echoing at the far end of a tunnel. After what seemed like an eternity, a liquid, hot and wet, came streaming down his neck. It must be from his ears. And then he was crying. No... he wasn't. It was the water, gushing from his eyes like some grotesque fountain. He was being power washed like a filthy car, he thought.

He blinked incessantly but it was no use—the yellow walls were waving, distorting. He told himself not to look down, not to let his eyes drift. It'd be over soon. But he couldn't help it. He glanced down and saw a flesh-colored bulge tenting up below his eye, moving with the pressure. It was the skin over his cheekbone, he realized.

When the needle was finally removed from his nose, he felt incredibly relieved, and strangely exhausted. But he was not too tired to dread what might come next.

He sat in a daze, exhausted, stuff oozing out of every hole in his face. The nurse dabbed at his ears, nose, cheeks. She appeared unfazed, bored even. Whatever he looked like, it must not be that bad. His fingers ached when he pried them off the chair. They must have gotten it, he thought. *Can I go home now?*

It was almost lunchtime when Dr. Alley returned. Unlike Gary's previous doctor visits, Dr. Alley did not talk to his mother while Gary looked on like a dog at the vet. He talked directly to Gary: "We have an important decision to make. And I think you deserve to have a say in what we do." The bone in the right side of Gary's face had been entirely replaced by a tumor. The standard treatment, Dr. Alley explained, would be to remove Gary's nose, right eye, right cheek, and his palate. He would have a prosthetic face made, which would just plug into the hole where his real face had been and be blended in with makeup. It would have to be replaced with a new one periodically as he grew.

Gary was crushed. He'd always thought he had an ugly face... but it was a face! Suddenly it seemed like a really wonderful thing to have a real face—any face.

But there was a second option. Dr. Alley thought he could cut the upper lip loose from Gary's mouth and pull the skin off of his face. Then he would cut away the tumor from where it shouldn't be and reshape the area like a normal face. He would sew the skin back on, and there would be no sign Gary had even been cut. It would have to be periodically repeated.

For Gary, there was not a moment's hesitation. Option two was the only choice. He wanted to grow up with a real face.

---

The next afternoon Gary's mother checked him into Vanderbilt Children's Hospital. When the paperwork was done and he went to his room, Gary found he was in a ward with a number of men. Although his admission was technically in the children's hospital, the whole thing had happened so fast there was no space for him. This meant his mother couldn't stay, so he was left alone in a room full of old men just lying there in their beds. Fortunately, he had brought several new books, so he was content to read until the lights were turned out.

The next morning started early with a couple of shots. Once the IV was in, Gary held his left arm perfectly straight. A shot was bad enough, but the IV was a needle *left* in his arm, and he was terrified that one wrong move could make it tear through his flesh and cause who knows how much pain.

The shots gave everything a dreamlike feel. As he was wheeled to the operating room on a gurney, he watched the lights pass overhead. Moving through the double doors into the operating room was like passing through a portal into a different world. There really was a big, bright light over the operating table, and people in scrubs were silently bustling around making preparations. In a scene he was coming to dread, a nurse pulled a table up next to him and began arranging various shiny, stainless-steel instruments. It reminded Gary of the preparations for the torture in the yellow room. There was a lot of ribbed tubing that he was curious about. Later he would ask and find out it was so air and not blood would go to his lungs.

Mostly he was concerned that they would start surgery while he was still awake. He might be the object of all this activity, but no one spoke, or even looked at him. So, when one of the masked figures came over and looked down at him, Gary immediately told him; "I'm still awake!"

The man chuckled into his mask and said, "I'm here to fix that." He instructed Gary to "count backwards from 100."

"100, 99, 98, 97...."

Gary became aware of murmuring voices and people moving around. Dimly he remembered that he had lost his count. Then he opened his eyes. He was on a gurney, in a room with other motionless people on gurneys. Nurses were circulating through the room checking on them all. *The surgery must be over already.*

For the first time Gary realized only one eye was open. He reached up and found the right side of his face was covered with some kind of pad. It was sore. Sort of like someone had punched him with a brick.

It wasn't long before they wheeled him down the hall. Once more the lights passed overhead. He was expecting to return to the ward, but instead he had his own room, where both his parents were waiting. His dad was poker-faced, but his mom's expression told him he must look pretty grim.

A little later, and more fully awake, Gary went into the bathroom and looked in the mirror. He found there wasn't anything covering his face. That was his face! A small bloody gauze pad was over his nose, but the right side of his face looked like someone had bisected a softball, put one half on top of his face, and blended it in with purple, green, and yellow makeup. The eye itself was just a tiny seam in his distorted features, recognizable only because the ends of his eyelashes were sticking out. He looked a hundred times worse than he felt. Yet he also saw it as only a 12-year-old boy could, that it looked "so cool!"

The next day Dr. Alley came with good news. The tumor was benign. Gary had always assumed everything would work out. Over time he came to realize how lucky he'd been. The initial prognosis, he'd find out, had been a 99 percent chance of malignancy—the same cancer that had killed Babe Ruth.

One morning Dr. Alley stopped in to say, "It's time to remove the packing." Gary was blithely oblivious to what was coming. He didn't even wise up when the nurse set a tray on his bedside table and began setting out stainless-steel instruments. Even when Dr. Alley had him lie down, put his hands over his head, and the nurse grabbed both his wrists, he had no concern...

Then Dr. Alley reached into his nose with a pair of hemostats and grabbed the end of an endlessly long strip of gauze. The moment he began to pull, Gary's mind blanked. A suction near his eye seemed to draw everything inside out. He screamed, but they kept pulling. When the packing caught on a sharp piece of cartilage, Gary thrashed like a wild animal, trying to get his hands on Dr. Alley. The nurse shifted all her weight onto his wrists. Gary's mother had to leave the room.

For the next six years, having his face overhauled would be a regular part of life. It might be twice in a year, or two years apart, but there would always be another surgery. Every time, he tried in vain to negotiate over the packing removal. He begged them to put him under. Too much risk to avoid a five-minute procedure, he was told.

For teenage Gary, there was no getting away from the reality of his condition. The usual stressors of high school and dating and "making something of yourself" would all pass through his now alien filter of being the outsider with the lopsided face.

# 17

# Just Lie to Us

***CREEP*—THE TITLE CAUGHT HIM** right away. The novel by Jeffrey Frank follows Bartholomew, a drifting outcast in an unnamed city who spends his days wandering from diners to bars to random parties, desperately seeking connection while convinced the world despises him. His mind twists every interaction through a lens of self-loathing and paranoia. He only approaches women he deems "ugly" enough to accept him, imagines strangers plotting his death, and sabotages any genuine chance at friendship with his consuming insecurity. When Gary picked it up from the Tullahoma library, he wasn't reading fiction—he was reading his new existence.

He entered high school at eighty pounds soaking wet and was "insanely not popular." He scored high on aptitude tests, but class was boring, easy, pointless. "There was nothing creative about it," he'd remember and admit he had "some objection to getting along with teachers." Reading aloud in class was the worst. He couldn't sit there and be bothered to listen to some kid stumble at seven words a minute.

So, he'd jump ahead. After hearing his name called repeatedly, again and again, he'd come out of it—fifty pages along but utterly lost. *Where are we?*

At home, Frank was obsessive about Gary's schoolwork. As far back as second grade he'd told him he'd end up homeless if he got a B. The more Frank complained, the worse Gary's grades became. The house was always quiet, orderly. Andy Williams' version of *Moon River* was put on the turntable once a year during the holidays. Dinner was at 5:30 sharp, Frank always in a white T-shirt, tucked in, belt. His fastidiousness was unrelenting; there was a correct way to do everything. He was a fanatic about shaving. "I never grew a beard," Gary would later say defiantly. "I just never shaved."

Religion was another sore. After coming to Tullahoma, Earlene took on the role of secretary at the local Baptist church. And church was Sunday morning, Sunday night, and Wednesdays. To get through it, Gary read the bulletin. "I hated church like it was prison," he'd say. "It's inside, boring, and you have to sit still."

From the age of eight, Gary had plans to slip away, make a break for it, see if he could really escape the adults. They had too much control over him and thought they knew everything. Just where he planned to go was anyone's guess, but he'd memorized every alley, fence line, and ditch. Sometimes he did get away, on his bike or hitch a ride... but he always came back.

His room was his fortress at home. Since he was little, he'd stay up late, reading under his bedsheets with a flashlight. Once, he constructed a miniature Museum of Natural Oddities on a piece of Styrofoam, with rows of neatly pinned bugs arranged like jewels. "And here," he'd say, gesturing grandly over the display, "is where I house the unfortunate." His small group of friends would lean in with wide eyes while he rattled off bug facts with the solemnity of a general cataloging his troops. He kept it. A recent storm in Tullahoma had blown in a rhinoceros beetle, and it became his trophy piece, sitting taller than the rest with its long horn stuck out like some insect unicorn.

After the yearly surgeries, he'd retreat there for days until he was presentable. Often, his face was still swollen when he went back to school, but he acted like he didn't care. Hardened from all the moves, there had never been much use in making friends. Still, he was full of lust for the opposite sex, and he spent hours ironing his curly hair to try and straighten it.

Gary's answer to his social awkwardness was sports. While regular conversation was foreign territory, sports teams offered a social structure he could grasp. During his time in Norman, he'd gravitated toward some of the Oklahoma players who taught him football basics—how to throw, how to punt. He nursed dreams of playing for the Sooners. But his family's constant moves, always landing mid-school year, kept him from joining any organized teams. By the time high school rolled around, he was determined to change that.

Reality hit hard. At just 80 pounds, he couldn't even get permission to try out for football. His only chance came from Coach Carden, who oversaw the track and cross-country programs. The coach was willing to take a chance on him. Running, Gary discovered, had multiple benefits—it kept him out of the house and kept his mind off the fibroid.

Carden's training was brutal but creative. A former Navy man, he'd carry the team in the back of his truck to a hollow to do half-mile repeats. He'd put them out at the bottom and make them race up the hill. They'd rest on the ride back down and then do it again. Gary's lungs burned and his legs screamed, but it was the kind of pain he could control.

Another way Carden made practice competitive and fun was to set up a mile loop and split the team into pairs. Two runners would take off in opposite directions. "You'd learn where the mid-point was," Gary remembered, "to check whether you were ahead or behind. Then, you'd come into sight of each other on the final stretch."

Like his father, Coach Carden was someone Gary wanted to impress, but their relationship lived entirely within the boundaries of sport. During track season, Gary would quit booze, even soda. He observed Carden intently, how he paid attention to each team member and motivated them differently. He used both positivity and negativity. One kid struggled under pressure, so Coach would agitate him before meets. The kid would externalize his anxiety onto Carden and run better.

While Gary was slower than most, Carden noticed that the longer practice went, the more Gary caught up. Seeing his potential at distance, Carden fought to get Gary into meets in Alabama for two-mile races, which they didn't have in Tennessee. Coach also began having his best runners race Gary for 1,000 yards at the end of practice. "Catch Gary!" he'd say. Back in his car, Gary's leg would quiver so hard he couldn't depress the clutch. Sitting there one afternoon, soaked in sweat, a thought came to him. If practice just kept going, he'd be the best on the team. If they all ran four miles an hour, every hour, he'd be the last one standing. It was just a dream but one that stayed with him.

Though Tullahoma High was the smallest school in the state with a cross-country team, Carden turned his athletes into a standout squad. When other runners glanced back and saw that reddish-purple uniform with the black stripe coming, the fight in their eyes gave out. Despite being a "little bitty" school, the Wildcats made the state meet each season Gary was on the team. His senior year, they were back, but like the other years, Gary was eliminated in the early heats. Running was finally over, and he knew he'd miss it. Dressed in street clothes, he sat in the stands and watched his teammates run their last races.

Then he saw Coach Carden coming up the bleachers toward him. A runner in the two-mile relay had gone down, he said. The final heat was coming up, and he needed Gary to run the first leg, an 880. Carden could have called on a half dozen people to do it, but Gary didn't hesitate. He borrowed shoes and a uniform and headed to the track cold. He told himself not to go out too fast, to try his best not to doom his teammates. "You don't need to be a hero," Coach said. "Run *this* pace. Finish your leg in *this* time."

When the gun went off, Gary bolted. While he ran the slowest leg of the heat, he got the baton passed and stood catching his breath while his teammates circled the track. One by one, they retook position until they came across the finish line first. He stood on the podium for the first time with a gold medal around his neck. It was one of the greatest feelings he could remember—reaching a level he'd never achieved on his own. He took home a medal in a race he'd never run, never trained for, wearing someone else's gear. Gary would later say, "Everything I'd do in my races, in some way, came from Carden."

---

Dr. Alley's theory proved to be right—the tumor stopped growing just as Gary finished high school. For the final surgery, Gary convinced Dr. Alley to try decomposing packing instead of gauze. The smell was unbearable, like something dead and rotting. Still, Frank insisted he get his hair cut right way. *It was too damn long*, like a hippie freak. Gary gave in, covered the bandage on his nose, and went to get it cut. In the mirror, he watched the barber gag, his face twisting in disgust. He'd never forgive Frank for that.

Traumatized by years of uncertainty and procedures, Gary refused reconstructive surgery on his last visit to Dr. Alley. He chose instead to live lopsided, his right cheek slightly larger than his left.

Without the structure of school and track, the war over Gary's appearance and behavior worsened. His parents didn't give a lot of freedom, "so I did a lot of shit," Gary would say. He got some grass and drove up toward Manchester at night, where a streetlight made a local legend of a leaning cedar tree. The shadow would cross the road as he hit the curve, hunched over like a witch—the witch Sadie Baker.

The weed didn't do much at first, but it grew on him, and soon he found a like-minded crowd of hippies, loners, and oddballs. One night, he and some buddies ran nude, just to see what "the Greeks must have felt."

One evening Gary tried mescaline. Nothing happened for an hour, so he went home. He was sitting in the living room with his parents when the world began to distort. He tried to remain cool as Frank and Earlene grew, shrank, zoomed in, and zoomed out. The house seemed to breathe, so he retreated to his room, and when he woke up, he wasn't quite the same, never would be. In a messy, creep world, the drugs brought some sort of clarity. He loved it. Wanted more. "I always felt my head came out in a slightly better place," he'd say.

He was careful about the drugs, had a secret place in his car where he kept them. The cops pulled him over regularly but never found his stash.

Frank, however, picked up on the changes and began riding him constantly about his hair, his grades, his clothes. "He wanted me to be an action figure that represented the ideals he valued," Gary would say. He could feel his father's growing disappointment. He was supposed to become an engineer, a mathematician, not the Creep. "You're breaking your mother's heart," Frank would say. And Earlene would echo it back: "You're breaking your father's heart."

One night, he came home late like always and slipped in through the back door. But this time everyone was up—Frank, Earlene, and Gary's brother, Doug. They were in the den, waiting. It had the feel of an intervention. Frank said they'd gotten a call and had learned Gary was involved in drugs. He'd admitted to smoking weed before, but now Frank was asking if he was *involved*. The implication was clear. "Is it true?" he asked again. Gary looked him in the eye after a long pause and said that it was. *Why drag it out?* he thought. They were here to get it out of him one way or another. Might as well admit it. But he wasn't going to narc on his friends or give any direct answers about what came from where or how.

He could see the shock on their faces, the horror in Doug's eyes. There they were, in the den where they'd watched Oklahoma football on Saturdays, shelling pecans. The den with the short-pile carpet, the breakfast bar, and the mantle topped with family pictures—where they'd spent so many family evenings together. Now, accusations were flying, voices rising. Finally, Frank said, "Just lie to us so we can go to bed."

Gary let it hang for a moment, then relented. "No," he said with a smart-ass grin. "None of it's true." Frank lowered his head in exhaustion, and they all retreated to their rooms.

That summer, it came to a head again. "Cut your hair or move," Frank demanded angrily. "Okay," Gary fired back, and without a word, he went upstairs, grabbed a change of clothes, a toothbrush, and stuffed them in his green Boy Scout backpack. He wadded up a hundred dollars, threw the bag out the window, and heard it thud on the lawn. He walked downstairs, his heart thumping when he passed the living room with the Queen Anne furniture, spotless but never used. He dashed by Frank in a whir. "See you later," he said, and didn't look back. He heard the door slam behind him. The air was tingly and alive in his lungs.

Days later, his tan Mustang was found abandoned by the highway. One less possession to weigh him down.

---

"NO SHIT!" Gary was genuinely startled. "I went to high school with a David Patton." The odds were extraordinary, and for a fleeting moment, he allowed himself to believe in fate, that this was a sign of good portent. The first car to stop after an hour of having his thumb to the wind.

"Where you headed?" David asked, smiling but keeping his eyes forward.

"West, I guess... nowhere in particular."

Hitchhiking was still commonplace in the early '70s, but Gary knew how he must look—hippie hair to the shoulders, a rucksack, a thumb in the wind. So many cars had breezed by without a thought.

It was already feeling like a journey run, like the time he ran eight miles to Estill Springs when he was 15 or the time he biked 70 miles to Shelbyville to see a girl's smile. And he'd hitchhiked before... just around, nothing serious. But this was different. This time, he wasn't going back.

The first couple of days, he got picked up by a lot of teenagers. Short rides to the next town, sometimes the next county. Conversations were all over the place. They bitched about their parents, injustice, freedom, politics. But they seemed to understand what he was about—freedom, the open road, the thrill of the unknown. Some had read Jack Kerouac's classic *On the Road* and eyed Gary with envy, hoping, they said, to do something like that... someday.

After he got out of Tennessee, things got stranger by the day. A trucker picked him up one rainy afternoon. He had saucer-sized eyes and was popping speed with one hand, gripping a beer in the other, all while barreling the 40-ton eighteen-wheeler down the highway with his elbows.

Then there was the enormous man in the tiny car. The VW Bug had pulled up next to Gary and slowed, a faint whining from the engine as it eased to a stop. The driver had a fun-loving, live-for-the-moment kind of grin that didn't quite match his rigid brow and dark eyes. But beggars couldn't be choosers, so Gary climbed in anyway.

The man was on his way to California, he said, and they drove for hours shooting the shit, the windows down, the sun fading in front of them. Eventually they pulled off an exit to get gas, and Gary got out to stretch his legs. It felt good to move around after a long spell riding. His friend was inside talking to the filling station attendant as he paid, and when he came out said, "There's a place up the road we can get a couple of beers."

Gary mentally checked his schedule. Yep, today's itinerary is go where the wind takes you. Same as yesterday, and same as tomorrow.

"Sure."

After a short drive down the two lane, they came to a two-story clapboard building. The front yard was a gravel parking lot, and the number of cars flagged this as a popular hangout. They pulled in and took a random parking space like everyone else.

Inside was your usual country bar, thick with the smell of stale roses and cigarette smoke, pierced by the murmur of chatter, laughter, and the clacking of pool balls. His ride headed for the pool table, and Gary headed to the bar. He spent his money sparingly on the road; a little cash was the ticket to keep from being picked up as a vagrant. But the occasional handout had kept his funds stable, and he was ready for something cold to drink.

The bartender was an older woman dressed in faded western attire. She took his order and his money and came back with a tall, cold one.

"You got a date, honey?" she asked, and winked.

"No, I'm just passing through."

"Do you need a date?"

Another wink.

Gary was perplexed. Did she have a tic? Was she picking up on him? He decided to be noncommittal.

"Probably not. I can barely afford my own beer."

The woman laughed and went to get someone else a beer while Gary took in his surroundings. The place was full of cowboys. There were tables with card games going on. His ride was engaged in a game of pool. Men went up or came down the stairs at the back, where he assumed the bathroom must be. Nobody had a date.

After a short time he saw the bartender hang up the phone, and she came over and leaned her elbow on the bar, putting their heads close together.

"Honey, in about five minutes the police are coming in the front door. And everyone in here is going to be arrested. There is a window at the top of the stairs and you can go out the back way."

Gary mentally checked his schedule. *Arrested?* No, that was definitely not on the agenda. So, he scampered up the stairs. At the top, a hallway ran in either direction, and in front of him was an open window. He climbed out, hung from the sill, reached for the ground with his feet, and let go.

He ducked down behind a parked car to stay out of sight while the police pulled up and shined their spotlights on the building. All that light just made the shadows darker as he made his way to his ride and reached in to grab his backpack. The police cars had come from one direction, so Gary slipped away and took the other.

Hours later, he hitched another ride. This guy seemed nice too—all smiles and a thick yeehaw accent—so Gary hopped in. But quickly he sensed something was off. The guy kept sizing Gary up and stealing glances at his hair. Eventually, the man smiled and said, "You wanna get in a fight? I know a place where we can get in a fight." There was fire in his eyes now, like a kid about to steal his first pack of smokes.

"What kind of fight?" Gary asked, just to see where this was going.

"Knife fight, gun fight, fist fight, any kind of fight you want." The man slapped at the wheel. "With your hair, we can get in a fight no problem."

"Oh, man," Gary replied with a tone of regret. "That would be great!" He held up his right hand in a fist, rubbing it with the left. "But I just broke my right hand in a fight two weeks ago. It hasn't fully healed yet, and I'm afraid I wouldn't be able to pull my own weight."

His ride, it seemed, wasn't afraid to take on the full load, but Gary convinced him that he couldn't just stand by while someone else fought his fight. And if he broke his hand again so soon, it would never heal. "Yeah, that wouldn't be right… but it sure is a shame."

"Don't I know it!"

When they reached Sallisaw, Oklahoma, Gary couldn't hop out fast enough. But he hadn't gone more than a block before he heard a voice call out, sharp and derisive, "Where'd you come from, hippie?" Before he could answer, a police car materialized. Rough hands, a shove into the back seat, then a silent drive to the county line where they dumped him like roadside trash. It wouldn't be the last time.

Standing there in the dark, watching the taillights disappear, Gary understood something about the road and about life. You have to be adaptable, to go with the flow, but be ready to dip your paddle in the water just enough to keep from crashing into the rocks.

He'd stay out on the road less than six months. But the feeling of freedom—that jolt of escape—would linger. It was something he'd keep chasing. When he finally returned to Tennessee, it wasn't to go home. He'd seen too much, learned too fast, to ever step into that life again.

# 18

# The Business

hello, my name is big.
and I am a very lucky dog.
i have come home.

i was living on a chain in the yard.
There was a man who fed me,
but he did not want to be my master.
No one had work for me to do.
No one petted me.
No one told me I was a good dog.
It was not a happy time.

But one day the man took me for a long ride.
I was worried because long rides always mean my life
is going to change.

—LAZ, *THE BIG DOG DIARIES*

**THE FALL AFTER BIG LEFT,** signs of trouble appeared in Shelbyville, and by the start of 2011, Laz was facing a new reality. Two new council members had gotten rid of the city manager, and the new guy wanted to clean house. Laz had been working as city treasurer, which he took pride in. But he also liked to draw caricatures of the local politicians, which a secretary friend kept locked in a drawer. Informed that he would be let go, he agreed to stay on until they found a replacement. But he'd also need a new job.

With a stiff mortgage on the new home, he applied for work in earnest, much the way he had in his thirties and again in his forties when he was laid off. He cut his hair, shaved, and sent out dozens of applications. But no one seemed interested in a 56-year-old.

Desperate, he drove thirty minutes to Murfreesboro and applied for a job at a local Fleet Feet running store. He'd do whatever they needed, he said. He filled out the application, and the young man disappeared with it behind a door. When he returned, he apologized and informed Laz he wasn't a good fit. *What?* He had forty years of putting on races and just as many as a columnist for *Ultrarunning* magazine. Honestly, the young man told him, management was "afraid he'd scare the customers."

On the ride back, he passed Walmart and wondered what greeters made per year. When he checked online, he found the average was $15,000. That, he figured, was all he needed to get by.

He was used to finding ways to make do with very little. He bought his beef by the cow, gave his kids toys he found on the side of the road, and never spent more than $50 for a car. "At one point he drove some old stick shift, three-speed Camaro," close friend Dirt Thompson recalled. "Nothing worked but the drive train. The passenger side floorboard was up to the seat in cans and bottles. I couldn't hardly get my legs in."

"I drove it into the river," Gary said, retelling the story with some flourish. "Some douchebag, lazy asshole drudged the ford. I came to it, about twenty yards across, a wide piece of water, but shallow. It floated for a minute then sunk. A geyser shot out of the stick shift in the floor, and all the electronics started shorting. So, I rolled down the window and climbed onto the hood."

After thumbing his way to nearby Flat Creek, he convinced a garage to pull the Camaro out of the river with a tractor. A tube of water shot out the tailpipe when it started, "but it ran." Gary took out the seats to let them drain, only to find the cardboard on the ceiling was warped. So, he cut a circle out of it for his head.

Later, a man hit him in a parking lot, busted the grill, got out, and said, "I can't believe I'm gonna have to pay to fix a car like that." Gary jerry-rigged it with five dollars' worth of chicken wire. When he drove the Camaro to a race in Florida, a runner in a custom-outfitted van commented, "You actually drove that car all the way here?"

Gary employed his practiced smart-ass grin. "I got a screwdriver in the glove box. If it breaks down, I just take off the plates and go home," he said. "You guys, if you break down, are dead." Over the years, his Datsun fell into such disrepair that to get the windshield wiper moving, Laz rigged up a wire system, threading it through both windows so he could yank the blade back and forth himself.

But by the spring of 2011, Laz still had no luck on the employment front, and the couple contemplated buying a tobacco store. Ultimately they opted not to, as the upfront money needed for fees and licenses was too much. Sandra got consistent work as a tax accountant. Laz, however, was barreling toward retirement age in bad health and with no insurance. "You're good at organizing races," Sandra said one day on a lark. "Why don't you do something with those instead of giving 'em away?"

At the time, Laz only had three—Strolling Jim, The Last Annual Vol State run across Tennessee, and the Barkley (which he still charged just $1.60 for). He also hadn't created a new race in twenty-five years. The year before, he did have a one-off dawn-to-dusk run behind his home. That had him thinking now of an old idea, and in a single, determined night, he distilled his musing into something that seemed inevitable—a set of deceptively simple rules that would once again upend the ultrarunning world—the Backyard Ultra:

A four-mile loop run every hour till only one soul remained. Each hour could be the last, every lap the bell lap in track, so he'd ring one to send them off. Victory demanded an extra loop after all others had crumbled—or there would be no winner. But no more than one. In the end, only the leader would fail to find the limit of their endurance, hemmed in by the breaking points of those chasing them.

Soon, he was spending hours in the woods with his loppers, clearing away the brush and connecting trails. A four-mile path emerged. Rolling and narrow, it wound through the rocks and roots, climbed up the hills, and navigated to Laz's favorite parts of what he was calling his "farm." This new route needed a name, and when he thought of it, he couldn't help but smile: The Big Trail.

---

"I said 'BIG!' and then I was down on the floor." Laz's daughter Aimee was back from Nashville with a sad tale. She'd gone to visit friends only to find Big. He was staying with Tony's sister, not with Tony out in St. Louis as Laz had arranged. From what she could gather, Big had become a monster.

When Big had first arrived in Missouri, he was "something of a celebrity." At Tony's college parties, Big was the star of the show, leaning his head on someone's leg; he always got petted. He also got lots of exercise—hiking, swimming, and strolling around campus. But Big "slowly turned from a campus celebrity to a campus terror, and one day he found himself campus banished."

He'd taken to stealing food, destroying furniture, and his walks amounted to "being dragged down the street to wherever Big wanted to go." He barked constantly if left outdoors, and the neighbors grew terrified of him.

"I feel so sorry for him," Aimee said. "He just goes from person to person looking for attention, and everyone pushes him away." Apparently, Tony had brought Big for a visit to Nashville and left him. When Laz heard talk of putting Big on Craigslist, he'd had enough.

"He sure does remember this place," the man who returned Big said, standing on the porch with the dog on a leash. "His tail was wagging all the way up the driveway." Laz opened the screen door, leaned over, and Big was in his arms "in a flash."

In the days that followed, Big fell back into his old routines, jumping high as a man's head doing flips. Laz got him a new igloo doghouse, which he dubbed the "Bigloo," and showed him the trails he'd been working on while he was gone. That October, 33 runners came to run a race in his honor, the first Backyard—Big's Backyard. The last runner standing went 18 hours.

But the real winner was Big. Not long after he'd been back, he sat on the porch in front of the door, pleading with his big yellow eyes. Sandra eyed him back. Then, she opened the door and let him in. "You have won, Mr. Big," Laz whispered in his ear. "You're home to stay."

---

That year, Laz quietly jackknifed ultrarunning onto a crooked, deeply personal fault line. He began by once again letting the media into the Barkley—this time it was Leslie Jamison, a promising fiction writer from New York. There primarily to crew her brother Julian, she came away with a provocative piece for a literary magazine, The Believer. The 2011 article was titled "The Immortal Horizon." The subheading in bold read:

THIRTY-FIVE RUNNERS FACE HOLLERS AND HELLS, A FLOODED PRISON, RATS THE SIZE OF POSSUMS, AND FLESH-FLAYING BRIARS TO TEST THE LIMITS OF SELF-SUFFICIENCY.

Though he'd used "Laz" in his emails, this was his first appearance in the media, and Jamison couldn't help but think of Joseph Conrad's *Heart of Darkness* and its main character. "Like Kurtz," she wrote, "Laz is bald and charismatic, leader of a minor empire, trafficker in human pain. He's like a cross between the Colonel and your grandpa."

The article caught the attention of two camera assistants in Los Angeles, Tim Kane and Annika Iltis. When they approached Laz about shooting some footage, he agreed. Their film premiered at the Austin Film Festival, where it earned the audience award for documentary feature. In 2014, *The Barkley Marathon: The Race That Eats Its Young* was released, and in 2016 it hit Netflix. Suddenly, the Barkley was officially known.

For the first time, a wider public got a glimpse of Lazarus Lake. In one scene, Iltis is riding into town in Laz's revamped Willys truck when she notices the gas gauge on empty.

"Is your fuel gauge broken there?"

"No," Laz says, looking at it. The camera zooms in on the orange indicator firmly on E. "E means excellent," he says with a grin. "F means you're fucked. Why? How does yours work? Backwards?"

There had been media attention before the Barkley movie, but after that, it exploded. Laz had a theory as to why. It was the same focus that had so often gotten him in trouble when he was so single-minded that he was unaware of anything else. The media could cover the real workings of the races, because he hardly noticed they were there.

As word spread, Laz gave numerous interviews to media in the United States and Europe, and thousands started applying for Barkley's forty spots. While he kept its application fee at $1.60, he implemented higher fees in his other races, which he and Sandra were now calling "the business."

And he began creating more events. One was born from a mistake.

His Last Annual Vol State race had been growing since 2007 with its ferry-ride start and its "crewed or screwed" journey across Tennessee. After the documentary, so many people tried to enter the race that it blew up the entry website, which malfunctioned and let in twice as many runners as Laz had space for. Rather than tell half the people they couldn't run, he came up with a second journey race, one that would be more of a challenge for the experienced journey runner—the Last Annual Heart of the South.

The runners would show up on a Wednesday, park their cars in a cornfield in North Georgia, and pile onto a tour bus. They'd be driven to a secret location some 300 to 350 miles away. There, they would be dropped off, given a map of a route back to their cars, and allotted ten days to get there. Like Vol State, the prize waiting for them at the end was to sit in the chair of honor, a lawn chair that would become so sweat-soaked and stained, it was thrown away after each race. Laz called it sitting on the "Thrown."

He stuck to a bare-bones budget, and the model became profitable. No crews would be allowed and no aid stations—runners would carry what they needed or scrounge for supplies along the way.

He also enlisted volunteers and co-directors. Steve Durbin helped him bring about the Barkley Fall Classic—a chance for the average runner to get a taste of Frozen Head by attempting an approximation of a loop. Inspired by the Barkley, it was made to be (just barely) runnable. The race strictly stayed within the park's trail system, which in turn allowed for a much larger field and proper entrance fees. Runners were given a check-down choice: Do the full 50 kilometers and receive the "Croix de Barque," or stop at the marathon mark and return in the "Bus of Disgrace."

Carl Laniak helped with Vol State and the Barkley, while Naresh Kumar, who'd recently left Silicon Valley, worked to get a website up for the burgeoning races. Naresh became so valuable helping with odds and ends that Laz and Sandra wanted to formally adopt him. "But Gary," he said to them, wide-eyed, "I already have parents."

In 2015, Laz created A Race for the Ages, and when COVID shuttered most of his races in 2020, he and Durbin took his Vol State run across Tennessee virtual. They hoped to have 200 sign up, but when registration went live, they got that much within an hour. Eventually, 19,000 from all over the world participated. Runners logged in daily to input their miles, watch their icon move, and try to "catch the leader"—the Gingerbread Man. But he was merely an icon put there by Laz like a carrot. And he couldn't be caught. *Run, run, as fast as you can, you can't catch me, I'm the Gingerbread Man.* The success of the race allowed Laz to donate $250,000 to food banks and $100,000 to animal shelters.

But by 2022, it was Big's race that was making the most waves. The human animal running against itself in this quirky 4-miles-an-hour race had become its own format, with over 70 countries around the world now holding their own Backyards, from Papua New Guinea to Japan to African countries like Morocco and South Africa. Some of the best ultrarunners in the world were competing, including Courtney Dauwalter, Johan Steene, and Harvey Lewis.

Laz's Backyard mantras entered the ultrarunning lexicon with "Speed kills," "You're tied for first until you're out," and "Just one more loop." However, he was charging mere pennies for countries to be certified—he didn't want anything to get in the way of their growth.

He was also taking what he earned from the business and throwing it into Big's, spending as much as $35,000 to have it live-streamed by a French camera crew. Thousands more went to putting it on. He worked doggedly to get international runners visas, helped them find sponsors, and even gave their admission fees back if they could make it. The Backyards became a singular focus, and to keep up with the influx of new countries, Laz began handing off most of his other races, even the Barkley. "I think Backyards is a version of running that has a place for people at all levels to succeed and to accomplish something," he told economist and podcaster Tyler Cowen. "It just seems like a worthwhile place to apply my time."

---

In October 2022, Laz held the second Backyard Satellite Team Competition. In an endeavor to be held bi-annually, the total loops of one country were tallied against the loops of the others. In 2020, there had been 25 countries. Two years later, there were 37. It seemed almost farcical in scale, but there it was, a last-nation-standing Backyard, run simultaneously around the globe.

In Malta, the event started on a sunny afternoon in a windswept park on the coast of the Mediterranean. Runners huddled together in a circle, arm in arm. In New Zealand it was nearing midnight, and the Kiwis were dining on late-night snacks. Team USA was scarfing a small breakfast in Bell Buckle, Tennessee. In Vietnam, the mood was festive near a tented pavilion in the jungle, with Christmas lights and dancing. Rain peppered the German runners gathered inside a soccer stadium, AC/DC's "Hells Bells" blaring over the sound system.

In a gymnasium in Mexico, a man wearing a blue bandana and a long white robe moved a chalice in a series of circles. Incense wafted from it in whispers of smoke. When he raised it even with his eyes, he blew the smoke over the runners, some of whom, like him, were Rarámuri. The legendary tribe also known as the Tarahumura were the best extreme distance runners in the world. They stood solemn and quiet beside a makeshift boxing ring, their hands clasped in front of them.

"This event is going to be one of the biggest ultrarunning races ever," declared team leader Michael Miller. His voice was steady and commanding, his eyes earnest and focused. "You're going up against the world's greatest endurance runners. The best of the best," he said, and held up a finger. "But this is the most important thing. This is not a race against each other. We are a team. We run together. We want others to do well because it will help you. And..." He tightened his grip on the microphone. "This will be the hardest race you've ever done."

Laz offered a different point of view in Bell Buckle, posting before the race: "it sounds easy... it looks easy... it is easy... until it's not." At exactly 7 a.m. CST, he rang his Swedish cowbell and boomed, "Happy Time!" With that, 37 nations—from Malaysia to Mauritius to Morocco—trotted simultaneously onto their first loops.

Under a bright, fall sky, Ukrainians ran past concrete pillboxes and retreat ditches full of tires. Tibetan prayer flags hung from the team's camouflage timing tent, and their clock was covered with netting. There was no cowbell, no music. Crew captain Polina Melnyk merely whispered, "One, two, three, start," and, wearing uniforms hand-sewn in Kharkiv, they dashed into the woods to run till they could run no more. For Oleksandr Slipets, who had spent months fortifying his neighborhood in Kyiv, the Backyard made him feel human again.

Ukraine's race looked to be over after the first hour. The police were on scene, declaring they didn't have the proper permits. But the runners kept running anyway, their pace steady, determined. The debate went on for hours until a compromise was reached, and base camp was moved deeper into the forest away from the eyes of kamikaze drones.

In South Africa, a brush fire rose up, orange tongues flapping higher than the trees. The director came up with two alternate routes, but the runners were being singed, and their race was ended. Canada breathed in smoke from their own wildfires. And an almighty storm hit Finland, tearing down trees and powerlines. Their race was halted with three runners still out there—hoping to run till they could move no more.

The days passed, the loops accumulated, and the US locked up the team competition with a score of 860 combined loops. No team had enough runners left to catch their totals, but runners were still out there, and all eyes turned to Western Europe, where Merijn Geerts and Ivo Steyaert of Belgium were still going. They'd surpassed the world record of 90 loops, and a palpable shift had occurred. The hashtag "#Break100" began to trend, and the possibility of reaching 100 loops became tangible.

Then, the duo shocked the ultrarunning world by surpassing it. They surprised again when the two stood in the corral for loop 102, embraced each other, and let the clock run out. In a moment of solidarity, there would be no individual Belgian winner.

Both men would go down as record holders, but they were also DNFs. You either win or you DNF—there are no ties.

For many, the ultimate goal was Laz's golden ticket. If they won their country's Backyard, they earned an invite to the 2023 Big's Individual World Championship, for a showdown against the other national champions. Filling out the field would be an equal number of at-large runners, Backyarders who'd gone the farthest in the last two years. It would be an international battle royale set in the rolling hills behind Laz's house.

When I arrived at Big's, twelve years after the first Backyard, and one year after my disaster at Little's, the tables felt like they'd turned. This time I'd come with a secret of my own to keep from Laz. Over the summer, I'd been contacted by Davy Crockett (real name). He asked me to do a write-up, in secret, for December, when he would induct Lazarus Lake into the Ultrarunning Hall of Fame. Laz would be the first to achieve the honor, not as a runner but as a race creator.

19

# Normal Rules Don't Apply Here

**ORGANIZED CHAOS WAS THE FIRST THING I NOTICED** when I came in. Empty Dr. Pepper cans grouped here, a pile of race paraphernalia stacked there, every surface in Laz's home claimed, purposed, used. A round table set against a wall was also piled with stuff—an open bag of potato chips, a carton of Camels, spreadsheets, a 3-D model of Frozen Head State Park, a tube of arthritis cream.

Laz showed no interest in a home tour, instead shuffling to a desk in the corner, so I was left to wander. A Christmas tree was already up in the living room and stood behind a sagging couch, a white baseball cap at the top in place of a star. Tucked in a chair beside it was a grey book Laz had written, *The Big Dog Diaries*, but otherwise, the theme of the room was boxes—it was stuffed with them. I peeked in a few by the hearth. One held race bibs and old timing sheets, another a plastic doll for the grandchildren on Sundays. Most were labeled "Barkley" or "Strolling Jim."

Two large bookcases, built into the wall and bisected by a mantel, were crowded with photo albums, signed baseballs, and books—books on Native American history, rock formations, and plate tectonics. One shelf propped up a child's drawing of a schoolhouse and a swing set beneath a bright blue sky. The sun was also blue. Beside it were photos of Laz's three kids, who all grew up thinking it was perfectly normal that their father made people run hundreds of miles until they quit.

Nothing about their education was conventional. His daughter Chrysalis remembered him teaching her Yahtzee and backgammon, but it wasn't just about playing games; he made her do the math fast, turned every moment into a lesson. When the others were watching TV and the dice got too loud, he created "quiet Yahtzee" on an Excel spreadsheet.

There was always a method to his madness, his kids agreed, even if it wasn't obvious to anyone else. For example, he didn't always tell the truth, in order to make them think for themselves. He often told Chrys if the groundhog didn't see his shadow, she couldn't have birthday presents. "He did lots of stuff like that," said Case, their son. "He was making it up, but he was stone-faced serious."

"There was no set bedtime," Aimee remembered. "If you got to bed late, you had to deal with it the next day."

When I walked into the front (back) of the house, I came to what appeared to be a long-lost dining area. But in the place of accent chairs and a sideboard was a sprawling map of Tennessee—thirty feet across. Over the years, Laz had taped together more counties until the entire state was formed, thoroughly veined with orange. He still hoped to do more—to do them all, he said. Of Tennessee's 95 county seats, he'd run to 90.

The races weren't just their father's hobby—it was woven into the fabric of their childhood. At eight years old, Chrys was already manning the timing clock in the back of Barry Barkley's pickup truck. Case would help mark the course and sometimes ride in the lead car with his dad, stopping every five miles to take splits. He'd try to run with the leaders and loved the rush as they blew by him even though they'd done 30 miles.

All of the kids manned the Coke trailer at the finish line of Strolling Jim. At a young age, they had to explain to flushed, overheating runners that if they gave all the runners ice, they would run out of cold drinks. Chrys earned the right to create her first taunt on the course, "It's fun to run in the sun," and would later become the first "Jeerleader" at Big's. "They will think we are assholes," she worried, but her mom and dad just laughed, and she soon began creating even more zingers to tease the runners.

Nonconformity ruled the house, even when it came to answering the telephone, Case remembered about his dad. "He'd pick it up and say, 'Hi, Kampala airport, this is Roberto.'" When a Hungarian runner watched Sandra spooning salsa on top of her steak, he did the same. She stopped him and said, "No, no, you don't have to."

But nothing was done without some kind of educational or functional purpose. When Case graduated high school, Gary rented an Impala and took them on a vacation of ten states in ten days. Each day was the pressure to make the next state, but he'd show them the wagon ruts where people had gone west and the hill he'd sledded on as a kid in Oklahoma. Chrys remembered a day trip when all they did was drive around looking for grey historical markers along the road and learning the history of Tennessee.

The kids would pile books into grocery bags to take to the races, and all three would go on to earn either academic or athletic scholarships to college. "They were big on reading," Aimee said about her parents, but there was also a perfectionism with her father that bordered on "insane."

"There is a wrong way to do a lot of things," she remembered. "It never occurred to me how to fold a tarp." Mowing the lawn was the worst. He'd come up behind her and tell her what she was doing wrong—how to go around objects, how to divide sections. "I'm never doing it again," she said finally, and paid a neighbor a case of beer to come do it.

They all agreed the documentary in 2014 changed things, and the races became jobs. "Oh good, you're here," a worn-down Aimee recalled saying when Chrys arrived to help with a race. "Now I can get some sleep." One upside was they didn't have to explain anymore what their dad did. But Dad also changed, they said. He became "the Barkley guy," an almost mythic hillbilly who enjoyed chewing runners up just to see them writhe in pain.

Laz the sadist was not someone they recognized. "He does get emotional," Aimee told me, and believes a lot is buried behind the persona. She often saw him come back from races and talk about the runners' struggles. One year, she remembered seeing him make a point to comfort a distraught Japanese runner. He put a hand on his shoulder and told him that he'd done better than anyone from his country ever had. "It's entertaining to hear that they think he's a madman," Chrys said. But "there's my dad and there's Lazarus Lake. That's a different person."

---

A 9,000-piece jigsaw puzzle—a globe with travelogue vignettes in different sections—dominated the dining room, and I was staring at a big hole in its center when Sandra appeared. "He's never going to finish that thing," she said with a look of despair. Pieces lay in assorted piles along the edges—white, red, blue, ground colors. "And I'm not going to get my table back for Thanksgiving."

We'd met briefly at Little's, but this was my first chance to spend some time with her. Dark-eyed with grey medium-length hair, she wore a pleasant yet worried look.

"I guess Gary didn't tell you where you're staying," she said, rolling her eyes.

"No. He hadn't gotten around to it," I replied, smiling.

She sighed. "Well, the French film crew is taking the big bedroom upstairs, so... I guess you could take the bedroom next to it. When Naresh comes, you two can figure out who gets the bed." She threw her hands up in the air as if bowing out of a fight, then proceeded to give me a tour of the rest of the house and apologized for the mess.

I followed her past more boxes on the stairs to the top, where a tall stack of *Ultrarunning* magazines was on the verge of spilling over. "This, of course, is all Gary's stuff. Things get crazy around here for Big's," she said, flipping her wrists like shooing away flies. She passed a nook of various household items and came to a railing overlooking the living room. "Call me old-fashioned Southern, but I believe when someone comes to your house, you show them around. Well, someone I know never thinks of things like that." She rolled her eyes again and pointed toward the floor. I could hear the faint tap of Laz typing below.

"But I designed this house," she said, lifting her head and looking out over the sprawling A-frame living room. "And I'm darn proud of it."

It was a beautiful design, a blend of modern and rustic. It had the look of a new home, albeit one that had been squatted by a mob of ultrarunners. "How long have you been here?" I asked.

"Oh, gosh... twelve, thirteen years." I imagined Sandra with blueprints, setting out to build a dream home, now resigned to nothing but the frame of one.

"You know one thing I've always wanted to do?" she said, her voice softening. "I thought it would be the coolest thing if we framed Gary's map of Tennessee and put it on that wall." She pointed at a large space over the entryway. "We could even build him a little ramp where he could get up there with his markers." She cocked her head and lit up with a smile.

"That would be impressive," I said and realized that in many ways, Sandra was the house—a sort of framework for Laz's operations. When he coached, she ran the scoreboard. If a runner needed a ride, she was there. On Laz's long runs across Tennessee, she let him out and picked him up when he was battered and broken.

"Well," she sighed and slumped her shoulders as she stared at the blank wall. "Maybe, one day. We'll eventually get around to it."

When we returned to the living room, she hit me with a question I wasn't ready for. "So, what do you think about this whole Laz thing?"

I just shrugged my shoulders. I wanted to ask her.

"I don't buy it," she whispered. "That he just found the name in some phone book." She cut her eyes in Laz's direction and a frown tugged at the edges of her lips. She then leaned in close. "You've seen the documentary, right?"

I nodded.

"Well, look at him." Her voice was so soft, I could hardly hear her. "All this... it's aged him. Look at him!" She rolled her eyes again and moved toward a shelf of books, continuing to talk out of the corner of her mouth. "So many people want something from him. They're good people. Well, they're family. But honestly..." She smirked and her gaze turned sharp. "Sometimes I think they're a cult."

All I could think to do was smile.

"Anyway," she said, perking up. "Gary mentioned something about you looking for a photo book. There's one up here somewhere." She pointed to a white binder. It was thick and worn and heavy when I pulled it out. We sat on the couch, and it sank under us like a sponge. "Gary's mother's," she said and grinned.

Sandra rifled through a blur of images while she narrated, and I tried my best to keep up. "... and this is the old, haunted house. That place was spooky!" *Flip.* "And that's Gary taking a bath with the kids in a washtub. We had to heat the water on the stove." *Flip.* "And this is Frozen Head." *Flip.* "I don't know what year, but we would take the kids Easter egg hunting." *Flip.* "And that's Gary trying to run the Barkley." Flip.

"Whoa," I said, shocked. "Can you go back to that picture?"

"What, this one?" She turned back a page, maybe five.

"That one." I squinted close. "That's Gary at the Barkley?"

She smiled like she was reading my mind. "Yep, that... is... him."

Pictured was an outlaw, perched precariously on a slope, caked with snow and ice. He was decked out in blue jeans, a duster down to his ankles, a Stetson hat, and what looked like cowboy boots. "He ran like that?" I said, incredulous.

Sandra grinned till she laughed. "If you call that running." A gleam of teenage impishness lit her eyes. "He was always a rebel."

"That's long before Laz," I said.

"Oh yeah." *Flip.* "And here's Gary and his brother, Doug." I stopped her before she turned the page.

"Wait, that's Gary?" I put my nose into the binder. It couldn't be. I could make out the familiar devilish eyes, but otherwise this was a completely different human being. An afro of curly brown hair touched with hints of blond; clean-shaven; big, handsome smile; a trim mustache. He was wearing a tight-fitting, button-up denim shirt, untucked, hands behind his back.

"And in the middle is his father, Frank," she said.

Frank was in a white T-shirt, tucked in, belt, hands behind his back in the same way as Gary. They looked proud, delighted even, standing on a porch, a white house in the background, double doors, sidelight glass panes bordering each side.

Sandra tapped a finger on the photo. "That's him," she said, chuckling. "That's Gary."

---

The next day, I returned from a supply run to find the scene had grown. Flags now hung on the barricades, one from each country participating, and stood stark against the white of the tents. The black, red, and gold of Germany formed a doorway on one tent, the Union Jack of Britain on another.

A finger of smoke brought the smell of charred meat before breaking up in the breeze and flittering up to the sky. A group of runners drank beer by a cookstove while others sat on the edge of their tents, chatting.

"Has anyone seen Harvey?" I asked, but no one had. He and his expert handler, Judd, were the only ones in the race I'd ever met. Judd had come in early, fixed up the tent, and jetted off to emcee an event. Word was, Harvey would be coming in the morning. That meant a six-hour drive from Cincinnati straight to the start line. Or maybe he was staying in a hotel nearby, I thought, trying to get one last good night of sleep.

"How far you think they'll go?" asked a voice from a face half lit under a tent flap.

"Oh... 96 hours?" I said. "Maybe." The course record was 85, but that was Harvey, and he wasn't getting any younger. Whether he could do it again at 47—that was another question entirely. Phil Gore of Australia had the current world record at 102, but I was confident these guys were in for a surprise on Big's tricky course.

The corral had been spray-painted on the grass in a soft red. "From their chairs to here," Laz had said, was the most difficult section of the course. "The hardest spot to keep going." After forty years of making races more intricate, he'd found some simplicity in his old age, whittling away the excuses of failure to highlight a simple choice: to quit or push on.

Laz called Backyards a "blood sport," but looking over the sprawl of tents, the camp had the feel of a peaceful little village. It was easy to be lulled into the illusion this was nothing more than a Cub Scout jamboree. One juggled under a tree. A young Japanese woman danced merrily around a cookstove. There was little sense that tomorrow morning, an infinite loop would begin, a run that could last for days without sleep, distance unknown.

---

"Wanna go cut some wire?" Laz was standing in the door frame, a lighter in one hand, a cigarette in the other. A pair of diagonal pliers stuck out of his flannel jacket. "You can see the improvements to the trail."

I had already set my things up in the bedroom—a carry bag, groceries, charger, the leather satchel I liked to sniff to remind myself I was a writer—so, I said, "Why not."

Dusk was setting in as we walked, falling leaves trickling from above like large snowflakes. The softening light filtered through the trees, casting "the farm," as Laz called it, in hues of gold and orange and stretching our shadows long and thin. Little led the way, following some instinctual homing beam to the exact spot where the downed fence was jutting over the trail.

We followed behind, Laz kicking stones and fallen branches from the path. "Now, this wasn't here when you came for Little's," he said, pointing to a raised walkway of neatly trimmed wood that crossed over loose rocks and thickets. "I wish I had two more months to prepare." He tapped the wood proudly as we walked over it.

Little was lagging behind now, trotting into the forest to sniff and mark. "She knows every inch of this trail," Laz said, not looking back, trusting she'd catch up when she was ready. We passed deer scratch on a sapling, and Laz paused to look at it before moving on.

We finally came to a spot I recognized. The tree stood in the center of the trail, with two trunks—one dead, the other clinging to life. It was two trees, Laz explained. "You must remember The V Tree!" he snorted. "Did'ya go around it?"

"After the first loop, absolutely."

"Not this time." He pointed his prod at some rocks and logs to each side of it. "No choice but to jump through it now." He laughed. Then suddenly his brow wrinkled, and he cocked his head toward the canopy. When thoughts hit him, his features shifted like fast-moving clouds, changing shape in an instant.

"You know the difference between old forests and new forests?" he asked and flashed a knowing grin.

"Is this a trick question?" I felt like I'd arrived for a test I hadn't studied for.

"The evergreens grow fast," he explained, "and drown out the briars and weeds. Eventually, the hardwoods take over and shade them out."

He took out his pliers and leaned down to a fence laid over part of the trail. He snapped a link, then another, and we pulled the wire fence off the trail.

"So, a tall hardwood forest is old," I said and he nodded. "By the way, I saw a picture of you and Frank, back at the house." I tried to catch his eyes to gauge his reaction.

"Oh yeah?" Laz said with little hesitation. "Frankert." He laughed. "That's what his mother called him."

"You looked happy."

He stilled for a moment. "Oh, we got along fine after we were living under different roofs," he said, kicking a rock off the trail before meeting my eyes. "It wasn't easy raising me." He smiled for a moment, then it was as if the expression were suddenly washed over with a rag, replaced with a serious, thoughtful look. He gazed at the trees and said, "This is a cedar glade," as if he hadn't missed a beat. "The normal rules of age don't apply here."

Both sides of the trail were full of cedars and carpeted with dry, crusty moss. These evergreens were not very tall, somewhat stunted, and spread over a rocky slope. "From what you just said, I assume this is a young forest."

"The opposite," he said, brimming. "It's quite old. It's the soil. It's so thin, only the cedars can grow."

On the way back, the trail twisted sharply, and Laz stopped at a small clearing. "This is where the trail first started," he said. "I was working on these trails before the house was even finished." His eyes lit up like a child's. "From the beginning, this was my goal, my dream. Can you imagine? Tomorrow, 75 runners will toe the line from 37 countries.

"As a fan of competitors and competition," he went on, "I've never been this excited." He paused for a moment and eyeballed the trail. "How many really have a shot in a world championship marathon? Maybe four? Of the 75 tomorrow, I'd say 60 of them could win."

Little was suddenly back and squatting to poop smack-dab in the center of the trail. "Uh-uh," Laz barked and gave her a poke with his prod. She looked up, agitated, and scooched to the edge, her butt tucked under her. She then laid three steaming logs on a rock. And Laz walked on without a second glance, leaving it there—a little gift for the runners to see every loop.

# Part IV

# LAST ONE STANDING

## 20

# Happy Time!

**THERE IT WAS**... one year since I last saw it, the arch, inflated and straddling the gravel. It rose over the tents and cut against the dull lavender dawn. The flags were up as well, hung from the barricades on both sides, with every color of the crayon box. Laz stood silhouetted underneath in his faded flannel, like guarding a portal. Above him in the dim light was that familiar sign, written in magic marker—THERE IS NO FINISH.

They came in twos and threes, shuffling in the chilly air, a small United Nations of ultra-athletes. Their faces were flushed and their eyes narrowed with a kind of raw, focused intensity. Half were national champions. The rest were at-large runners, the best Backyarders of the last two years. But when they stepped into the corral, they became a single-minded horde, prepared to run until they could no longer move.

As they waited for the bell, some hugged themselves to stay warm. Others looked down at the ground or stared blankly ahead. They wore shorts and jackets, sock hats, caps. A few opted for tights. Shifting their weight as they waited for what came next, they were a nervous collage of smiling faces and worried brows.

"From here on out," Laz shouted in his high-pitched coach's voice, "once the whistle sounds, if you're not a runner, get out of the corral. Make room for 'em. We have a lady assigned to yell at people." He threw a smirk at Sandra. "And you do not want to cross her."

JP was right there in the thick of it, among the huddled crowd edging in toward the starting line, a big-boned journalist from *The Guardian* with dark eyes and a heavy cream sweater, the color of sun-aged parchment. He had that Hemingway air about him—gruff, solid, and romantic in a roving kind of way.

We'd met pouring ourselves coffee at the same large rock. We remarked on the strangeness of it—two lone journalists in a race with no end. JP also had a cosmopolitan vibe, the kind that suggested an ease with languages and a life spent adrift in foreign lands. Now, he was chewing gum, arms crossed, looking on like something spectacular was about to happen at any second. Something about that warmed me. He'd obviously never seen a Backyard. He wasn't even a runner.

"Remember the rules!" Laz said, pacing in front of the horde. "This applies to the crew maybe even more than the runners. It's really simple. Be in the corral when the bell rings." He pointed like a runway technician to the red rectangle spray-painted on the grass. "If you're not inside the red lines when the bell rings, YOU'RE OUT! *Start* when the bell rings. You *can't* hang around. You *can't* go back to your tent. Once the bell rings, *you gotta go*!"

A drone hovered overhead with the insistent whine of a mosquito and broadcast the scene live to some distant audience. Below it, a French film crew threaded their way through the corral with hulking cameras. Meanwhile, photographers materialized in odd nooks and corners—crouched behind stacks of water jugs, lurking near the shadowed line of porta-potties, half-hidden beneath folding chairs—all aiming for that one fleeting, revelatory moment.

"We're strict here!" Laz continued, his eyes growing fiery. "And a lot of it will be on video. So, if you're caught breaking the rules—YOU'RE DEAD!" I noticed a runner with one foot lazily outside the corral. When his crew pointed it out, he yanked it in like a whip.

"We don't want to disqualify anybody, but every race... we end up disqualifying someone. It breaks my damn heart." Laz softened his tone. "Everyone here has earned their place. It wasn't easy, but you did it. This is the best of the best. It's an honor and a privilege to ring the bell for you guys... I stand in awe of what you've done."

If some emotion crossed his face, I didn't see it. Instead, he walked over to the new feature this year, a Swedish cowbell hanging from a rope strung between two pieces of plywood. "When you've run the longest distance you've ever run..." *Ding, ding*—he rattled it with purpose. "... ring it out. Seventy-five times we want to hear that bell ring!" He concluded by lowering the white sheet of paper in his hand and catching any eyes he could. "In the US," he said, smiling, "we like to say good luck, but I like the way the Japanese say it. May you run the race you prepared for."

A ripple of applause crackled through the camp, and crews began gathering outside the barricades, phones held high. The runners grew still, bracing themselves. You could sense it—something unspoken beneath the hugs and handshakes—a thought rolling over in the eyes. *How far? How long? How much of myself will I have to give? If I push that invisible envelope deep inside and break it open, what will I find?*

Mike Melton stepped onto the gravel, microphone in hand. Good Mike was tall, bespectacled, hair high and tight, and spoke with the rich voice of a DJ as he laid out the basics. "The way it works is you are gonna go out here to the first turnaround on the road and run right back underneath the arch. You're gonna run up to the trail. You're gonna come around the trail and finish here."

He paused, then went on. "The way the night loop works is, you go all the way to the turnaround, 2.08 miles out, and so you finish coming in this way." He gestured toward the road.

This change would happen at six o'clock in the evening before reverting back to the trail at seven the next morning. The two loops couldn't be more different: twisty and technical in the woods, flat and boring on the pavement. While the trail claimed more runners, the road was sneaky. Its lonely, hard surface at night brought on hallucinations. It was here that Courtney Dauwalter saw a giant Mickey Mouse beside the road. But it was common knowledge that the most brutal loop was the return to the trail in the morning. The mere thought of heading back to the roots and rocks and the 470 feet of elevation gain was demoralizing.

Three whistles cut through the air, signaling three minutes to the start. The shiny metal object was between Laz's smiling lips. He blew it with the practiced expertise of a referee. "You're going to grow to love that sound," he said, chuckling. Handlers handed over last-minute water bottles and clothing items. Then, the second whistle, two minutes. "Crews, *crews*!" Laz shouted. "Get away!" After the final whistle, he stared at his watch then called out, "Thirty seconds!"

The horde became restless like a rodeo bull, and the final countdown began: "Ten, nine, eight..." Claps and cheers erupted. The onlookers yelled at the runners in various languages. "Vamos," a voice cried. "Ganbarre!" said another. Laz lifted the cowbell over his head and rang it full bore.

"Happy Time!" he shouted at the top of his lungs, and the horde surged forward. The bell was still echoing as they turned the corner, gone in a cloud of dust.

---

Ringside! I set my lawn chair and bag right in front of the firepit, three feet from the gravel. JP settled into a chair beside me, and we both put our feet up on the stones of the pit. "How long do you think this is gonna go?" he asked.

"Well." I thought for a moment. "Three have gone over a hundred yards—two Belgians and one Australian."

He cocked his head. "Yards?"

"Yeah, all things Laz involve some lingo."

"Argots, I get it." JP nodded.

"So, one loop, one hour, is one circumambulation of Laz's backyard. I'm sure he'd tell you that it only makes sense to call them yards," I said, opening up my phone to look up *argots*.

"Jesus." JP was rubbing his chin. "A hundred hours? My rental is for three days."

I grinned. "But here's the thing. Those three have never run here."

I explained that Harvey Lewis had the course record at 85 yards, but Laz believed he had too much frost on the side of his head now. "Who knows how far they'll go?" I said, tilting my coffee mug in his direction. "But you might want to extend your rental."

Five minutes after they'd left, the runners started coming back through. Some of the heavy hitters were at the front. There was Ivo, the Belgian who'd run 101 hours and stopped in a show of sportsmanship. He wore black sweats, a red top, and black gloves. He was taller than I'd imagined and seemed to want to get to the front for the first trail loop. A technical course can be a nightmare if all you see is a butt in front of you.

With him was the Mexican runner, Rodolfo Ramírez. Dark hair. Good looking. Full of pride. I could hear his mother shouting in Spanish when he passed. He was decked out in solid black. Just behind them was Phil Gore, the man with the target on his back—the current world record holder with 102 yards. He was easy to spot with his colorful sunglasses perched atop his head.

It took two minutes for them all to come through, a testament to the many approaches of Backyard running. If you ran it fast, you had more time in camp but wasted more energy. Run it slow and there'd be little time to recover.

"That's Harvey," I said to JP when the teacher came in toward the back of the pack. I took out my phone and shot a video of him passing.

Since the Barkley article, *The New York Times* had shuttered their sports desk, another casualty in the ongoing journalistic apocalypse. Fortunately, *Ultrarunning* magazine had given me control of their social media and wanted updates with video, pics, and some words along the way.

"He looks pretty rough," JP said, his PC open on his lap. "Is he always like this?"

I watched as Harvey went by. JP was right. He looked stiff, like the Tin Man with no oil. Something about the way his head was down, face grimacing. It reminded me of how he'd described his peculiar entry into all of this—with a neck fused with titanium and cadaver bone.

---

It was 2004, and Harvey was merging his Saturn onto I-74 on his way home from a four-mile race when suddenly the car in front of him came to a dead stop. Harvey slammed the brakes, locked up the wheels, and went into a ditch—then airborne. While the car flipped and rolled and wrenched, he heard his neck crack.

When he came to, the world was still spinning, and he realized he was upside down. It was like a movie, and in the movies the next thing that followed was always an explosion. He quickly undid his seat belt... dropped down to the roof... and kicked at the front glass. But it was already a web of fractures in the safety glass, and he couldn't get through. When he noticed the back windshield was busted out, he crawled out, lay on the grass, and wondered if he was dying.

The doctors tried traction first but ended up fusing his fifth and sixth vertebrae. Four days later, Harvey left the hospital and refused to take any more pain meds. He taught school that summer and walked in the afternoons to feel better. He reread *The Count of Monte Cristo* and promised himself to keep chiseling. Two months later, he was running slowly, and after a year he was back to normal speed.

But he found his goals had shifted. If he could make this kind of progress when he was down, how much more was he capable of when he wasn't? While he'd done well in 24-hour races, he wondered if the longer, tougher events might suit his skill set better.

Harvey was a vegetarian but also had a rock-solid stomach that could take a ton of food and not get upset when he ran. That helped him when, a few years later, he ran Badwater, the notorious 135-miler through Death Valley and up to Mt. Whitney—*in summer*! Arguably one of the toughest races in the world, it can literally melt your rubber soles to gummy slabs of goo.

It helped him even more at Big's Backyard. He twice finished runner-up, one year coming in from a muddy loop with seconds to spare. One other runner remained and looked on as Harvey slid across the line and rolled back into the corral with one second to go. Laz rang the bell, and Harvey was up in an instant and running.

He didn't win, but he came back. He kept coming back. On his third try, he won it and set the course record.

But nothing ever came fast for Harvey. It took him five years to break five hours in the marathon and seventeen years to qualify for Boston. It took four tries to win Badwater and six more to win it again.

Before the car crash, Harvey had just a single win to his name. Now, nineteen years later, he was one of the most accomplished runners in the sport. He seemed to thrive on hardship. "When things get really tough in Death Valley," he told me, "I just try to make it to the next telephone pole."

---

Two hours had gone by, and JP was getting restless. "I'm going to go into town. Want anything?"

I thought long and hard. "Yeah. The biggest box of brown sugar cinnamon Pop-Tarts you can find." I reached for my wallet.

"No, no," he said. "You can get it to me later."

After he was gone, I noticed a rhythm to the race taking shape. First, the three whistles, followed by the bell, then the horde would lurch forward in a trot. In they'd come from the out-and-back, and off they'd go onto the trail. Forty-five minutes later, the first runners would start to filter in. The last would come in with four minutes to spare.

Each time I saw Harvey, he looked worse. His aw-shucks grin was nowhere in sight, and the lines about his mouth were stretched and taut. He'd grimace to his tent, then frown back to the corral.

By midafternoon, the sky had cleared and the sun began to cook—the runners were dripping with sweat. They'd been doing loops for seven hours, had covered over a marathon now, but in Laz's quixotic crucible, were all tied for the lead.

# 21

# I Think It Will Catch

**IT WAS LATE AFTERNOON** on the first day, and Kartik Joshi lay on a cot, a blanket pulled up to his neck. The last whistle had sounded, then the bell, but Kartik wasn't going. I was told he'd fallen and injured his ribs. But the look on the Indian's face suggested something more painful—the kind of burn that comes from the inside. It was a sullen look, his blank eyes staring into the fabric of the cot. As I walked back to the fire-pit, I realized who it reminded me of... myself, after my own Backyard.

The sun crept beneath the tree line, and Laz started work on the fire. He hauled four massive logs from the pile, refusing my help. "You're on stroke watch," I said, "remember?"

"Yeah?" he muttered back. "Not supposed to lift more than ten pounds." He stacked the logs on the grey ash—two east/west, and two on top north/south.

"These look about thirty pounds each," I said.

He looked at them and bobbed his head. "Yeah."

I sat down.

Laz was just beginning to explain how to build the perfect fire when Kartik's handler approached. The runner stood three feet back, head down. "He wants to apologize," the handler said. "He needs to do better." Before the two left, the handler shook our hands, pointed to his head, and glanced back at his runner. "Got to do better."

Laz continued as if nothing had happened, explaining how the perfect fire would last the entire five days the race would take, and he believed without a doubt that Big's would go that far or further. "We will only need one match," he said with a grin.

"You're going to keep the fire going during the day?" I asked.

He laughed. "No, why would I do that? There should be enough heat left over under those grey ashes to catch. If..." he said with bite, "... somebody doesn't fuck it up, like try to make it too big or produce a lot of fucking smoke. It's your job to make sure they don't." And like that I was given a role for the entirety of the race, firewatcher. No one was to touch it. I felt honored.

After ringing the bell, he smoked a cigarette then went in the little green house and wrote up the drama that had unfolded over the last hour. He then posted it to the Backyard website. Reappearing fifteen minutes before the bell, he shuffled over to the firepit and sat next to me. This became his rhythm. Conversations were broken by the start of new "yards" (loops), only to be picked up upon at some undetermined point.

I watched the firelight illuminate the runners coming in. Some moved stiff-legged like walking on stilts, while others tapped the gravel so lightly, you imagined they were on an afternoon stroll. "There's something primal about it," I said to Laz, "being the last one standing when the dust settles. I don't know if I'd call this a race. It feels a lot like the Barkley that way."

"The Barkley requires strength and speed and woodsmanship," he said, poking at the fire with a stick and opening up an orange tunnel of heat. "Here it boils down to pure will. Backyarders are survivors." He glanced over at a group of runners and leaned back in his chair. "Most Backyards go less than twenty-four hours," he said. "Anyone can do them. The biggest mistake I made was tagging on the word 'ultra.' If your longest run is a 5K, then one yard is a personal best. I never imagined Backyards would catch on like they have. I just didn't realize how fun they would be."

"But at this level," I said, "it's gonna get merciless."

"Yeah," Laz said, stretching his back. "It doesn't always have to be fun to be fun." He was laughing at the thought when an air-raid siren screamed from Bad Mike's phone in the timing tent. "My alarm in case I doze," Laz said with a defeated groan. He was about to plod back toward the corral when a French girl came staggering toward the arch. She looked whipped—half-lidded eyes, shoulders slumping, shoes worn and dusty.

Her name was Claire Bannwarth, and word was she'd done a hundred-miler out West the week before. She'd finished the first loop with mere minutes to spare and had been at the very back ever since. The Backyarders called it "circling the drain." But she kept coming in, kept stepping into the corral. "Damn," Laz said, flicking his cigarette into the fire. "That girl's a Danny."

---

Principal Danny Rucker at Pigeon Forge Junior High School phoned me back an hour after I'd left a message. "Gosh, I haven't talked to Coach Gary in thirty years," he said with some surprise. "I guess I've known him since I was eight years old."

He'd heard of the Lazarus Lake persona but remembered him most for the traveling basketball team he'd created for the elementary school kids. "Gary did all of it," Danny said. "He just took time out of his day. Organized the practices, set up the games with other towns, and drove us around in a white Astro Van. The middle was torn out where a seat used to be, and it had an Oklahoma Sooners tire cover on the back. He'd take us to Winchester and Tullahoma, Manchester, Fayetteville. Sometimes we'd get our doors beat in, but he kept at it.

"I could tell he was very intelligent," Danny added, thinking back. "People thought he was off, or a bit eccentric. He was off the cuff but had an unorthodox style of getting to you. He challenged us." Coach Gary was strict—assigning them tasks to keep them occupied, making kids run laps if they goofed around, always drilling them on fundamentals. Even after Gary's son, Case, moved on, he kept coaching, creating a pipeline for the junior high teams.

Gary eventually became a mainstay as an assistant coach for the high school basketball team. "He was always there early. Always looking at things analytically. Very smart, psychologically, with the kids," said Coach Mike Edmondson. "He was known as the Godfather because he'd been around so long the kids assumed he came with the school.

"Players loved Gary," Coach Mike continued. "He would write things for them for each game—what they'd learned, how they could improve—and would read it to them before practice."

When I told Danny that he'd become the archetype for Laz's latest race, he was stunned. At the same time, he said after a moment, he could understand. Before becoming a principal, he'd coached basketball, baseball, football, volleyball. "If a me had come up and wanted playing time," he admitted, "I'd have looked him off."

Danny was always the smallest kid in class. With reddish-blond hair, a round face, and lots of freckles, he was "the kind of kid that never fit a uniform." He tried out for basketball in the seventh and eighth grade but got cut both times. Too short. So, he became the equipment manager. He went out for baseball in the ninth but got cut there too. When he finally made the team in the tenth, he was early to practice, last to leave, first to rake the infield.

"Coach Gary did the books while Case was on the team," he told me, and remembered Case being on the low-cost lunch program when his dad got laid off one year. "His equipment always looked like hand-me-downs," Danny said. "But he loved it, played with the same glove and bat since he was twelve. And Case had the highest GPA I've ever seen."

"He kept books like major league baseball," Case would say of his dad. "He was big on giving errors. If you got a glove on it, you're getting an error."

While Case turned into a star baseball player, earning a scholarship to play college ball, Danny lost his spot his senior year to a freshman. Still, when the games were over, he was the first one out of the dugout to shake hands with the players. It wasn't until the fourth game of the year that things changed for him.

Several players were out, and everything was going wrong. In the sixth inning, they were down 6–1. Coach was wringing his hands in the dugout. He called Danny in to bat with two outs. He swung at the first pitch and drove in two runs. When he came up again in the next inning, they were down 6–5. Again, there were two outs, but the bases were loaded. Danny swung at the first pitch again, rifling the ball into left field and driving in the game's winning run.

He got his spot back, and he never gave it up.

He learned something out there on that field that went beyond baseball—something about showing up, about earning your spot. His parents had always taught him nothing was given. Now with four daughters of his own, he watches with a sense of bewilderment as coaches drag the fields themselves.

His senior year, the team pushed further into the regional tournament than the school had ever been, but they finally came to a juggernaut pitcher with a 0.25 ERA. Though they lost, he and Case got hits off him—the only two that did. "You didn't need to be able to hit it hard," Danny said, his voice catching. "You just had to get the bat on the ball."

---

Laz rang the cowbell over his head and the race churned on with predictable regularity for the next two days. The air-raid siren, his whistles, the bell, and off they'd go.

Fifty minutes later, the whole mob would march back to camp as if on a conveyor belt. Night would fall again, and Laz would rekindle the fire by placing small skins of bark on the grey ash. He'd blow on it, then let it sit till it caught. Each time, it erupted into a roaring masterpiece. And when the flames were licking four feet high, he'd smirk and say, "I think it'll catch."

The moon was waxing crescent above them as they came back from the road, their headtorches bobbing and weaving. But sneakily passing by was the fact that 72 runners had made it 24 hours and 100 miles—then 47 reached 48 hours and 200 miles. For those of us that follow multiday running, it was unprecedented.

It was hard to find any race where more than three runners had reached 200 miles in 48 hours. The strategy for most had always been to build a lead, then hang on. Here, there were no leaders, and each hour they were made to stop. Speed was the enemy in the Backyard, and its controlled throttle, like governors on a car, was providing miraculous results.

But by midday Monday, the Tennessee sun had begun to broil the depleted, sleep-deprived runners. Many slowed, sweat beading and forming rivulets down the backs of their necks. As they waited for the 54th yard to start, the large triage tent was filling up. Many simply hid from the sun, while the Belgians, all in their red and black, were worked on by their crews. A Japanese runner lay face down, his wife beside him monitoring the electrified needles poking out of his legs.

Laz blew the second whistle, and someone yelled, "Come on, Jennifer!" A spot of orange appeared out of the haze, Jennifer Russo. The 57-year-old mother of three was dashing toward the line, sweating profusely in the glare of the sun. She'd developed the dreaded leans—her legs continued forward but her torso tilted sideways. There are many theories as to why this occurs, from a weak core to an imbalance of electrolytes. But once it shows up on a run, it's insidious.

She stumbled at the line, but by the time she hit the seat of her chair, Laz blew the last whistle. She groaned and tilted her head back to get air. Even the way she did that was classy; she carried herself that way. She held her hands in her lap almost politely and said, "I can't breathe." Her crew handed her an inhaler, and she held the air in her lungs as long as she could, then coughed into her sleeve.

Earlier in the year, Jennifer had upended preconceptions of what a woman of her age could do. She ran 74 yards in The Capitol Backyard outside DC—a new female world record, becoming the first American woman to run 300 miles in three days in any format.

"Thirty seconds," Laz's voice pitched high and sharp. When he rang the bell, she trudged forward with the rest till they were out of sight. When it sounded for the next hour, she was nowhere in sight. Neither was Tokimasa Hirata.

He came in twenty minutes late, inching toward the line like a defeated warrior, his gait heavy and labored. He removed his black cap, and his bald head, soaked in a sweaty sheen, glistened in the last bits of day.

Laz handed Hirata-san a silver coin, the same one he gave to all those that didn't win, and the 55-year-old from Fukuoka bowed and devolved into tears. I'd met the Japanese team early in the race. In a previous life, I was a bilingual tutor for Japanese media companies, so I'd agreed to translate if needed.

Hirata-san was standing under the arch when I got to him, bowing and searching for words. Behind his thick, black-rimmed glasses, his eyes were pressed tight with emotion. His thin body wavered as if a wind were hitting him from different directions. "*Saikō no hitotoki deshita*," he said, smiling. "It was the most incredible experience." Then, he lowered his head in disappointment. "*Nanimo motte nai kedo*," he muttered. "I guess I'm not that special." And then the emotion became too much, and his voice rose to a high-pitch cry. "*Hontō ni, Nihon kara ōen to shinrai o itadaita noni, konna fugainai kekka de mōshiwake arimasen deshita*—For those in Japan cheering me on, I'm so sorry for letting you all down." A smattering of applause broke out, and he turned, composed himself, and bowed in all directions.

The next hour claimed the South African, Thembinkosi Sojola, who fell into such a state that he had to be picked up—chair and all—and carried out to his handler's car. Before he was hauled away, he was seen clapping for the others. One was the Frenchwoman, Claire. She walked in as Laz blew the first whistle. But there were more behind her now, struggling to get in, and when the bell rang, she went out again with them.

At this point in the day, all the runners wanted was to get to the night loops and to the pavement—none more so than Canadian Amanda Nelson. She'd just finished 56 loops, tying the most she'd ever done, and sweat was flowing between her eyes and down her cheeks. She passed me on the way to her tent, her muscled legs as tight as a drum, her eyes fixed in a tunnel.

Amanda had large blue eyes, bright blonde hair, and looked younger than her 35 years. For two days she'd run like she'd been shot out of a gun—near the front of the pack, every loop. *She can't last*, I thought, as she came in consistently under fifty minutes. But when Laz rang the bell for the 57th yard, she sped away again.

Rodolfo, the Mexican runner, breezed in calm, to a handful of lazy claps, and his mother—a chorus of one whenever he was in sight—danced, sang, and shouted. Not far behind was the German, Hendrik Boury—erect, not a drop of sweat. He eased to the line, waved at Laz, and calmly walked back to his tent.

Fifty-three minutes went by, then Canadian Ihor Verys came out from the trees with Amanda hanging onto him. The usual energy she sprinted in with had bled out. She trotted slowly to the personal best bell, rang it loud, then dropped like a marionette with its strings cut.

Thor, a dropped runner from Iceland, got to her first. Then her own crew was there rubbing her legs. "One more loop," her handler said with a stern voice, employing Laz's mantra. "You can do this," she said, looking into Amanda's sparkling blue eyes. "One more loop." But the rest of Amanda's face was pallid, drained of something or everything vital.

*Tweet... tweet... tweet*—the whistle, and Laz standing there blank-eyed. Three minutes.

She didn't stir. More prompts from crew and helpers. "My legs won't work," she said, pushing a gel away, her eyes bulging as if she might puke.

*Tweet... tweet...*

"You are amazing." Her handler shifted to an upbeat tone. "It's going to be dark soon, going to be a lot cooler." She rubbed furiously at Amanda's legs.

*Tweet...*

Scared confusion spread across Amanda's face while Thor tried to get her to her feet. "I can't stand," she insisted. Naresh arrived, and the two tried to lift her, but she insisted she couldn't and fell back on her butt. "Thirty seconds!" Laz yelled. "Cameras have got to get out of the corral!" They were swarming now, sensing blood, sensing a cover shot.

*Ten... nine...* "Get her feet up!" a voice shot through the crowd, then Laz rang the cowbell and screeched "Happy Time!" and the horde passed her one by one. A few glanced over, but most didn't want to see.

Laz stood motionless as she sat broken after two and a half days and 235 miles—the brim of his cap casting a thin shadow over his eyes. Thirty-three were left.

# 22

# Heredity

**IT WAS SIXTY YARDS,** I speculated, from the edge of the driveway to the last tent. My firepit home was in the center of it, three feet from the gravel of the course. For days I sat there, letting the cacophony of languages mingle in my ears. When I closed my eyes, I was in the East Village, the Bowery—the sounds of Italian, Japanese, Portuguese; the smell of charred dogs and Halal food. Then, I would open them and remind myself that this was actually Tennessee.

One evening, early, I shivered awake from a nap. I was still in my shorts from the day and scooted up to the house to change. When I opened the door, Little raised her head from her blue La-Z-Boy and thumped her tail. I ran a hand along her back. She was full of lumps but narrowed her eyes when I rubbed her. I let her out to pee before I left. Before going back in, she perked her ears and looked down the hill—she seemed to know what she was missing.

I was just coming into the firelight when I saw him—a small, dark figure trotting in from the road. He moved toward the Mexican mother, but something didn't quite add up. The language didn't fully fit. JP understood why—I was looking at a real-life Rarámuri, a Tarahumara Indian, the legendary tribe of ultrarunners from the Copper Canyons of Mexico. They had become mythic to me. JP was equally intrigued. We both sat quiet, watching the Rarámuri return to the corral with the others, sweat beading on his wrinkled brow, exhausted, human. He left for the next yard unrushed and held a steady pace, his feet beating in time like a metronome. It made me think of the broad-shouldered Latvian and Laz's Backyard saying, "Speed kills." On the third yard, he'd taken off in a show of power. He set an all-time record on the trail loop—31 minutes, 58 seconds. He beamed a cocky grin to the rest of camp. The next time I saw him, he was a shell of his original self, his butt sunk in a pink pool floaty. He'd quit over a day ago.

By the third night, things were getting weird, heightened, my mind buzzing in a warm, fuzzy cloud. I'd grabbed snatches of sleep at the house but it was never any good. The sense that you were missing something was overwhelming. What yard we were on now, I couldn't remember. I laughed at myself when a photographer showed me some shots of the race, and I realized I'd been wearing the same shirt for days. It had a quote from Melville's *Bartleby* on the front: "I would prefer not to."

The race seemed to have reached an inevitable rhythm. Those that had made it this far were good enough and determined enough to go much deeper. To me, they'd begun to move on autopilot, drifting into the background while the characters around camp came to the fore.

Beside me, the man from Rome talked music, sport, culture. I listened to him for hours. He reminded me of the old Italian actor Marcello Mastroianni—suave; jet-black hair that was always in place; deep-set eyes; and moist, tan skin. His name was Mauro, and he liked to sleep by the fire, leaned back in his ergonomic chair. For twenty-nine years he'd worked as a flight attendant and run when he could. Now retired, he wanted to see Big's for himself.

At fifteen minutes to the hour, the Roman's phone would erupt with "All Along the Watchtower"—Hendrix version—and he'd come to, clear-eyed, quickly gathering supplies for his runner, his friend Antonio. But when awake, he lounged as if sipping espresso by the glowing streetlamps of Piazza della Rotonda.

He was sitting exactly that way when Laz settled in a chair on my right. He leaned back, groaned, and stared at the stars. He hadn't missed an hour, and it was taking a toll. His face sagged as the firelight moved over the hills and valleys of his face.

"You know, Pop-Tarts aren't food," I finally muttered, thumbing open another box of brown sugar cinnamon. "If I keep eating like this my mouth is gonna go to shit."

Laz turned his head like a robot low on batteries. "You just got to wiggle 'em till they get loose," he whispered, "and they'll come right out."

The Roman cocked his head at that. I marveled at the difference between the two. One had a long leg crossed over the other as if in repose. He held his phone with a limp wrist, cool, relaxed, as if the world were in it. The other would be on the edge of delirium one minute, a cigarette thick like a swollen bumblebee between his fingers. The next minute his eyes would brighten, and he'd gaze into the fire, playing with some idea he wouldn't tell you about unless you asked.

"I suppose you're gonna say pulling your teeth wasn't real pain." I cut my eyes in Laz's direction.

He brought a cigarette to his lips but paused. "Dammit, it hurt," he muttered. "But I ate the rest of that burger."

I pulled myself up in my chair. "You lost me."

"The first one, at Hardee's," he said, shaking his head. "The first bite was beautiful. It was the second or third bite that there was this crunch." Rather than face a dentist, he said, he grabbed the tooth with his fingers and started jiggling it. He thought it would come out easy but was worried what he'd do if it started bleeding nonstop. He finally got it out in the bathroom at work, when he was Shelbyville's city treasurer. He held it up to a coworker. "You're just pulling my leg," she said. He opened his mouth to reveal a pool of saliva-tinged blood.

"How many total?" I asked.

"Thirteen." He twitched his mouth in thought. "It hurts like a bitch till you break the nerve."

I noticed my Roman friend had been listening. He'd shifted his legs to the other side, a slight look of horror etched on his face.

"All my teeth were big, healthy teeth," Laz continued. "I didn't have any fillings. They were perfect." He let out a long sigh. "Heredity." He took a final drag on his cigarette, then moped up to the corral. When he rang the bell, thirty survivors trudged off into the dark in utter quiet.

Every night, two or three would call it quits on an easily walkable four-mile stretch of pavement. Comparatively, the out-and-back of the road was a cinch. But coming from the trail, the stiff road had a way of making angry feet scream. *Who would it be tonight?* we wondered amongst ourselves.

The whistle blew and the bell rang for yard 68, but the Rarámuri hadn't come in. The wife of the other Mexican runner went out for him. She came back, bracing the runner's weight with an arm around his back. Laz appeared from the grass and handed him a silver coin. The Rarámuri started to smile, but it crumpled into a wince. "*Muchas gracias*," he said, and the entire Mexican crew embraced him. Before he retired to his tent, they pointed to the personal best bell. He'd forgotten all about it.

"You can't have a bad hour," Laz said, sitting back down instead of going into the house. He'd been awake for all of them, catching a few minutes of sleep here and there in the little house. I asked him how he managed it. "I have the short sleep gene," he bragged. "When you need only three hours a night, it leaves a lot of time to think up stuff."

The Roman didn't come back after taking care of Antonio. Instead, JP appeared with a plastic sack and took his chair. He looked fresh, like he'd just toweled off from a shower. "I've got a bit of bourbon in the tent if you gents would like some," he said in his rapid-fire way. He thought fast, changed subjects fast, and, like Laz, enjoyed digging into the meat of a topic.

He sat with one ankle propped over the opposite knee, idly resting a hand on his foot. "So, Laz, this math problem," he said. "It's quite the mind-melter." I'd given him the same puzzle Laz had given me the year before, just to see how it would land with his brain. He'd been on about it all day.

Laz raised an eyebrow with what seemed like considerable effort. "Yeah," he groaned. "I can't remember right now."

"Have you always done ultramarathons?" he asked Laz in a burst, almost tripping over his brain. "Did you develop some disdain for conventional marathoning? Or—"

"Not at all," Laz cut in, suddenly awake and sitting up in his chair. "I was a mediocre marathoner at best. I just figured if I couldn't run a marathon in under three hours, I'd have to reevaluate my situation." He drew a cigarette out of the pack in his pocket.

"So, I assume you didn't." Like Laz, JP had an accent all over the place. At the moment, the American sounded British.

"My goal was to do the first 10 miles in 70 minutes, then let it fly." Laz stretched his bad leg out and flexed it. "I was right on pace through mile 20, cruising, confident. After that someone attached an Oldsmobile to my ass, and I think it was in neutral." He chuckled out a cloud of smoke. "At mile 23, they shifted it into park."

“Was that one of your illustrious 3:17s?” I said, trying to prod him. “One theory out there is you created Lazarus Lake because you didn’t want your slow times to be connected with your fast times as Gary.”

He laughed but didn’t—just a hitch in his chest. “What fast times? That one was 3:20.”

“That’s a totally decent time, man,” JP said, rubbing at his trim beard. He looked even more like Hemingway in the firelight.

“I believed the old adage that you can achieve anything you set your mind to,” Laz said, eyeing the journalist. “My father dreamed of running an eight-minute mile. Never did.”

For the first time, JP didn’t have another question ready in the chamber. There was a long silence, and a few minutes later, the journalist retreated to his little green tent by the woodpile. I didn’t have the heart to tell him that rattlesnakes had nested there one summer.

Laz was hunched back down into his chair after the start of another yard. His lids were heavy and falling, and I thought he’d nap right there. But he raised his head with a start, picked up his walking stick, and stood. He looked down at his cigarette as if remembering a chore he’d forgotten. “Yeah,” he said before making his way back to the little house. “I was a total failure as a marathoner.”

He had explained to me on several phone conversations his talent for running 3:17—on the nose. In one marathon, he was on pace to run a sub-three when his stomach turned frisky. He saw some people standing in a yard chatting and asked to use their toilet. Relieved, he hit the road and picked up his pace. He finished in 3:17. In another, he was on fire, he said—till mile 20, when he came unglued, quit, and hitched a ride back to the start. “Oh, that air conditioning felt great,” he remembered. But the guilt was stronger. He asked the driver to stop the car. And he got out, hitched another ride back to where he’d stopped, and continued on. He finished in 3:17.

There was also the time he got shot mid-race.

Gary was making the second of two loops at the Chattanooga Marathon when he turned under a hill. He felt it before he heard it. It bounced off his jacket, but his exposed left leg was sizzling with "dozens of little wasp stings." *Must have been birdshot.* There they were up on the slope—stupid, dumb-ass quail hunters. *Have you got no brains!* He was yelling and pointing his finger when they plugged him with a second round, and the boom echoed over him.

His legs were on fire, but he was over the fence and running toward them. He got close enough to see the man's squirrely little eyeballs grow wide, he said. But when the man raised the tip of the barrel toward his chest, he stopped. He imagined the pellets splitting him open, carving up his innards. So, he backed away.

Luckily, there was a policeman at the next intersection. "I want to file charges," Gary said, pointing to the hunters still crouched in the field. "They shot me!" The officer looked at the blood dripping down Gary's legs and into his shoes.

Gary continued on with the race. Maybe it was the burning in the legs, the BBs squirming in his skin that he'd pluck out later with his fingernails, or maybe it was the red in his vision that made the road look like a punching bag—but whatever it was, he was flying. He came to the line in a blur of sweat and blood in 3 hours, 17 minutes.

The whole story was too incredible to be believed. So, I started nosing around till I came across this:

> *The Leaf Chronicle*—Nov. 11th, 1979. Headline: MARATHONER SHOT. "Police said a runner in a marathon race was struck by shotgun pellets, but not seriously injured, while running near a wooded area Saturday. The runner, 25-year-old Gary Cantrell

> of Shelbyville finished the 26-mile race in suburban Ooltewah, the Hamilton County Sheriff's office said."

*The Jackson Sun* ran the same article but added that Sheriff Lt. Mike LeVan believed "it was an accident."

Gary wasn't quoted due to a run-in with the reporter. "My first experience with the media," he told me. At the finish line, he'd gone hunting for a cop. He expected there to be a slew of them. They were nowhere to be found, just a damn reporter. "They said you were shot with a shotgun." The man took out a pen and pad.

Gary let the question hang there for a moment before looking down at his bleeding legs. "No," he seethed. "I just have a bunch of holes in me."

# 23

# Rules Are Not Suggestions

**IT'S OFTEN HARD TO PIN DOWN** the moment change comes—like the precise second when a passing curiosity ignites into passion, or the sharp edge of hate dulls into forgiveness. But it's as clear now as it was hazy then that Big's started to slant with Hendrik Boury.

The German had been the picture of discipline, his movements deliberate and precise. You couldn't miss him; his tent right behind the firepit was marked by a regal German flag hung for a door. Day and night, he came and went with quiet determination, his hair perfectly trimmed, his face suggesting a mind that thrived on order and forethought—the kind of person who knew the answer before he asked the question.

But sixty hours in, something in him slipped. After changing his shoes for the road loops, he left his ankle timer behind. He was half a mile out when he realized it and frantically doubled back to his tent. I, like everyone else, watched the clock tick away. Five, then eight minutes—lost. Yet, in the next breath, he was back out on the road, hunting down those four miles at a furious pace. When he returned, leading the pack, the camp collectively exhaled—a sigh brief as a heartbeat.

"You need to talk to Laz." Bad Mike's voice was clipped and direct. He repeated it again, "You need to talk to Laz." No further explanation, no added urgency, just the directness of someone who wasn't going to get involved. The German gave a tight nod and muttered a pair of "okays" and "thank yous" before pivoting back toward the firepit.

This all went down while I was crouched next to the timing tent, trying to get a clear read on another runner's situation. I didn't think much of it until Bad Mike fumbled behind him for a bottle. "I'm gonna need booze for this," he said, his normally deadpan expression cracking. "You want some?" He tilted the bottle toward me, and I thought I saw a flicker of something raw in his eyes. "This is going to be talked about for a long time," he said, and I got what he meant—another controversy.

Then I was trailing Boury—the warm burn of alcohol seeping through my chest—and took a knee in the grass when he came up behind Laz. The rest of camp seemed to freeze and grow quiet.

"Laz," Boury called, his voice soft and deferential. "Sorry, Laz. Sorry."

The old man finally swiveled his head around and muttered, "Yes?"

"The Mikes told me I should talk to you about the timing chip." After the German turned off his headtorch, the two stood bathed in the red light of the race clock. "I forgot my timing chip in the tent, and uh..."

"Yeah, you can't," Laz said matter-of-factly. "Remember the instructions at the start. Get nothing. You can't go back." A heavy pause followed, and a thin smile tried to form—the one Laz used to defuse tension. "You can't go back." His tone was lower now, with a sense of finality. Hendrik's face tightened, a storm gathering in his eyes. He was speechless, searching for a way out, until finally he stammered, "Can... I..."

"It wouldn't matter what it was," Laz cut in, tilting his head slightly to catch the German's eyes. But Hendrik's gaze faltered, drifting away as if he couldn't bear the truth settling in front of him—that he was out. "Then it's an endless series of 'well, but,'" Laz continued, his voice rising with confidence. "Because it happens. It happened two years ago. And the guy went back to get headphones. It was just headphones."

In the pale red light, it was hard to make out anything beyond his mask of race director. This is why he had rules, to save him from moments like this. Clear cut. No grey area. No discussion. If a runner could go back to the tent, they could get aid. Boury hadn't done that—camp knew it, and Laz knew it. But moving the goalposts now would put in debate other slipups and he'd be faced with more situations like this. No, he couldn't give.

"There's nothing I can do?" Hendrik pleaded, desperation creeping into his voice. "I got like an eight-minute time penalty. I ran forth and back to make sure I was compliant..." He tugged nervously at his headband as his words trailed off into a mumble.

"There would become endless discussion," Laz said, searching for the right thing to say. He was always better when he had time to write. "Not with you," he went on awkwardly, "I mean... I am beyond... I feel so bad. You can't imagine. Well, you *can* imagine." His gaze dropped to the ground.

Hendrik held his hand to his cheek, his wedding band glinting crimson under the glow of the clock. "Maybe you could ask the other runners how they feel about it?"

Laz stiffened. "Then, this becomes a protest committee."

The air-raid warning blared by the arch. The sharp whine seemed to unnerve the German—the clock ticking—hope dying. *Four minutes.* He ran his hand over his mouth, eyes darting around, for someone—anyone—to step in and help. But help wasn't coming.

"I don't know what to say," Laz said, the smile back under his thick beard. Across from him, Hendrik's face seemed to crumble in slow motion. He blinked and turned away as if looking for a tribunal. Laz stepped closer and placed a hand on Boury's shoulder. "I'm sorry," he said softly. "You were doing so fucking good." Hendrik pulled away, no longer able to look at him, then buckled from the waist as if gut-punched.

The sound of the whistle cut through the air, but not from Laz. It was Bad Mike standing in the timing tent, eyes large, the shiny metal pressed between his lips. He kept it for emergencies, and now, after sixty hours, he'd used it. *Three minutes.* Hendrik staggered when Laz walked away, then crept slowly back toward his tent. He paused by the fire and stared through the smoke at the glow of the coral-hued embers.

The second whistle came, and a lone runner eased from the shadows and into the corral. He pulled on a flimsy jacket. Then Laz blew the third with command, a piercing screech that stirred the rest from their tents. And one by one they gathered in the red corral, their shoes softly rustling over the gravel. Just beyond the start line, two women with silver pom-poms took up their posts as Jeerleaders—volunteers whose sole function is to taunt the runners. They eyed each other, nodded, then began to jump up and down, shouting, "Around the world. You're tied for first. Who's gonna last when the pain gets worse?"

Laz began the countdown—*ten... nine... eight*—and his voice was crisp in the cool air. He raised the cowbell over his head, rang it, and hollered, "Happy Time! Ho, ho, ho, hey!" Twenty-nine lumbered forward into the night, a thin cloud of grey dust when they were gone.

"The damn thing is," Bad Mike said, his eyes filling, "he had a second chip in his bib."

---

Controversies—Laz isn't sure when they started, but it could have been the time he outwitted a lady on the course with nothing more than the promise of a breakfast muffin. Or it might have been "The Death Match on the River," as he calls it—the time he tricked a 12-year-old girl to take a nap so he could jump ahead. There was also the time in the late '80s when he promised ultra-legend Ann Trason (after she'd asked) not to write about her. After her dominating performance, he didn't—and found himself blasted for being sexist. But certainly the times he said that women were not strong enough to finish the Barkley created Laz's longest-standing row, and a perception that he was somehow anti-woman.

His first wife, Mary, never felt he was sexist but wasn't surprised that he'd made such a statement. "He always wanted to shock people," she said.

"To be honest," filmmaker Annika Iltis remembered, "I thought he would be a misogynist." She'd seen bits here and there of Laz saying women could never finish the Barkley, but when she arrived in Frozen Head, she said she "quickly figured out the little hot-button statements are really to challenge people." Her co-director, Timothy Kane, felt the same. "No one would be more excited for a woman to finish."

Having grown up always doing the opposite of what he was told, it made sense to Laz—telling someone they couldn't do something to get them to try. Reverse psychology—nature's way to sure results. In private, he had a different tone. "We really need a female finisher," he told Amelia Boone when she came to Frozen Head. And when Jasmin Paris was tapped out in front of me, he whispered to her, "Please put this to bed."

Writer Leslie Jamison found that Laz intimidated people, but "it didn't seem like it was coming from a mean-spirited place. There was kind of sparkle in his being concealed behind this reputation of a taskmaster. There was a tenderness at the core."

In recent years, he's taken heat for not creating a separate division for female Backyard runners. He was sexist, they said in forums and chatrooms. Laz shot back by reasoning that the Backyards didn't require speed or strength. "Women's divisions depress women's results," he wrote. "The Backyard is all about that challenge of keeping on stepping into the corral. Being told that you've already won just sucks the life out of a competitor."

When the prolific ultrarunner Maggie Guterl began running Backyards, he told her, "I would give anything to see a woman win Big's." In 2019, she did just that, beating the men.

The following year, Dauwalter did the same. "All of us in every avenue of our lives can raise the bar," she told me. "His events are doing that in running but apply to life in general. Big's is four miles an hour till you give up on yourself. That's really representative of other areas of life. You can always give it one more lap.

"And I know he believes a woman can finish Barkley," she went on to say. "He thinks we all have more in us than we think is possible."

To his detractors, these were outliers, and they pressed for more inclusiveness. As far as Laz was concerned, however, these individuals were not superhumans, they were products of willpower. Winning and losing, equality versus equity, and broader ideas of fairness were good arguments, he believed, for most sports—and in most of his races. Just not for what he was doing with the Barkley and Backyards. "For those who think it should all be put to a vote," he'd say, "it is. But if you don't do the work, you don't get a vote."

He took other shots over the years, but nothing prepared him for the social media era. Using Facebook groups to unite runners of his various races, he believed he could keep sport groups confined to the topic of sports, and his creations in their own universe. By 2020, the political climate for many was getting too hot to stay quiet. Fake accounts and bots were also punching out hard-line propaganda. Laz responded by getting more moderators to delete posts, but that caused a greater problem.

When a runner posted a photo wearing a Black Lives Matter T-shirt, arms raised high, the response was immediate and toxic—in Laz's words, "typical white supremacist bullshit." Though he didn't consider the original post overtly political, he says the vitriol in the comments forced him or one of the moderators (he doesn't remember) to delete it entirely.

A month later, angered by what they saw as censorship, several runners attempted to enter another of his races under the team name Black Lives Matter. Laz wouldn't allow it, just as he wouldn't allow a MAGA team. Change the name or drop out, he told them. They chose to leave.

"I am 1000% in agreement with the movement," he told *Outside* magazine, "but this is not a political site. If I thought one heart would be changed, it would be different. But all that would happen is the race would fill up with the same crap that permeates everything." One blogger fired back, calling his stance "typical racist non-racism. Just keep it about running, and check racial politics at the door."

"Cancel Laz? Can't say I agree with that," said Jameelah Abdul-Rahim Mujaahid when she found out about the backlash. "Let me put this in perspective. I used to know I was the only Black person there. Now, it might be five of us."

I'd interviewed her earlier that year, after she talked a gunman down while working at a Waffle House. She was a mother of five who worked three jobs but made time to run ultras on the weekends. Once after work, she'd driven out to Death Valley and run across it in flip flops. She'd also been a regular at several of Laz's races. "This man has let me stay in a hotel for free because I was too tired to drive home," she told me. "He's sent rescue squads when some true racists were stalking me through Tennessee. And he never talked to me like I was Black Jameelah. He talked to me like Jameelah. He interacts with everybody there. Laz is all about the pure essence of ultrarunning. He taught me to dig deep."

The racism controversy resurfaced in 2023 during my coverage of the Barkley when my editor asked, "So, what's with the flag?"

"What flag?" I said, unaware.

"The Confederate flag."

"I didn't see one." Back in my car, I scoured my GoPro until I came to what had ignited the hubbub—a novelty license plate, a joke given years ago by a Barkley virgin. In the middle it read, "Darn tootin' I'm a rebel." Laz subsequently took it down.

"He is a master of ambiguity," said former plasma physicist and ultrarunner Blake Wood. "He's comfortable doing that. He can stir up something controversial, then doesn't resolve the issue." Wood had particular insight; he was involved in a situation that nearly ended the Barkley. "It's still personal for me," he told me over the phone. "Quite painful, and Gary didn't do anything to ease that pain."

The year was 2001—Laz was still Gary then—and Wood was making his fifth attempt on the race that eats its young. He had been stopped the year before at mile 90 by New River guzzling up in life-threatening torrents of floodwater. Now, a stronger storm was about to erupt, one that had been churning for thirteen years.

"You do what you have to do," Tom Possert murmured in 1988, sprawled across the ground, sucking in jagged breaths. "I know what I did." It was the third year of the Barkley, and he had been poised to become the first finisher. It was an honest mistake. Those cryptic course instructions—he'd misread them, hadn't gone past the aid station to the top of Frozen Head, because he thought he didn't have to. Which meant he skipped almost a mile per loop. Which meant, he was out.

When he returned in 2001, he spotted two potential finishers, Blake Wood and David Horton, on the wrong side of a ditch. He quit in camp and raised "a fuss," according to Bad Mike. He ran that year and described the situation this way: "There was a little part where you could cross over on a creek by Beech Ford," he said, and admitted that many were oblivious to the fact that it was no longer part of the course. "None of us realized that," he said. "I did it. Everybody was doing it." The written instructions said otherwise. The problem was many veterans no longer read them.

"Between the keyhole and beech fork there is a trail on the south side of the creek that people could take," Gary would say. "Somewhat longer, but much easier than the boulder field. The year before some found it and took it. The easy way to control that was to simply require staying on the north side of the creek. Where Horton and Wood crossed the creek was inconsequential. Not the purpose of the rule and did not cut off any distance. It actually added two creek crossings."

Laz recorded them both as finishers in *Ultrarunning* magazine, believing the oversight to be minuscule. Possert's response was swift, firing off a letter to the editor. "To my surprise," he wrote, "Gary has ok'd the course cutting and cheating."

Because of Possert's '88 DQ, pressure mounted on Gary—the line he'd drawn in the Tennessee dirt, sharp and inflexible, was staring him down. On one side stood admiration. In the fifteen years of the Barkley, only one had finished the full 100 miles. Now, two in one year—and these were the first Americans. On the other side was the letter of the law, and it had been broken.

Gary sent an addendum to *Ultrarunning*, but the editor posted only the second part—the part that backed Possert. Horton and Wood both wrote letters in their defense. (Years later, Wood returned to the creek and ran up and back twice on each side. He estimated the difference was eleven seconds.) Still, Laz officially disqualified the two finishers. "It made no sense," Bad Mike opined. "It was the only time I saw Laz buckle to pressure. Usually what he says goes."

Privately, Gary was inconsolable and wiped all his records of the Barkley—the entrants, the finishers, the splits, his papers, his maps. Even his hard disk. He inserted it in his ancient PC and hit reformat. No more arguments. No more hassle.

Then, something shifted—a change in him, one that, looking back on years later, seemed inevitable. If it were to continue, he thought, it would have to be on his terms. He'd lean on a new name, Lazarus Lake, and he'd never use "official" again. If asked, he'd say Wood and Horton were finishers. And yes, he'd admit, they were also disqualified. Both could be true. "The truth," he'd now say, was "malleable."

People could believe what they wanted. He'd believe what he knew.

---

There would be no Boury controversy. The German runner was back in the corral, alone, looking out toward the road as the dust settled at his feet.

I'd watched him circle back around to Laz and embrace him tight—the old man squeezing him back. I fought the urge to get closer and instead let them be, retreating to my spot by the fire. The air was suddenly a growing chill and the fire felt like warm hope under the empty void above.

I sat alone for an eternity, probably ten minutes, letting the front of my pants get crispy. I tried to imagine what Boury must be feeling. Then, there he was—coming close on the way to his tent. I stood and reached out my hand. He took it. There was nothing to say. The anguish was misty in his eyes, and I knew even the best-intentioned phrase could spill him over. But he held himself erect and bowed his head before retiring to his tent. I doubted if I would have been so composed.

Not long after, I heard shoes on gravel coming closer. It was Sandra. She plopped down and sank into a chair beside me. We both stared at the fire in quiet with our tired faces. "That's a tough one," I said finally, rubbing my chin.

"What's that?"

"Boury," I said, "the German getting DQ'd."

She raised her eyes as if to say, "I know," but instead said, "Oh yeah. He's that way with everybody—with his kids—with himself."

"I get it. If you bend the rules for one, you have to..." I stopped myself and leaned over my knees. Boury had passed by me for days, and an unexpected sense of loss was welling up in me. Odd, I thought—I didn't know him at all.

Sandra sat back and crossed her legs. "Gary's a lot better now," she said with some enjoyment. "Once his thyroid was radiated, he became more mellow. Lost some of that 'it's got to be just so.'"

"Sometimes I call him Gary and sometimes Laz," I said. "Both seem right but odd. Does that make sense?" I was stoned from fatigue and wondered if I really believed what I was saying. Then, I repeated what Bill Schultz had told me, that there was a separation in his view, that "the Gary everyone knew and loved no longer existed."

Sandra's mouth dropped open and her eyes flared. "What?" she said, in a long, drawn-out sigh. "Call him whatever, he's the same guy. He's always been this way, the way..." she gestured with her hands at the tents and the cigarette butts in the fire, "you know... the way he is."

## 24

# There Might Be a Body in There

**IT WAS THE DEAD OF NIGHT**, and Laz was a mere outline in the dark, a cigarette burning softly between his fingers. For the last hour he hadn't said a word, only poked at the glowing embers with a stick. Then, he lingered around the tents by himself, lost in some train of thought. Now, his face was half lit, one side touched by the orange glow of the fire, the other side dark like the far side of the moon.

"God, that never gets any easier," he said, finally.

I had nothing to say that wasn't obvious, so we sat quiet for a moment. When I looked over, he seemed to be sinking in on himself, small flames flickering across his glasses. "This could all be over tomorrow," I said, trying to take his mind off of it.

He looked up slowly. "We'll know a helluva lot in the morning," he said, tossing the butt into the flames, where it shriveled like a marshmallow. "That will be 300 miles in three days. God, I could never do it."

The thought of this all being over was bittersweet. A full night's sleep would be welcome. At the same time, I'd become attached to the race's rhythm, the ebb and flow of the runners returning and going like the tide. They were familiar faces and strides. Some nodded at me each time they came in. Then there were those that seemed impervious to external stimulus. Boury had been one of the former, wrapping himself in decorum despite the miles. He would give a brief, economical wave when the claps came. The toll never showed until it was over, and I couldn't get past his ultimate acceptance of his fate; the better part of my nature was not as good as that.

"I think I expect things to play out in some kind of order," I said, stammering to fit my words with my feelings. "Maybe that's why I tend to bow out when I feel they're not."

Laz sank deeper into his chair. "My mom used to say, most of the time when things go against you, it's not fate or the universe, it's collateral damage." He chuckled under his breath, then sighed. "Spend any time in a hospital, and you'll see that play out every day."

His time working as an orderly was something we'd touched on occasionally, a period in his life that felt like a mismatched puzzle piece. With nothing but hours in front of us, I decided to ask him about it again, about Memphis.

---

After hitchhiking across the country, Gary reluctantly returned home and enrolled in the University of Tennessee in 1973. He'd already paid for a quarter in advance and hated squandering money. While he didn't attend class, he did meet Mary Wells—first standing in line to get a student photo, then at a party. They married in a Catholic church. He was 19. She was 18.

When her quarter was up, they strapped their furniture to the top of the rusty Mustang and headed for Memphis. A new town on the other side of the state—away from parents, away from anyone that knew them—seemed like a fresh jolt of freedom for both. The agreement was she'd study at Shelby State to become an X-ray technician, and he'd work doing whatever.

Memphis was riddled with crime, and their cheap duplex on the south side of town seemed to be smack in the middle of it. The sound of gunshots and sirens was a part of the nightly ambience. Early on, Gary picked up a game of basketball only to see a kid, "eight, maybe nine," pull a knife on another kid and rob him.

Gary was aimless. Getting stoned was a daily thing, and on the weekends, he'd drive down to Mississippi and pick shrooms. He'd try anything once. Crack, he didn't like. Cocaine? Too dangerous. Once, full of LSD, he told Mary he had a mind to paint the living room black with little white dots for stars on the ceiling. She refused. When her parents paid them a visit one weekend, Gary was tripped out on shroom tea. He got goofy, then paranoid and quiet, anchoring himself on the couch.

He would only hint about it later, but his foray into the drug world was more than experimental. "I might have done something illegal," he'd say. Mary admitted they'd gone further than they should have. "We were just dumb kids," she said, and she got out first and was on him to quit—though telling him to do anything only ensured he wouldn't.

To help with expenses, Mary took a part-time job at McDonald's, and soon the excitement of a new start faded. He tried to cheer her up by getting her a motorcycle. She loved engines and going fast, but the cheapo 125cc wouldn't do much. It was also temperamental and liked to cut out on her after work. She'd push it back to the duplex, wearing her flat, black, leather-soled McDonald's shoes.

Gary worked in construction at first but then got hired on as an orderly at Baptist Memorial Hospital. Part of the new job involved transporting bodies to the morgue. During orientation, he and the other trainees were taken down to the basement, to a chilly room that buzzed with bright, florescent lighting and smelled like a Band-Aid. The instructor lined them up in a semicircle, pulled a body out of a drawer, then with a swift, casual motion removed the sheet. The newbie next to Gary was a relapsed Catholic and nearly fainted, crossing himself frantically. It didn't bother Gary though. "It was a body," he'd say. "There was no person there anymore."

He started on the orthopedic floor, where a big part of his job was making sure that people pooped every day. He dispensed medication and quickly became known as one of the best at inserting catheters. He often joked with the patients to keep them talking until, "there you go, all done." His favorite part was the old people. They were often alone and with no pretense, and they reminded Gary of his grandmother Mama Lou. He'd eat his lunch with the ones that never got in visitors. Mostly, he just listened as they talked.

Mr. Putnam had been there for weeks, and Gary had grown to like him. The old Black man was kind and appreciative, though a deep sadness hung about him. It showed in the wrinkled places under his eyes and his sunken cheeks. It wasn't fair what had happened to him. He'd worked into his retirement years and liked doing it. Then came the day he was changing the tire of a big rig, and the wheel exploded. The metal shards from the rim "smashed his legs to smithereens." Now, he was no good to anyone. Each day he'd ask if anybody had called for him or if his children had come by while he was sleeping. They hadn't. Gary would hang around on his lunch break, listening to stories about his working days, watching the way his eyes drifted to the door whenever footsteps passed by.

Gary's own health was taking a slide. He was smoking five packs of cigarettes a day and drinking gallons of sweet tea. He also hadn't run in six months and was starting to miss it—miss the feeling of cruising along the road effortlessly, the rhythmic flop of his hair on his back, the sweat pouring down his body on a hot, sunny day. He missed the soreness after a hard workout and the devastation after an even harder race. But most of all he missed having a goal.

When he read an article on Frank Shorter's Olympic gold in the 1972 marathon, Gary's course felt set: He would someday do the same. The next afternoon, he climbed in his Mustang and measured a mile on a series of neighborhood roads. If he wanted to win the Olympics, he'd need to average 4:50 a mile, so he decided to start his training with one 4:50 and build from there. The first hundred yards went really well, then he was gasping and leaning on his knees. He stopped eighteen more times before he hit a mile and finally headed home, bathed in sweat. It seemed possible his training method might have to be adjusted.

He discovered an abandoned track near the duplex, started doing intervals, and was soon expanding into treks across the city. They were gritty runs. Good neighborhoods, bad neighborhoods, it didn't seem to matter—there was danger everywhere in Memphis.

One day, finishing up a long run in Overton Park by the zoo, a motorcycle gang swarmed him. Decked out in matching black leather jackets, they gunned their engines beside him in stops and starts, soaking him in fumes that reeked of oil and metal. When that bored them, they swerved their fat hogs and drove him into a ditch. He climbed back onto the road, but they buzzed him again. He retreated to the trench, hurling obscenities at the receding thunder.

It wasn't until he was running again that he realized they still weren't done with him. The bastards had formed a line and were leaning into a curve as they came back around the giraffe enclosure. Gary screamed at his legs to move—he had to beat them out of the park. But the bikers sped up. It was a race... until *whoosh*... they wiped. The leader went first—a crunch of metal on pavement, man and bike sliding, bouncing, slamming into a tree. The gang broke up, braking and skidding. Number two laid his down and away he went... zipping along the asphalt like a bowling ball... his machine ahead of him until they crashed into the leader.

Gary stopped to look out of curiosity, his lungs tight and burning. The guy was in bad shape, blood everywhere, maybe some broken bones. But Gary didn't spot any arterial bleeding. Anyway, the EMTs would get to him soon enough, and the hell with those punks.

Another day, he stopped at the intersection of Cleveland and Thomas, and a guy leaning against a building suddenly jumped out with a knife and said, "Give me your money."

Gary looked down at his skinny shorts and running shoes. "Where am I gonna have any money?"

"Yeah, you're right." The man shrugged and went back to leaning against his corner.

Gary was undeterred. He'd run at night—he'd run whenever he could—that feeling coming alive again, of being in shape, of being able to cross vast distances on your own power. He ran all over the city and saw sights and sounds of an urban landscape under siege with poverty and chaos and change.

One night, running under a film of dirty air, he came to something truly strange—another runner on the road. *So, there are people like me.* He sprinted past the intersection to catch him, and when he did, the man seemed equally shocked. His name was Arnold Weiner, and he belonged to The Memphis Runners.

Within a week, Gary was surrounded by a band of like-minded individuals and had his yellow singlet—the twelfth member of the first running group in Memphis.

---

Gary's image of farmers was one of hard men, with gnarled hands and weather-beaten faces, who could fix anything with baling wire and duct tape. Working at the hospital in Memphis, farmers came in from Arkansas, Mississippi, and West Tennessee, and they did nothing to dispel that image. All they wanted was to know what they had to do to get out of this place and go home so their wives and neighbors wouldn't have to do their work for them.

So, it was no small shock when a young farmer arrived at Baptist Memorial with a broken femur, whining and crying about everything, not willing to do anything for himself. It wasn't an insignificant injury, but the farmer's wife and mother hovered over him like he was a wounded butterfly. When it came time for physical therapy to prep him to go home, he got worse—like working with a rag doll. When he left the hospital, he had to be wheeled down and lifted into his car.

Gary had seen people come in with thirty broken bones and walk out six months later, and his expectations of what someone *could* do became what they *should* do. After months of watching patients work hard to get back to life, their victories felt like his own.

Meanwhile, Mr. Putnam was improving day by day, and Gary was glad to see that. The old man was determined—did everything the doctors said. He pushed through the painful physical therapy sessions, rested when they said, and took all his meds. He endured all the probing and pressing from the nurses with one goal in mind—to get out of there.

Finally, he got strong enough to leave, but the hospital wouldn't release him. The problem was he had nowhere to go. Mr. Putnam had hoped somebody would take him in. He couldn't understand what had changed in people. His kids lived nearby but "didn't want an old, broken-down man to take care of." They had busy lives. "Everyone would be better off if I just died," he told Gary one day over lunch, his voice flat and certain.

With nothing to shoot for anymore, a light went out in him. "He decided he was done," Gary said and remembered watching him fade away. Through sheer will, the man had overcome his injuries and now, each day, his body was listening to that will. His blood pressure got lower and lower, his heart rate slower and slower. And the day came when he reached his goal, and Gary was on duty. He lifted him up, laid him gently on a gurney, and took Mr. Putnam to the basement.

---

It was in Memphis that Mary remembers Gary's drug involvement stopping abruptly, and she never knew why. He would say that he outgrew it. There was also a story he never told her...

It was a bright summer day, and Gary was planning on doing his longest point-to-point run to date: an 18-miler up to Shelby Forest Park, then just north of the city, where Mary and friends were waiting with blankets and beer. The heat was growing oppressive when Gary crossed the Wolf River, and a foul odor wafted over him.

Gary stopped and looked off the bridge, expecting to see a deer. But all he saw was a recliner, a mattress, and a couple of large, black trash bags tucked in a thicket of weeds. "Must be a body in one of those garbage bags," he told himself and chuckled.

The next night he was watching the TV news, sipping a mason jar of sweet tea, when he heard them say a body had been found in a trash bag by the Wolf River. The blood drained from his face when the video came up—a police car and an ambulance parked at the exact spot he had looked off the bridge the day before. Then, three more bodies were pulled from the Wolf River.

All were reported to be drug related.

Gary would keep that to himself and simply say something had to go. The all-night carousing and the running till the sun came up—it was untenable. "I just couldn't give up running."

---

One Sunday, he was in front of the TV thinking about longer running routes when a new miniseries came on, *The Olympiads*. He'd still smoke a joint and rolled one as the first sequence opened to a woman in a Greek toga, passing a torch to a runner. There were triumphant horns and a flyover of a modern-day stadium, a brown track below, striped with white lines—the roar of an enthralled crowd in the background.

Then, Gary's TV went on the fritz—a Goodwill job, twenty-five bucks, black and white. He slapped it and a line moved up and down the screen but cleared just in time for the narration.

> On the fifth day of September in 490 BC, Persian ships anchored here off the shores of the small Greek village of Marathon. Their mission? The conquest of Athens, 26 miles to the Southwest... Athens was outnumbered two to one... and then it was written that Miltiades dispatched an unknown runner... from where the mountains look on Marathon and Marathon looks on the sea... And he ran the mountains and hills with steady stride... under a hot sun and his feet were cut by agate stone... until Athens came into view. He moved to where the people waited and could utter but one word, *nenikekamen*, "Yes, we are victorious!" Then he died from exhaustion...

Gary watched, transfixed. "Today," the narration continued, "from Australia to Ethiopia, from the United States to the European Continent, from Japan to the British Isles, men continue to run the hills and valleys of their homeland, preparing themselves for the most grueling event of the Olympic Games."

Video images cut across the screen of Dorando Pietri from 1908, running the first marathon ever filmed. He stumbled into the stadium in the lead, turned the wrong way, and collapsed four times before being helped to the line.

Then, there were the wobbly legs of Jim Peters as he reached the stadium in 1952. He was 17 minutes ahead of the second-place runner when his limbs softened into noodles. Over and over, he collapsed on the track. It took him 11 minutes to make 200 meters, and he was finally stretchered away without a finish.

Gary sat in awe of the guts of John Stephen Akwari, who ran it in 1968. The Tanzanian had fallen early, dislocating his knee and injuring his shoulder. Bandaged and bruised, he hobbled into the stadium and crossed the line in last place. Asked by Bud Greenspan why he kept running, he said, "My country did not send me 5,000 miles to start the race: They sent me to *finish the race*."

These runners gave everything, spent it all, and were still crawling ahead. That was life. That was *Gary's* life... right in front of him. Here, too, was the struggle he witnessed day after day over hospital lunches, packed in a single sporting event—pain, courage, grit, willpower. The last bit of the show's narration would play on in the back of his mind on runs: "Silent, alone, these men are of a special breed, with three adversaries to overcome—the land, the competition, and perhaps most important, themselves."

---

Laz stared at a ball of sap, sizzling on a log in the fire. "One man was just mowing his yard," he said, still talking about the patients. "He did nothing wrong. Some idiot came off the road and hit him." He chuckled and groaned, amazement in his eyes. "They put his shinbone together like a jigsaw puzzle. I thought if he just kept his leg, it would be a miracle."

The air-raid siren whined, and like an animatron, Laz plodded up to the corral, rang the bell, and returned 45 minutes later.

"So?"

Laz shifted slowly to glance at me. "So, what?"

"The man hit on his lawnmower..." I said, pulling my shoe off the stone of the pit to see smoke curling up from the toe tip.

"He was there a long time. But he eventually walked out," Laz said, resting his cattle prod in his lap. "Most people defeat themselves."

I gazed into the fire the way I used to as a boy, letting the tongues of fire dance through my squinting eyes. I had to hand it to Laz, he was an artist with a fire—no smoke, it burned long, and here it was in the small hours of Tuesday, and he'd only used one match.

I'd stopped thinking in terms of hours but rather yards, and they passed quietly—the crews speaking in hushed tones to runners who said little, or nothing at all. The tent village lay mostly in darkness, their tops touched and blued by moonlight, their insides glowing softly by the occasional pool of light from a headlamp. Those who remained in the fight appeared from them like apparitions. They walked gingerly over the gravel to start the next yard but often returned from the road jogging in thin cones of light from their bobbing headlamps.

The Japanese contingent ran together and strong, consistently back to the line first. Maeda-san rang the personal best bell while their national champion, Shibawaki-san, casually retreated to his own space separate from his teammates. He was tall with chiseled cheekbones and carried himself with a clear sense of pride. "*Honti ni sugoi*," I said as he passed me in a shadowed alleyway between the tents. "Absolutely amazing."

Most runners aimed for three to seven minutes of sleep per hour. As soon as they entered their tent, they'd sit, throw a cloth over their face, and their handler would cut the lights. The faster you finished the yard, the more time you banked for sleep. Slow down, and you'd steal those minutes from your own recovery. It was chess, but the board was in constant motion, and every move carried a cost.

"The thing about the day and the night," Laz told a cameraman, "is they're both worse." Standing under the arch, he waited to see who came back for more and who stayed in the comfort of their cots. He blew the obnoxious whistle, and slowly the horde trickled back toward the corral, eyes drifting and wanting to shut.

Laz sounded the bell full force, and two dozen or so lumbered back into the night. "Hey, hey, hey," he yelled at them as they passed. "Here we go. Where it stops, nobody knows."

# 25

# Can We Go Get Him?

**MY WATCH READ TUESDAY MORNING,** 6:55. We'd started this time Saturday. No one could grasp this, I thought. I couldn't get my head around it myself. I watched with groggy, disbelieving eyes as they came in one by one from the road, their shoes crunching on the gravel. There were 23 of them. Twenty-three still alive, having just finished the 72nd yard—300 miles in three days with no sleep.

There was a time in this sport when only a handful in the world could do such a thing. It was unthinkable that so many had done it here and on such a tricky trail by day and on a bland, lonely stretch of road at night. On top of that, they'd been forced to stop every four miles, in a way finishing and starting again 72 times—all within the same race.

Before the next bell, the survivors bunched in tight on the timing strip. There was an energy among them, almost an excitement, as if the peloton had led the best out to this point and now, the real race would begin. I made my way to the back of the corral and spotted Ivo, the

Belgian. He tossed something to his handler, looked right at me for the first time in the race, his eyes bright and fiery, and said, "It's on."

Laz rang the cowbell and yelled, "Happy Trails! Till we meet again," and I was sure I was finally hallucinating. A streak of yellow zipped toward the road. Nothing could possibly be moving that fast at this point. It was Harvey, jetting away, sprinting, his arms pumping like pistons. He was wearing a floral-patterned, short-sleeve button-up and bright yellow shoes. His legs stretched out like a footballer's as he bolted full bore all the way to the road. Day four had begun.

It had been another sleepless night. Laz didn't miss a whistle or a bell, but somewhere around three a.m., I moped back to the house to rest, feeling guilty. I plopped onto the mattress on the floor and wrapped up in a blanket of Barkley shirts Laz's mom had stitched together. I rolled over on my side and saw a girl staring back at me—a prom picture probably, or a high school portrait. She wore a formal dress, flashed a big smile, had Laz's eyes, and looked down-to-earth and smart. On the shelf next to it was a cheerleader's bullhorn. *Hi Mr. Cantrell, I'm here to pick up your daughter.* I snickered at the thought. *We won't be out late.*

I finally gave up on sleep, the fear of missing out still too unrelenting. When I clambered back toward camp, the sky was pinkening like Valentine candy. The thought of not seeing the runners reach 300 miles was too much to ignore. Beside the timing tent, I spilled half my dark roast over my thermal mug and thought I heard Bad Mike laughing at me as I mixed in some almond milk. But he wasn't there. "Absurd," I heard someone say behind me. It sounded like Tracy Outlaw, the volunteer who kept everything supplied, but again nobody was there. "Life is absurd," I agreed, then darted my eyes around to see if anyone saw me talking to myself.

By ten a.m., it was clear the day was going to be a scorcher, and Italian runner Antonio Di Manno hobbled in from the 75th yard, bitching and throwing up his hands. He braced his weight with wiry, heavily tattooed arms and lowered himself into a chair as one would a tub of boiling water. His handler, the Roman, was not having it. He was in his face, speaking in fast torrents of Italian, slapping one hand in the other, spit flying.

Whatever he said had some effect, as Antonio soon limped to the line, wincing and shifting his weight from one foot to the next. When Laz rang the bell, he death-marched off with the rest.

Back at the firepit, my Roman friend (who went by Mauro) explained. "I told him, you want to quit a race, run a marathon." He spoke as if Antonio were still there, a vein the size of a large earthworm throbbing in his neck. "Not here!" he yelled. "Look at what these people go through just to get to this place. No. You are going back out there or I'm through with you!" He spat on the ground. "You go out there and you die on the course. That's the way it's done here."

This was a marked change. I was well acquainted with hot-blooded Italians from restaurant work in the city, but Mauro had so far been steady as stone. His sudden fire suggested a point had been crossed, a firewall breached. Systems were glitching, and there was no turning back till they crashed. When the Italian limped in from the next yard—well over the time limit—Mauro hugged and kissed him. There were tears and sweat and dried blood. This was no longer a race; it was a reckoning.

As a journalist, I try not to get emotionally involved. But those practiced walls were poised to come tumbling down. The sun certainly played a part; the raw, unfiltered rays had us in a mood. It seemed to blank the mind and open nerves, radiating the countryside in a sharp contrast of shadows and washed-out pastels.

By midafternoon, it was a bright, broiling 83 degrees when I began holding my hand over my eyes, looking for any sign of Ivo Steyaert.

The Belgian Backyard hero had missed the third whistle. With less than a minute to get to the line, his crew scoured the woods with worried glances, their faces distorted with fatigue and stress.

This couldn't happen. Not to Ivo. Thinking that, some kind of compulsion pulled me out of my chair, my gut folding in on itself. I wandered to the edge of the tents and looked up toward the trail. But all I could see was his smiling face under thick glasses from the year before—he and Merijn capturing the world record and quitting in solidarity. They'd sent a message that day to our sport, if not the world—that humanity was the ultimate goal, not miles or medals.

Ivo had struck me as a thoughtful person, sensitive but not pensive. Now, the unforgiving clock was ticking down on him. I glanced at it. Only 45 seconds to get to the corral. Through a gap in the trees, I saw a spot of red. "Ivo," I yelled, my voice cracking. "Come, Ivo, come."

He rounded a stand of hickory and oak, the bright sun shining in his glasses. Behind me, the camp erupted with claps and shouts. "Ivo! Ivo! Ivo!" The urgency seemed to hit him then. His face scrunched up as he sprinted into a jog, dust kicking up beneath his feet, sweat glistening on his arms. He crossed the line, mere seconds left, and staggered backwards into the corral. Laz rang the bell. Ivo stumbled. A competitor caught him, pulled him across the start line, and gave him his own water. Ivo ran on.

The next forty-five minutes stretched into infinity, full of fraught glances and blank stares—paranoid, all of us, frayed at the edges. Across the dusty gravel, Ivo's wife was cupping her face with her hands. There was quiet desperation in her eyes as I approached—of a wife, a mother. "He hasn't made the halfway point," she said, wiping under her glasses. "Can we go get him?"

I walked up the wooden steps and into the little house for the first time. Laz was seated at a kitchen counter, typing on a computer. "Ivo's wife wants to know if someone can go get him," I said plainly.

He kept his eyes on the screen. "Who?"

"Well," I said, trying to think. "There was a runner there with her. He offered to go. Not sure who he is. He's dressed in black."

"Johnny Cash?" he asked and kept typing.

"I don't think he's much help to us now," I muttered.

He didn't respond to that but turned slowly and nodded, "Yeah."

It seemed like forever before a hobbling Ivo was finally brought out of the woods. He was under the shoulders of the two dropped runners. They inched slowly up the slot till it curved into the corral. Ivo's wife clung to his middle. He appeared drunk, elated, childlike. "I remember you," he said, pointing at someone. Then another. "Yes, I remember you."

Guilt began to well up heavy in my gut. What did that extra bit of running mean? If I hadn't urged him on at the end of the previous yard, I reasoned, maybe he would've just timed out. And he wouldn't be in this state. I sat by the grey ash of the firepit and put my head in my hands.

Moments later, Naresh pulled me out of it. "Hey, can you come to the timing tent?" There was urgency in his voice. When I got there, he and Bad Mike were pointing at the live stream. I squinted at the monitor, and there among the brown and yellow leaves I saw Japanese champion Daiki Shibawaki, spinning in small circles—looking down one minute, talking to trees the next.

The Japanese media had lauded him as "the last samurai standing." And he'd carried himself that way at all times, stoic and strong. In his introductory video before the race, however, he was childlike. Dressed as Harry Potter, he struggled through English for the sake of listeners. He had three teenagers and managed the repair department of an electronics company. He'd started running seven years before, the way many of us do, overweight and approaching 40. When he first heard of Backyards, he thought, *What a stupid idea*. Then, the eccentricity of the idea grew on him. "The most attractive thing," he explained in his video, "is you will never lose if you don't give up."

Now he was helpless out there, and I was being asked to get him out. The news hit the Japanese crews like a full-force body blow. When I told his handler, her tears came in an instant. Barely 20, her head and shoulders slumped as she buried her face in her hands. "Shiba-san," she cried, "Shiba-san."

Laz pulled me to the side of the driveway. "Listen," he said quietly. "If you can, ask him whether he wants cameras or not." A wave of pain crossed his eyes. "If he's bad off and doesn't want them, I'll make sure there aren't any on him." He paused for a second as Sandra scooched up against his shoulder. "His dignity is paramount here."

There was some debate among the Japanese as to who should go with me. I sensed they were concerned whether his handler could compose herself enough to help. But Chi-chan, as she was called, insisted—he was her charge.

We started toward the woods in a brisk walk, and once we cleared the corner, we ran. Immediately, a figure came bounding toward us with a white singlet smeared with blood—Harvey. He passed as if we were invisible, blood oozing out of his left nostril. Not far up ahead, a figure lay sprawled on the ground amidst the leaves and rocks.

When we reached Shiba-san, Chi-chan crumpled at his side, repeating his name over and over, apologizing and sobbing. She'd failed him, she said. The girl who had been so giggly in camp was now a rag doll, limp and defeated. She couldn't even bring herself to look at his face.

Shiba-san's knees were bandaged over. A dark-red cauliflower of dried blood spread out from under them—fresh, bright blood trickling down his shins. His elbows were also scabbed and taped with thin Band-Aids. His eyes swam with the falling leaves overhead until finally, they centered on Chi-chan.

"It's okay," he told her, his voice faint and wispy. "It's okay." He lifted a hand and placed it around her neck. "*Daijobu desuyo. Daijobu.*"

The look on his face struck me. It was peaceful. I had wondered since seeing DeWayne Satterfield choose the icy mud over the grass why they do it. But in this Japanese salaryman's eyes there was some kind of answer. More than pride, a boundless release burned there. From what, I did not know. Each person has their own menagerie of reasons, but Shiba-san had searched for his edge, found it, and come out alive. He kept choosing to go—to move forward as long as he could. In the end, his body had quit, but his spirit hadn't—and there was honor in that. He could die here and die happy, I thought, on this rock with the smell of dry, crispy leaves filling his nose.

I touched his shoulder and told him how impressed I was by him. He turned toward me, and I could see dried salt on his hat, his parched lips, and his hazy eyes forming tears. When the bell sounded in the distance, it seemed to rouse him. "Is your brain working?" I asked in Japanese. He nodded and said it was. "Where are you, then?" "*Jaa, koko wa doko?*" His eyes fluttered at that for a moment, then he looked up at the canopy of trees above, their arms swaying in the breeze, and said, "Tennessee."

I let him lie there a moment before giving him the message from Laz. He nodded yes, cameras were okay. I called Laz and told him we were coming. Then I hoisted Shiba-san up, shocked at how light he felt for his size. Chi-chan got the other side, and we started the slow walk back.

When we came around the trees, harsh rays of sunlight blazed down on our faces, and soon runners trickled in from the road and turned onto the trail. One was Japanese. I felt the weight of Shiba-san's arm pull away from my shoulder to reach out a hand for his countryman. He then stopped, leaned against me, and clapped softly until the last of the remaining twelve had passed and disappeared into the hazy woods.

# 26

# Speed Kills

**"OH MY GOD..."** The voice was familiar but distant as I drifted on paper-thin sleep. I was floating, picturing Naresh on a tandem bike riding alone. "Oh my god, oh my GOD." It buzzed in my mind like a warm blur. I pressed my eyelids tighter, wanting nothing more than to lie there indefinitely. Then my name cut through, loud and stark.

"Who is it?" I asked, jolting back to Wednesday morning, to the race. "Who won?" My first guess was Ihor. He'd been a machine. If so, I could fire off a tweet and crash back onto the mattress.

"It's really unbelievable, man." Naresh's face was blue in the light of his phone. "Eight."

"What do you mean?"

"Eight runners are about to make the 400-mile mark."

The gravel sounded like Rice Krispies under our shoes as we bounded down the driveway in the dark. When we rounded the corner, the sky was unfurling a dull lavender over the white tents. The firepit was a cold grey. After the carnage of the day before, there had been no fire.

In the timing tent, the live stream was scrolling down the list of drops. Their demise was recorded in specificity: *DNC*—did not complete loop. *Over*—had finished their loop but not in the time required. And the dreaded *RTC*—refused to continue. In total, the night had claimed four.

The survivors came in from the 96th yard surprisingly fresh. Phil Gore of Australia trotted up the last hill till he reached the driveway then walked it in the rest of the way. Ihor Verys came in running and kept running after he'd crossed the arch. He ran all the way down the hill to his tent. Mori Mori, the Japanese runner, however, was limping as if the driveway was full of wall tacks. He touched a foot over the line then retreated to get aid.

Next was Merijn, the other half of the Belgian duo; Fudali, the Polish runner; then the two remaining Americans, Jon Knoll and Harvey Lewis. They went to their tents muted by exhaustion. Last was Frank the Tank. Tall, big-boned, with his cap turned backwards and colorful arm tattoos—he'd been the class clown of the race, always making light of the hardship, high-fiving, dancing. Now, however, he was leaning to one side, his mouth slouching into a half smile.

"There's something wrong in their heads," Laz said, turning back to us with a knowing look.

Naresh nodded. "This is just insane."

A moment later, the air-raid siren rang out—four minutes. Laz looked rough. His face sagged, and his eyes sank like a sleepy beagle's. His resting homeless look, he explained. He'd struggled through the night to complete the hourly recaps without his head falling on the table. "I have the attention span of a fly right now," he said, his throaty laugh trailing off into an "ughhh...."

The paranoia of the day before was gone. What was left was primal—a reboot in safe mode. Eyelids heavy. Vison fuzzy. I was lining up my coffee mug with my mouth when I noticed Laz staring at my midsection.

"Is that a swacket?" he said.

I glanced down at my Eddie Bauer ensemble, a mishmash of patterns—one side polyester and green with horizontal bars, the other green and solid and cotton. I'd zipped my sweater to my jacket.

Laz twitched an eyebrow with some unspoken thought, turned back to the timer, then blew three whistles. They cracked like a whip. Yet, no one moved. "Every day this is the test," he muttered softly. "Can you survive the first trail loop?"

If the change from trail to night loops was a godsend, the return to the trail was daunting. No longer could you run without staring at the ground in front of you. The hours of mindless road would be replaced with rocks, roots, and twists.

"Alright, let's see who lines up," he said, staring down toward the tents. "Thirty seconds!" The coach's voice was now thin.

All eight came, Harvey in a grey T-shirt, VEGAN written in big letters across the front. He kicked his heels up behind him like a bull about to charge. Phil Gore had changed to green; the two Belgians wore red, always red. Mori Mori limped out with bowed legs like a bulldog, both knees in compression braces of various colors.

"Happy Time!" Laz shouted, ringing the bell. "Hey, hey, hey!" Like he had for mile 301, Harvey sprinted out, his yellow shoes a blur. A water bottle in hand. Five other survivors zombie-walked forward, two jogged—almost in place.

"I can't believe eight have gone over four hundred miles," Naresh said, tucking his hand into his yellow jacket to stay warm.

"If it weren't for the German incident," Laz mumbled, referring to Boury, "we'd still have nine here right now. No one could have possibly shown more class."

When he blew three whistles for the next yard, all were in but Frank the Tank. A minute later, he appeared, wincing but reaching out high fives. He swerved left and right as his crew guided him to the large triage tent by the corral. He apologized to his manager while the crew loaded up his pack and shoved food in his face. At thirty seconds, they hoisted him up, and he wobbled into the corral. He hugged Ihor.

Once again, Laz rang the bell. "Happy Time! Ooh-ho... each lap easier than the one before!"

A half hour later, Frank hadn't reached the midway point...

Frank wanted to run, but his lower body was wrapped in invisible rubber bands. He almost walked off a raised bridge, tripped on a rock, and stumbled down the trail. A cameraman kept following him as he weaved and stumbled. He looked at his watch incessantly. Each step slower now, like a toddler trying to move his feet with his brain.

Then, he stopped and crumpled over his knees. He looked at the watch again, just to see, to see if it was wrong. He'd been at this, he estimated, for almost 98 hours. "Finito," he said back to the cameraman following him. "Thank you, Laz." His voice was raspy, no more than a whisper. "This is Frank the Tank," he said, pointing to his chest. "Bye."

He glared down at the trail. Then, he slumped back over and glanced to the cameraman. "Do you know... where I can... go home?"

---

Ihor came in from the 100th yard easy breezy. He smiled at the timing tent and sauntered past the defeated Tarahumara standing in his jeans. Five others had come in too. But when the first whistle cracked, there was no Phil.

As it had with many others, this odd format had taken hold of him in unexpected ways. It started with an epic failure...

It was a cold night in Australia in 2020, and Phil was down. His headwrap and gloves were pressed against the smooth herringbone brick. Beside him his wife, Gemma, on hands and knees, had her head nestled against his neck. "One more loop," she said, her voice calm but determined. "One more. I just want you to get to that start line." Then more crew joined in. "Let's get you down to the corral even if you don't start. Come on, buddy—just take one step—one step over that start line."

Phil pushed to his feet and plodded into the light of the corral. Only one was left besides him. *Three... two... one,* and his competition dashed off, headlamp fading in the distance. Phil took three steps and collapsed. They wrapped him in a blanket, placed him on a cot, and carried him away. It was only his fourth ultramarathon.

Seven months later, he was at another Backyard. This time he won. "I just want to see how far my mind can go," he said. How far that was, was anyone's guess. Just four months before coming to Big's, he'd broken the world record, running 102 hours, 425 miles. But as in all Backyards, he was limited by the other runner dropping at 101. He could only do one more yard.

The edge was still out there, he told himself. If he was going to find it anywhere, it'd be here at Big's. But part of him hoped he didn't find it. The part of him that logged 5,000 steps up and down the aisle on the plane ride over. The part that wanted to win.

Laz blew the second whistle, and Phil appeared out of the wavering air, dashing awkwardly to the arch. Gemma handed him water and supplements. He drank too fast, spat it up. Unfazed, she got him more. He stared across the gravel and sized up Jon Knoll. The American was laid out in an ergonomic chair, getting his feet worked on while finishing a Pop-Tart. He didn't look rough; he looked dead. Their beleaguered eyes met for an instant as they shuffled into the corral.

Ihor was already at the line, his hands behind his back, waiting patiently. Harvey snuck in with three seconds to go. *Happy Time!* Phil trotted with the group but was soon walking, a bandage flapping from his left shin. He moved in short bursts. Run... run... walk... run... walk. One small comfort was others were suffering too.

Mori Mori pressed forward with the choppy steps, his face distorted with pain. Fudali looked tight too. Half of the field moved like the walking wounded, and Laz dubbed them "The Magnificent Seven."

The heat returned, a bright glare of sunshine shimmering across a film of dust in the air. Fifty minutes later, they were all back with iced towels around their necks. The Mexican mother cheered as if everyone were her son. In a bright-pink T-shirt and pink sweatpants, she raised her hands over her head, jumped up and down, clapped, and yelled.

When the next bell rang, Jon Knoll was timed out. Laz found him in the triage tent. "It was a helluva show," he said as he reached for Jon's hand and searched for something to say. "I don't know... words escape me." He then handed the runner a coin, blue on one side, silver on the other.

Only one would be gold. Only one could finish. Six remained.

---

Somewhere on the 100th yard, things went sideways for Phil. He was just getting into a rhythm on the trail when the ground suddenly rushed up to meet him. The dusty earth felt warm and gritty against his face, and he felt the sharp jab of a rock catch him in the chin. He spat out a mouthful of blood and pushed himself up, not entirely sure what had just happened. He didn't remember falling, but it didn't matter. He was alright. *Gotta keep moving forward*, he told himself. He wasn't here to stop. Not like this.

He was somewhere deep in the woods when the whistle blew, and the clapping began. He pushed forward, knowing that time was running out. "Come on!" He heard a voice, loud and desperate, and reached for another gear. But all he had was a hobbling, desperate trot.

When he reached the corral, he immediately wanted to lie down. But he clicked his watch and bent over his knees, the sun a bright fireball on the back of his world record "102" shirt. Gemma slipped a towel over his neck, cool and damp. When he tried to straighten up, she saw it—the line of blood trickling off the edge of his chin. "Oh shit," she said and wiped at it.

The whistle screamed right by his ear—loud enough to bring him back... almost. His head was spinning, his feet shifting as if he couldn't find where the earth should be. Someone handed him a Coke. He ignored it.

"Crews and spectators," Laz yelled, "get out of the corral."

Gemma darted for the grass, and Phil went with her. He wanted to lie down, he told her. A second later, it was time. "Get in there," she said sharply and pointed toward the corral. He obeyed. Then the countdown. *Ten... nine... eight...* "You're okay," she shouted. "Just start."

The rest stood in front of him like a wall in the sun. He staggered behind them. With the bell, he stepped forward and heard the old man say, "Each one is easier than the one before." Then there was nothing but silence and the wind and the dust.

Sometime later, he was on the ground—this time sitting. There were rocks scattered about and leaves. Had he fallen again? He didn't think so. But his head was dizzy, his vision checked with floaters. When he looked at his watch, the race came back in a shock—37 minutes. Where was he? Not even halfway.

He stumbled back toward a section where he remembered seeing spectators and spotted a car instead. It sat there, surrounded by leaves like it had sprouted from the earth. That made sense somehow. He reached for the handle, but as his fingers brushed against it, the car shifted, morphing into a large, shiny rock, its surface cool and impenetrable. He trudged on.

The funny taste in his mouth was beginning to worry him. *Why?* The fall—yes, that was it. *Or was it?* No... Finally, he limped into a clearing, and everything was green and bright and hot. A scattering of white tents. Tents! A music festival—he was sure of it—they'd have help. And he was desperate for help now. Something to do with this annoying taste, the gunk and the blood.

Then Gemma was there, and he seemed to wake up as if slapped. "I told you I was over," he said, head down, apologetic.

"I know," she said, softly. "But you had to try."

## 27

# The Barricade

**A ROW OF FALLEN RUNNERS** sat in the shade of the tree line like sculptures of exhaustion. One of them was sprawled with his legs stretched out, a beer cradled in one hand and a faint grin frozen on his lips. Nearby, another lay curled in the fetal position, oblivious to the persistent fly buzzing around his parted lips. Off to one side, Ivo rested in a high-tech lawn chair, reclined and seemingly peaceful. But when the shrill blast of Laz's whistle echoed through the air, he was startled awake, eyes wide and twitchy.

JP had disappeared. For all I knew, he'd left, and I hadn't even gotten his email address. It must have been the rental. My own car was coming due if tomorrow really was Thursday. And then, just like that—he materialized out of the dusty air, stripped down to a red T-shirt, pants rolled up to his knees, a pair of Birkenstocks on his feet, clapping emphatically for those that remained.

The whistle blew and five shuffled into the corral. I watched their haggard faces under the arch, hollow eyes glancing at Laz, who was already there—ready as always. He rang the bell with the enthusiasm of an eight-year-old, and off they went on the 102nd yard—the farthest anyone had ever gone. Surely, I thought, surely this must end soon.

When they were gone, I spotted Laz across the way. He'd found a quiet perch, leaning against a metal barricade. His eyes roamed past the road, out across the fields, and over the sun-browned hills. He had shed his flannel, leaving only a thin white button-up, which he had tucked into his jeans. One foot was up on the barricade as he squinted at the runners coming back. As they trudged past him, he barely seemed to notice, lost in his own internal geography.

I flipped through my phone to find his last post. "no one is running on physical capabilities anymore," he wrote. "that ran out several days ago. they run because their mind makes the body run. only force of will keeps them going. this race has become a contest of the will to win. a high stakes game of backyard poker."

His spot by the barricade, I imagined, was where he wanted to watch the final innings play out. I caught up to him there just as Harvey was making his way past. Harvey now looked forged from mismatched parts, his strides stiff and out of rhythm, his arms high and tight. "Fifty runners had looked better than him from the start," Laz said, watching the schoolteacher plod away.

Fifty minutes later, they came staggering back, faces dewed with sweat and contorted under the hot sun. The last whistle had just faded when Mori Mori appeared, blundering into the corral like a man whose body no longer listened. At the arch, he raised his arms to a handful of applause. With no time to go to his tent, he shuffled around the corral and began hugging the other runners.

"Thirty seconds!" Laz's voice cut through the dry air. Mori Mori struggled to stay upright. "*Saigo made*," a Japanese crew cried out. "Till the end." When they handed him a bottle of water, the added weight nearly toppled him. He glanced up at the sun, a glaring white eye above. "*Iiyo*," he said, defiantly. "Alright."

"Fifteen!" Laz hollered. Suddenly, a flash of red in the distance... Merijn... a hundred yards away... sprinting... but the bell was over the old man's head now, and he rang it. And the Belgian Snooker player turned ultrarunner was out.

Mori Mori tried to start but couldn't. He could make his legs move but had no steering—and he bounced from one barricade to another until he finally turned back. "*Muri muri,*" he said. "No more."

Then, there were three.

Laz returned to the barricade beside me, and we watched as the Japanese man was assisted to. We didn't speak. I didn't want to break the spell that seemed to be over him. He looked content, his eyes as bright as the first day—like Big's had just started.

Ihor and Fudali returned in 54 minutes and moved as a single unit. But Ihor's stride! It was so easy, so effortless—his hands gently swaying at his side, as if he was composed of something other than mere bone and blood. It was clear he'd slowed for his Polish friend. The two linked hands under the arch and raised them to the sky triumphantly in some kind of statement. But what kind? Perhaps it was Fudali's last gasp, and Ihor was celebrating alongside him. Or maybe it was a shared promise, wordless and solemn. It could have been the fact that they'd just set a new world record. In the heat and the dust of Wednesday afternoon, that somehow felt distant.

When Fudali asked Laz for a private meeting, the old man followed to find Ihor sitting in the shade. "While Harvey is still in, we have to compete with him," he was saying to Fudali. Then Ihor asked Laz, "Can we share the win if we beat Harvey?"

Utter confusion clouded Laz's eyes. "Share the win?" He looked stumped at the thought that they wouldn't want to continue after putting Harvey away. The Belgians had quit in solidarity in the team championship, but this was Big's—last runner, singular, standing. He gave no answer and returned to our spot.

Not long after, Harvey trudged in, rivulets of sweat running down his taut face, his white singlet smeared with dirt. Laz's eyes narrowed as if inspecting a vintage Cadillac with a sagging axle. Then the old man's gaze softened as he turned away, moving slowly toward the blue timing tent. But something stopped him under the arch. He looked back at me with a crooked, curious smile. "This is how the world could get along," he mused almost to himself, a faint smile on his lips.

"Do you think Harvey feels that way?" I said, a laugh escaping me.

Laz arched an eyebrow, and that knowing smirk was back. "Oh, Harvey is doomed," he said softly. "He just doesn't know it yet."

---

*Q-U-I-T... just went down to only three.* The Jeerleaders jumped and waved their pom poms. *Q-U-I-T... just went down to only three.* With the bell, Harvey trotted onto the 104th yard. A spot of dried blood marked his chin, and dirt covered most of his left arm. There were cuts there too. That he understood—the fall on the rocks. But why his nose kept bleeding was harder to figure out. It flowed out of his left nostril, twice now—came on its own, stopped on its own.

He didn't see them stop behind him. Didn't see Ihor turn and wrap his arms around Fudali in a tight embrace. Or Fudali, his face squished with pain, whisper to Ihor, "Chase him." But Harvey knew after the turnaround that it was now down to the two of them.

The kid had twenty years on him and passed him in a breeze, his steps light, bouncy, a *tap... tap... tap* patting on the pavement. Harvey's own steps had an uneven racket, a *thud... thud... skid.* If only he could make it to the night loops. He'd have a chance then. But that was hours away.

He trailed Ihor like a caboose, and at the halfway point, passed him. Now, the kid was breathing down his neck, the pitty-pat of his strides almost even with his own. Every time he slowed to walk an uphill, so did Ihor. *Maybe the Canadian is playing with me.*

He sped up on the open stretch, but Ihor passed him anyway, and after a couple of turns, was gone. When Harvey finally came into camp, Ihor was sitting in the cool of the big tent, eating fruit.

As soon as Harvey crashed into his chair, the air raid sounded. In four minutes, he'd have to get up and do it again. Whatever happened, he couldn't make the mistakes of the past; he couldn't give up mentally.

The first time he ran Big's, in 2017, he had to admit, that's exactly what he did. The record was 200 miles then. "Do I really want to do this another night?" he'd asked himself, and stopped. He quit again in 2020 against Courtney Dauwalter. She was never going to stop—he could see that, believed it without a doubt. After following her to mile 280 or so, he decided he'd had enough.

Now, he was over 440 miles—roughly the distance from Columbus, Ohio, to New York City.

"Thirty seconds," Laz's voice echoed over to Harvey's tent. He pushed up and headed to the corral. The kid was already there, waiting patiently—no stress on his face, heart rate probably at 60 beats per minute.

*Look at this, we're down to two. If you lose, you'll feel so blue.* The Jeerleaders. The bell. The short out-and-back of the road, then onto the trail. If he could just make it to the road for the night. Two more hours.

Yard 105, and Ihor was by him again. He tried to stay with him, but the Canadian vanished around the turn to the trail. "Just keep doin' what your doin', buddy." It was Judd, Harvey's crew, down by the edge of the tents, cheering him on. He didn't usually do that. Harvey could feel it now, a dulled electricity, that this was finally a race. But he didn't see the kid the rest of the loop.

Camp again, 54 minutes again, the kid sitting there coolly again. Harvey lay down on the ground, poured water over his face, and told himself he'd been through worse. He waited until the final whistle, then made his way to the corral.

*Hey, hey, what-a-ya say? Once you quit...*

He couldn't pay attention to the Jeerleaders. That was an arm of the Laz mind game. The old man stood beside him in the heat. "Easiest lap yet," he heard him say after ringing the bell.

The kid quickly passed him, and Harvey was on the trail alone. The shadows grew longer, making the footing dicier. When he made the corral again, the camp was being disassembled around him.

The bell. The Jeerleaders. *Don't give up. Just give up, three more days... three more days.* One more trail loop—the idea was a jolt, and for the first time he blew by the kid—and when he hit the trail, there was no sight of him anywhere.

---

Harvey had been gone at least a minute when Ihor came back to the arch on the way to the trail. Amidst the cheers and yells for him to continue, he stopped and leaned against a barricade in front of Laz.

"It's the circumstances, right?" Ihor said. "I don't want to race... him." Whether Harvey's sudden burst had surprised the Canadian or the thought of another night on the road had him wanting to stop was unclear. But those of us around the timing tent could see the frustration in Ihor's eyes as he glanced away.

"I don't know what holds Harvey up," Laz replied, looking genuinely surprised.

"Someone's gonna fall asleep in the end," someone said. "Could be him. Could be you."

"I know," Ihor shrugged. He reminded me of something, I just couldn't place it.

Cheers rose from the crowd of dropped runners, yelling and pointing at the trail, while the Mexican mother jumped up and down. "Vamos!" she shouted.

Ihor turned with a reluctant smirk and adjusted his hat. Ice fell out and bounced on the dirt. He moved under the arch with 52 minutes to run the trail and get back. He did it in 44.

With road shoes on and ear buds in, Ihor entered the corral first for the next yard, hands behind his back as usual. When Harvey came to the corral, Ihor shook his head with disbelief, and then it came to me—Apollo Creed in *Rocky*; that look on his face as the Italian Stallion came out of his corner when he was certain he wouldn't.

*The road again. The never-ending road again. The life I hate is where the road is not my friend. It really sucks to be on the road again.* As the two trudged forward, the Jeerleaders tossed in a chorus of additional taunts—*Just quit now! Just quit now!*

Nine minutes later, Ihor could see Harvey around a curve, a couple hundred yards ahead, a white dot on a dimming horizon. And then Ihor stopped... stood there a moment... wavered on the breeze... pulled his left shoe off... then crumpled to the ground. He sat for a few moments, thinking. Then, he was up and headed the other way.

Harvey forced himself not to look behind him, then he made the turnaround—no sign of the kid. He came back to the bridge and the creek, up the hill, now a third of a mile from the arch. Still nothing.

*Is this really happening?* He slowed, wanted to stay in the moment—a moment that might never come again. He'd later tell me it felt like he'd been climbing a mountain his whole life, of doubts and weaknesses. Moments flashed through his mind—the mysterious blood from his nose, his shoes coming apart, falling down five times in one loop. He'd tripped again just a few hours ago, and when his face was planted against the hard dirt, he said out loud, "It's not gonna end this way."

Coming up the last hill, Harvey hollered and shouted the way he used to cheer for the Cleveland Browns as a boy. Finally, he came to the arch, and those that remained cheered as he stopped just in front of it. "A little farther," Laz said, laughing. Harvey smiled and tiptoed over.

He'd run 108 hours. 108 yards. 108 decisions to start.

He looked better than he had the entire race, his skin glowing in the red light of the clock. A chair was pulled up by the arch, and he sank into it. "I felt as if I'd won the lottery," he'd say later. "No, better."

"Hell of a job out there," Laz said, shaking Harvey's hand. "Unbelievable, 450 miles." He handed the winner the gold coin, and Harvey flipped it over in his hands. Big dog was engraved on it. The other side read, "Be your own hero."

---

The sky was dark now, my engine on and humming, the instrument panel aglow and somehow foreign. I hadn't needed a car for five days, nowhere to go.

I plugged the coordinates into my phone and almost left without updating the magazine with who'd actually won. It felt odd to think that way, that there had been a winner or a loser, like putting a ribbon on a painting. They were all so different. We'd been taught on schoolyards with our skinned knees that speed wins—that a race is about getting to the finish line as fast as you can. But here, and at the Barkley, the best runners finished last.

The numbers told the story: 72 runners made 100 miles in 24 hours, 47 of those made 200 miles in 48 hours, 23 made 300 miles in 72 hours, and eight made 400 miles. Over half the field had rung the personal best bell. Had Harvey? My sleep-deprived brain couldn't recall. Curious, I checked the Backyard website to see how Laz had summed this all up. "harvey lewis," he wrote. "too old. too slow. never had a chance. but he just could not get that through his thick head."

I came down the hill slowly and lowered the window to hear the sound of the gravel pop. I rolled softly toward the road and into camp, sucking in the smells of the last five days—the air crisp and cooling.

I stopped before the arch, where Laz was hunched in a chair, a collection of cigarette butts spread around his feet. I wanted to say goodbye, but his head was down to his chest, eyes shut tight, one hand still gripping his cattle prod. Through his beard, I spotted a pleased grin at the edges of his mouth. I let him be.

The moon was full and bright on the road, and I looked back to get one last glimpse of the sign, still lit in red. *There is no finish.* I eased forward till it was gone.

# Epilogue

**AFTER THREE FINISHED** the year before, the 2024 Barkley course was toughened up with a new section, the Rusty Spoon. Long, steep, and infested with briars, the climb was so brutal that no one was expected to make the fifth loop. So, when Jasmin Paris became the first woman to ever step on that final loop, thousands around the world became glued to their phones.

She'd started the loop in horrid shape, unable to keep anything down. Before leaving in the pre-dawn dark she'd ducked behind a boulder to puke. The expectations in camp were that she'd come far but not far enough. It was just a matter of where she'd stop. But when she was spotted at the Fire Tower midday, heading down Rat Jaw—and fast—the itchy-fingered internet erupted into full hysteria.

The hashtag #smalleuropeanwoman began trending in the top 10 on X (Twitter) in the US and the UK. Graphs, charts, and theories began popping up comparing her splits. Bad Mike had his own calculations, however, and he was not optimistic—the numbers didn't add up. She'd done the tower to the gate in 2 hours and 45 minutes on the first loop. But on loop three, it had taken much longer. And that was Thursday. Now, it was Friday, and she had roughly three hours.

There was also the severe nastiness in front of her: The Bad Thing, the Zipline, Big Hell. "She's not going to make it," Bad Mike declared, calmly. And time stretched on...

John Kelly, who'd finished a third time, and Jared Campbell, who'd returned and become the first four-time finisher, waited by the gate. So did Ihor Verys, who'd just conquered the Barkley on his first attempt. The rest of camp did likewise till there was a hint of a tunnel stretching down the hill. Laz leaned against the stone pillar and eyed his watch—20 minutes.

Online, it became a Baby-Jessica-in-the-well scenario—the world was watching, waiting and hoping for a miracle. A woman posted on Twitter that she "didn't know anything about the Barkley till today," and that Jasmin "is a complete stranger to me. But I can't stop crying."

In camp, all eyes were down the hill, where there was only stillness and the rustle of shriveled leaves. An ominous feeling moved through the veterans who'd been Out There—Frozen Ed, Gary Robbins, Tomo-san of Japan. They understood the haunting pain of days on end only to come up short. They glanced at one another with unspoken doubt and checked their watches as hope began to fade. Ten minutes came and went, then five, three...

Naresh was pacing by the gate, gazing over the runners and crews, when he heard a sound he'll "never forget"—a voice from far away, pitched high, piercing up through camp—"RUNNER!!"

From a brown screen of trees, a lean patch of red and black appeared. Jasmin. A chorus of voices erupted with whistles and cheers. Those who were sitting stood. Those who were standing leaned across the barricades. Camp burst to life with a roar of noise—an urgent clamor, phones thrust skyward, cameras clicking, hands clapped over mouths. Laz gazed at his watch. It was going to be tight.

Her eyes were almost closed as she sprinted up the hill—shins slashed from briars, tights splattered with mud, her face smeared with dirt. The trekking poles in her hands churned like pistons as she gasped and pushed. She would later say she was either going to pass out or finish. Damian Hall fell in behind her, yelling and cheering. Her husband, Konrad, was next.

She barreled to the gate till she hit it, right in front of Laz, and folded over it like a rag. She then collapsed to the ground and was caught perfectly framed under the gate by photographer Jacob Zocherman. His photo of her, crumpled in utter exhaustion, went around the world. A woman had beaten the Barkley. At last, Jasmin Paris was a finisher.

When ArtButMakeitSports.com created a meme of Zocherman's photo alongside Domenichino's 1603 painting *The Lamentation*, a woman posted, "Sweet God. My favorite account recognized a moment I have hoped and prayed for over the decades. I wept in public when she finished."

As Jasmin lay there beneath the yellow gate, Laz pushed the photographers away from her with his cattle prod. "Out, out," he barked. "Media out!" When he made his way over to Carl, he got the official margin of victory: 99 seconds.

---

Laz shifted in a straightback chair, searching for the right spot to ease his pinched nerve. After days of steep climbs and steeper descents, the world was again mercifully flat, if only for a moment. Somewhere out there, the Allegheny Mountains lay in wait. But Laz didn't want to think about that now; the pizzeria was filling up with smoke.

A 20-year-old scurried from the back to apologize while the man sitting next to us was still staring. He'd been speechless since Laz told him he'd just walked 17 miles to get here but "didn't smoke on the uphills." Under a farmer's cap pulled down to his squinty eyes, the man grinned, rubbed his jaw, and finally said, "Come again?"

"Yeah, I started in Delaware."

"I'll be." The man adjusted his cap. "And you're going where?"

"San Francisco." Laz let the pause linger till the man's eyes grew wide before adding his go-to response. "Doesn't everyone walk across the country when they turn seventy?"

He completed his first transcontinental trek in 2018. The self-dubbed Lazcon took him 126 days from Newport, Rhode Island, to Newport, Oregon. "I want to go another way, see a new way," he said. "A long trek alongside the great basin." The plan had been to head out on April Fool's, but he'd gotten itchy feet and started the day before. There was also another tenor to this walk—it was against medical advice.

The surgery on his carotid had been a success, but the images he posted after were frightening. He lay in a hospital bed, clean-shaven and swollen. His eyes were slits, his skin pale like outlaws in a Western, shot dead and laid out for viewing.

It wasn't long until he was doing his miles on the hospital floor, then back home increasing his daily distance, determined to go across the country again. But the first week of his 2024 walk had already taken a toll. While he was able to reach his daily goal of 23 miles for the first few days, his totals were shrinking.

We were holed up in a hotel room in Winchester, Virginia, after a merciless day of headwinds. I'd joined him to crew for eleven days, and the morning had begun outside Berryville, at sunup, with a deadly dance on a shoulder-less backroad.

The routine was I'd drive up ahead, get out, and run back. Then, I'd walk with him till we reached the car. Then repeat. But the road was getting too tight for that. Cars whizzed around corners in brilliant flashes of color and brushed us with hot air. I thought of something ultrarunner Rob Apple had told me, that he won't run on the roads anymore. "You used to could see the whites of the drivers' eyes," he said. "Not anymore. They're looking at their phones."

I also had flashbacks of Kim McCoy, a New York City nurse who'd lost her leg crossing a highway in Laz's Last Annual Heart of the South. Her attitude and determination had been unfathomable—she'd told me she couldn't wait to turn her primitive prosthetic into a lamp stand and one day return to finish the race.

So, I stayed in the car more, pulling ahead a ways, then watching with trepidation as Laz darted on and off the grass, dodging cars. After 10 hours of fighting the unrelenting wind, he was a meager 15 miles up the road. It was five o'clock—stopping time—and we were right beside our hotel. I assumed he'd stop. Instead, he leaned over his cattle-prod walking stick, his face like chapped leather, frustration rumbling in his eyes—then pressed on.

The wind rose up again and ripped at him in gusts. One was so violent, it brought him to a standstill. Certain he was ready to stop, I pulled a Dr. Pepper out, put it in the cup holder, and rolled down the window. He limped right by me, the bright, sharp sun in his face. I drove up to a deli and again turned to where I could see him back down the road. It was a good ways, and I was certain somewhere between there and here, he would stop. He didn't. An hour and a half later he slumped into the parking lot and collapsed into the passenger seat.

He didn't touch the soda, didn't reach for a smoke. He just sat. There's a silent reverence around someone at the edge of themselves. It's a space felt as much as seen. For several minutes, we just sat there. Eventually, he turned and said, "It's a hell of a thing getting old. You walk 150 miles in a week and your legs are tired for no reason." He chuckled, lit a cigarette, and stuck it to his lip. "I looked in the mirror this morning and saw a 90-year-old. I'm okay having a stroke and dying. I just don't want to have a stroke and live." He paused. "I'm still putting in applications for dying in your sleep."

That night we had pizza, and he seemed to recover, listening to music in the room while he chewed on dark chocolate. At first, I couldn't believe what I was hearing. *The world is a vampire.* Laz rocked slightly in a chair, his shoulders rolling. *Sent to drain.* It was alright, it was the Smashing Pumpkins, blaring on YouTube. I sat slack-jawed. "Music for your head," Laz shouted.

We found we shared a similar love for electronica. His taste, however, trended more toward an industrial grunge. Soon, a video was playing with a Rockette sort of dance line of kicking legs with ladies with cats for heads. Jake Fairly, Laz said. Then another tune, and he sang along. "Love is a bullet to the head, uh-huh."

Come ten o'clock, the lights were off, and we were in our beds on schedule. He moaned in his sleep from pain, his leg twitching under the sheets. When the alarm rang at five, he grunted to the bathroom and came back ashen and puffy. He sat in a chair and stared blankly at his box of foot-fixing tools. He looked worse than I'd ever seen him. He'd maybe better take the day off, he mumbled. Then, for the first time since I'd known him, his face drooped in what looked like defeat.

I had no idea what to do. What could I say that he didn't already know? Somehow, he began to ask me about my family. He didn't know my parents had already passed, and he seemed genuinely surprised. His voice was soft, and he made eye contact in a different way, vulnerable and listening.

Then, the whole day changes...

A sudden jolt—he snaps upright as if electrocuted. His whole body locks, from his toes to his fingertips. His head quivers. A nerve in his back has pinched, he croaks. In an instant of agony, his face fills with blood, his eyes brighten, and he's reborn.

A quick piss, then he cracks open a Dr. Pepper. Several gulps and a smoke, and he's checking his left pinky toe. A nail as thick as a throat lozenge is purpling underneath. (He cut a hole in his shoe so it can stick out.) On the ball of his foot, he attaches a small grey neuroma pad the size of a dime. It alleviates some pain, but "damn it hurts" as he pulls on his socks and shoes. In the car, he chugs a Bang energy drink, 16 ounces of purely legal, calcium-infused liquid speed.

A short drive to where he'd stopped the day before, and he's walking toward West Virginia...

My final day with Laz was spent mostly from a distance. In front of him was Corridor H, a raised four-lane highway that made it difficult at times to access him. It also climbed a continual grade into the tallest mountains we'd seen yet. More like a ramp to heaven than a road, Laz pressed up it for ten hours solid. Parked on a side road late in the afternoon, I watched him across a vast expanse, his yellow safety vest like a speck of lint inching forward against the landscape.

He finished the day at the top of the mountain, and I drove him into Morefield to the next hotel. After checking in, I got him a chocolate milkshake from McDonald's. For some reason, I felt like I owed him something. He was standing by the door, sipping it, when I pulled away.

I followed his progress online, and predictably, he began to slow. I messaged Sandra and found out they were having a hard time lining up crews because Laz wasn't where he'd planned to be. He pressed on through the Allegheny Mountains and made it all the way to Oklahoma before he finally stopped. He spent his last day of the walk trekking to his parents' graves and to the statue of Andy Payne in Foyil. The Payne legacy of running across the US in 1928 still stuck with him, of hearing Frank tell stories about the dogged Cherokee.

The Paynes were still there, running the family business—a funeral service. Somehow, Ryan Payne had heard about Laz's Walk, this stranger retracing his ancestor's ghost across America. And so, on his way to a funeral, he decided to take a turn and meet him.

Laz was waiting under Andy's statue when it came around the corner—something right out of *Harold and Maude*—a black, gleaming 2008 Cadillac Escalade hearse.

# Author's Note

This book is the result of hundreds of hours of interviews with Gary Cantrell—as well as with his relatives, close friends, race directors, and fellow runners. I also drew extensively from Gary's own writing: his monthly columns in *Ultrarunning Magazine*, beginning in May 1981, and his books *The Big Dog Diaries* and *A Season to Remember*.

Equally essential were the writings of the runners who lived these events firsthand. Jasmin Paris (*Talking of fells, ...*), John Kelly (*Random Forest Runner*), Damian Hall, and Aurélien Sanchez all documented their experiences with remarkable clarity—capturing what they felt, thought, and endured. Without their essays, blogs, and candid podcast interviews, Out There would have been impossible to reconstruct with any fidelity.

Numerous documentaries—often made by participants themselves—provided critical insight. These include *#17—To Finish the Barkley Marathons*, *The Barkley 2023 Documentary* by Pilot Field, *The Barkley Marathons: The Race That Eats Its Young*, and *Crewing for My Dad* by Chloe Reed. The books *Tales From Out There* by Frozen Ed Furtaw and Rich Limacher's *The Why of the Barkley* also served as useful references.

Sections set at Frozen Head State Park were written from firsthand experience, often in the freezing cold, with a recorder or laptop balanced on my knees. For *Big's Backyard*, I drew on my own observations, interviews with runners and crews, and the real-time race coverage on the YouTube channel *Conversations by the Woodpile*.

Additional details came from the documentaries *Unlimit and Phil Gore—Big's Backyard 202*.

Finally, I owe a deep debt of gratitude to the Barkley and Backyard veterans who welcomed me into their world. This story couldn't have been told without them.

# About the Author

Jared Beasley is a New York–based author and journalist. His work has appeared in *The New York Times*, *The Guardian*, *Canadian Running*, and *Runner's World*, where two of his features were named among the magazine's top ten stories of 2020. His column in *Ultrarunning Magazine*, "Detours of the Lost and Found," shines a light on fringe figures of the sport.

His first book, *In Search of Al Howie*, chronicled a lost piece of ultrarunning history and received the Kirkus Star for literary merit. It was also selected for Kirkus's Best Books of the Year. Beasley has published more than fifty features on ultrarunning in major newspapers and magazines and has been a guest on several popular podcasts, including *Ultrarunner Podcast*, *Author's Stories*, *Bad Boy Running*, and *The Shakeout Podcast*. He holds a degree in theatre and literature from the University of Alabama.